PREFACE TO THE EIGHTH PRINTING

This is *The Publish-it-Yourself Handbook*'s eighth printing.

From the modest beginnings described on page 363, *The Handbook* has become a "bestseller" according to *The Book-of-the-Month Club News*. Commercial publishers have offered to take over publication and distribution, but we have declined their good offers believing as we did at the start that this book should be an example of what it proposes—an alternative to large commercial and vanity publishers.

The item you hold in your hand is the homemade original. We have avoided temptations to dress up the published-in-poverty format, desiring instead to preserve the authenticity of that first 1,000 copy edition. We still type our own invoices on a cranky Olivetti portable, still hand address our mailing bags, still answer our own phone—indeed we still push our own cart.

We hope you will find the Handbook as practical and useful as previous readers have. Most of the step-by-step guidelines are in the "Assorted Tips" section at the rear. But it is important to consider all of the chapters previous to that section for there are no simple rules in publishing.

Three years after publication date we find there is little to add to what follows. As John Seelye said in *The New York Times Book Review:* "No review can do justice to the variety of experiences and the wealth of information recorded in this Handbook." And neither can this preface. If any of your particular practical publishing questions aren't answered here just write to Pushcart (enclosing a stamped self-addressed envelope) and we'll try to help out.

A few footnotes: since our 1973 publication date the small press movement has tripled in membership—about 2,400 presses now flourish. Meanwhile more commercial publishers have been conglomeratized and are run by accountants from movie, television and gasoline firms. The Literature Program of the National Endowment for the Arts now distributes financial largess directly to small presses (as does The Coordinating Council of Literary Magazines and other worthwhile people). *Margins,* a new small press review, is worth a subscription at 2912 N. Hackett, Milwaukee, Wisconsin 53211. Richard Abel wholesalers is sadly no more. A fine new bunch of information people called Poets and Writers is stationed at 201 West 54th St, New York, N.Y. 10019. And finally Pushcart now publishes an annual collection, *The Pushcart Prize: Best of The Small Presses.* We invite nominations from small press publishers every year—with an October 15 deadline.

Please use this handbook wisely, with common sense and imagination. We salute you in the democratic spirit of today's multitude of small press talents.

Bill Henderson

What This Book Is About...

A writer writes, a printer prints, a publisher publishes. "To publish" means *to proclaim to the public*.

This book is *not* about writing or printing; it *is* about proclaiming to the public--by yourself or with friends--*without the assistance of commercial or vanity (subsidy) houses*.

This book deals principally with the publication of many types of books, but information is included about magazines and journals too.

In the context of their personal experiences, the do-it-yourself publishers in this handbook tell you when to, when not to, and how to publish whatever you want to publish.

Pushcart illustration from The Bettmann Archive, Inc.
In December 1972, a group of authors demonstrated on
New York's Fifth Avenue, protesting the inefficient distribution methods of commercial publishers. The authors
sold their own books from pushcarts. Hence the name of
the press which brings you this book: The Pushcart Book
Press. Arnie Schaab, our lawyer friend, advised us to
enter the name with the county clerk of Westchester
County, N.Y., and thus obtain a business license for $5.
He helped us have the name researched to insure that no
one was using it already and to have it registered with
the U.S. Patent Office in Washington, D.C. (research
and registration cost $75). We had the above print re-
duced for our letterhead.

The PUBLISH -IT- YOURSELF HANDBOOK:

literary tradition & how-to

edited by
Bill Henderson

WITHOUT commercial
or vanity publishers ...

THE PUSHCART BOOK PRESS

Yonkers, New York 10701

Library of Congress Catalog Card Number: 73-76940
Copyright © 1973 by Bill Henderson
All rights reserved
Printed in the United States of America
First edition: 1973

Published by The Pushcart Book Press
            Box 845, Yonkers, N.Y. 10701

TO...

To writers
To mothers and fathers of writers
To the Russian *samizdat* movement
To the memory of Walt Whitman, who never quit
To the contributors to this book
To thinking readers, without whom it would all
   be useless
And to us, the fevered publishers, Bill and
   Nancy Henderson.

CONTENTS

INTRODUCTION:

A TRADITION OF

DO-IT-YOURSELF

PUBLISHING

Some writers imagine that they have only two options for publication: the commercial houses (McGraw-Hill, Doubleday, Harper & Row, and others of assorted shapes, sizes, and predilections) and vanity publishers (Vantage, Exposition, Dorrance, and more).

Vanity publishers issue just about anything that an author will pay to see in print. Consequently, nobody wastes attention on books that vanity publishers announce--even the rare book of merit.*

The commercial houses publish--"proclaim to the public"--about forty thousand books each year. Most of these books sell a few thousand copies, remain in print for a year or two, and disappear. It is no news that these publishers make public in order to make money. They are trapped in that financial situation by overheads, manufacturing costs, salaries, expense accounts, and by choice. Commercial houses seldom take a chance on a book unless it promises to show a profit. Commercial houses are followers: they go where they think the public is, or will be. Quality is important but profits more so.

Writers should not depend exclusively on money-makers to bring their creations to public notice. If writers and their friends hadn't decided throughout history to bypass the money-makers, form "small presses," and publish their own works, the manuscripts of many classics--and best sellers-- would have rotted away in basements, attics, and desk drawers.

Today this tradition of do-it-yourself publishing is too often ignored. Commercial and vanity publishers ignore the tradition because they prefer that a writer

*An inside report on vanity ("subsidy") publishers can be found elsewhere in this book.

create for their profit. They are only too happy to
teach a writer how to write, but seldom tell him how
to publish.

But the tradition of self-publishing is ignored
mainly because writers imagine that they must be commercially published in order to be proud of their work.
"If my manuscript is worth-while, why didn't a commercial house accept it?" the myth persists.

Thousands of authors have circumvented the assistance of commercial houses and the interference of vanity houses; they have been published by themselves or
with a little help from friends. Some of their books
were critically acclaimed, some made money, some did
both, some flopped.

What follows is a history of some notable do-it-
yourself successes, and a few flops, in England and the
United States.* Other countries--particularly Russia
with a vigorous *samizdat* movement under both the czars
and communism--have a long history of do-it-yourselfing.

Two centuries ago, Thomas Gray wasn't published--
because he didn't want to be published. Shy Thomas
worked for over eight years on *Elegy Written In A Country Churchyard* and sent a copy off to his friend Horace
Walpole. He didn't reckon on Walpole's enthusiasm.
Walpole, who later founded his own small press at his
Strawberry Hill estate, circulated copies of *Elegy*. The
reputation of the poem increased until it came to the
attention of a shoddy rag called ironically *The Magazine
of Magazines*.

Copyright protection in England of the 1750's was
not strong, and magazines often reprinted whatever they
fancied. *The Magazine of Magazines* thoughtfully informed Gray of the honor its editors were about to do him.
In horror, Gray wrote to Walpole, asked him to print the
poem first, and gave detailed instructions. Walpole
obliged. On February 15, 1751--one day before the *Magazine of Magazines* issued its sloppy version--Gray's

*Many names are omitted from this history because of
the limitations of space. Importantly, by starting
in the 1700's we do not include people like the printer William Caxton (1421-1491) who issued in 1475 The
Recuyell of the Historyes of Troye, the first book
printed in English.

poem was published: it appeared in the London bookshop
of Robert Dodsley as a quarto booklet.

Walpole's booklet was handsomely produced on good
paper with woodcuts featuring skulls, bones, hourglass-
es, pickaxes, spades, and other graveyard-poet paraphernalia. *Elegy* was reprinted four times in 1751,
twice in 1752, and five times thereafter. It was pirated by other journals; it was translated, parodied,
and paraphrased; it was quoted in sermons, at deathbeds,
on battlefields, and at gravesides long after the *Magazine of Magazines* had gone the way of all pulps.

Thomas Paine's first self-publishing effort, *The
Case of the Officers of Excise* (1772) got him fired
from his exciseman job. The firing was unlucky for England. Paine left home and sailed to the American Colonies looking for work.

When Paine's next self-published tract, *Common
Sense*, came off the press on January 10, 1776, not many
people were thinking of independence from England. Six
months later, largely because of this pamphlet, the
Declaration of Independence was signed.

Paine originally thought of having his opinions
published as a series of letters to the editors of col-
onial newspapers, but most editors would not print the
letters. At the advice of physician Benjamin Rush,
Paine decided to publish his views in pamphlet form.
He contracted with a printer,* Robert Bell, for a first
edition of a thousand copies of forty-seven pages to be
priced at two shillings each. Paine promised to make
up any losses that Bell incurred in the printing. Bell
would receive half the profits with the other half reserved for the purchase of mittens for the Continental
Army.

The first printing of *Common Sense* sold out in two
weeks. Paine said that Bell had made sixty pounds profit and demanded half of that for mittens. Bell insisted that he had made no profit and proceeded to print a

*In early America the practice of an author's going to
a printer with his work and then selling it to booksellers was not unusual. Often the printer and bookseller were the same person. Most commercial publishing
houses, such as Harpers and Putnam, were not founded
until the 19th Century.*

second, unauthorized edition. When Paine objected to
the second edition, Bell told him it was none of his
business.
Paine enlarged the pamphlet with an appendix and
an "Address to the Quakers." He paid two other printers to do six thousand copies of this edition and then
sold the edition to a bookseller, W. T. Bradford, for
eight and a half pennies per booklet, pledging the firm
to sell them at no more than one shilling so that all
readers could afford a copy. The printer Bell and the
bookseller Bradford began a battle of advertisements,
each claiming to have the authentic version.
Paine never made a shilling on *Common Sense*. By
1779 he was still in the hole by 39 pounds, 11 shillings
for the printing of the enlarged edition, although
150,000 copies had been sold in America and others were
sold in England, Ireland, France, and South America.
Total sales eventually reached over 500,000 copies.

Although his first self-published volume in 1783
was a disaster, William Blake continued to produce and
publish almost his entire life's work by himself and
with the help of his wife, Catherine. Like many other
self-published and self-produced authors, Blake learned
his production methods early, as an apprentice engraver.
When *Songs of Innocence* was finished in 1789,
Blake was without funds, without credit, without a pat-
ron, and without a publisher. Blake said that his dead
brother Robert revealed the solution in a dream: he
should engrave his poems and drawings on copper plates.
The next morning, Blake and his wife spent the last of
their money on copper.
He began the process that he would use with variations for the rest of his life. Blake outlined his
verse and marginal embellishments on the copper with a
liquid. The remainder of the plate was then eaten away
by nitric acid or other acid, leaving the raised out-
lines of letters and designs, like a stereotype. After
a page was printed from the copper plate, he and his
wife hand-colored it in imitation of the original.
Blake did everything but make his own paper. He
mixed his watercolors (preferring indigo, cobalt, and
vermilion), applied the colors with a camel's-hair
brush, and bound his books with diluted carpenter's
glue. Blake said this binding was suggested to him in

a dream by Joseph, the sacred carpenter.
The first edition of *Songs of Innocence* listed
"the author and printer, W. Blake, 1789." The book
contained twenty-seven engravings and was small, a mere
5 inches by 3 inches, in order to save money on precious copper.
Only once did Blake have a commercial publisher:
Johnson of St. Paul's Churchyard, London, issued Blake's
The French Revolution, A Poem in Seven Books in 1791.
Johnson published the first book but never got around
to the other six.
Blake was constantly hounded by poverty. Many of
his prints and poems have been lost to us because he
was forced to melt down engraved copper for new plates.
Blake published only to his friends and patrons. He
was stubborn about receiving money: if he suspected it
was offered as charity and not for his work, he refused
the donation. That he survived at all is due to the
patronage of people like Thomas Butts, who became a
steady buyer of Blake's books and engravings, and John
Linnell, who commissioned some of Blake's best engravings towards the end of the poet's life.

Bobby Burns, a poor Scotch farmer, was expecting
a child with a woman who was not yet his wife. When
Jean Armour refused his marriage proposal, he decided
to flee from his troubles to Jamaica, where he had been
offered a bookkeeper's job. But he lacked nine guineas
for passage.
His landlord suggested that Burns publish the poems
that he often read to neighbors. Burns protested that
no publisher would take on a book by an unknown farmer.
The landlord pointed out that there was a printer in
the nearby town of Kilmarnock. Why not self-publish
to raise the nine guineas?
Burns collected a list of 350 advance subscribers
and, in 1786, went to press for 614 copies of *Poems,
Chiefly In The Scottish Dialect*. Burns was acclaimed,
made 20 pounds profit, forgot about moving to Jamaica,
and went to Edinburgh instead. The next edition of his
poems in 1787 made 500 pounds in royalties, but Burns
was now contemptuous of profit, stating: "I'll be damned if I ever write for money."

The Reverend Mason L. Weems lost his pulpit but

soon became hell-on-wheels as a book peddler for the
Philadelphia firm of Carey and Lea. When not hustling
around the countryside from New York to Savannah with
a wagon load of books, Parson Weems was busy compiling
his own volumes of preachy "good books." His *The Immortal Mentor; Or Man's Unerring Guide to a Healthy,
Wealthy and Happy Life* was praised by George Washington,
who said he "perused it with singular satisfaction" and
found it "invaluable." Weems made good use of that
quote while peddling his book from farmstead to farmstead.

Weems' most important self-publishing success
("self-peddling" would be more accurate) was his imaginative biography of Washington, *Life of George Washington: With Curious Anecdotes, Equally Honorable to
Himself and Exemplary to His Young Countrymen.* In the
1806 edition, America learned for the first time about
George's experience with the cherry tree. Weems said
that George "bravely cried out 'I can't tell a lie, Pa;
you know I can't tell a lie. I did cut it with my
hatchet.'"

To publicize the book, Weems claimed that he had
been rector of President Washington's Mt. Vernon parish.
No such parish ever existed. The good parson's book
went into twenty editions during his lifetime and into
fifty more after his death, selling well over 50,000
copies.

On October 26, 1809, the New York *Evening Post*
printed a notice: "DISTRESSING--Left his lodgings some
time since and has not since been heard of, a small,
elderly gentleman, dressed in an old black coat and
cocked hat, by the name of KNICKERBOCKER."

A notice in the *Post* of November 6 reported that
such a man had been seen a little above Kingsbridge by
passengers on the Albany stage.

In the November 16 *Post*, "Seth Handaside," landlord
of the Columbian Hotel, announced "a very curious kind
of written book has been found in his room, in his own
handwriting. Now I wish you to notice him, if he is a-
live, that if he does not return and pay off his bill
for boarding and lodging, I shall have to dispose of
the book to satisfy me for the same."

With this hoax, Washington Irving publicized his
History of New York by "Diedrich Knickerbocker." Irving

had the book printed in Philadelphia in order to preserve the mystery in New York. His hoax was so successful that a New York official offered to post a reward
for information about Knickerbocker's whereabouts.

After the advance publicity, the two-volume work,
priced at three dollars, appeared in New York bookshops.
Irving was acclaimed "America's first man of letters,"
and the *History* was said to be "the first great book of
comic literature written by an American."

Later Irving self-published his *Sketchbook*, paying
a printer to produce the work, then selling the books
at discounts to various booksellers.*

A self-publishing mistake occurred in 1811 when
Percy Bysshe Shelley published his *Necessity of Atheism*.
Although the contents outlined a position that was
merely agnostic, the word *atheism* in the title was calculated to outrage.

During his first year at Oxford University, Shelley
had the pamphlet printed by the local firm of C. W.
Philips. He advertised the event in *The Oxford University And City Herald*, ballyhooing that the tract "speed-
ily will be published, to be had of booksellers of London and Oxford."

This was at best an overstatement. No bookseller
would handle the title. Undaunted, Shelley picked on
the Oxford bookshop of Munday and Slatter. While the
owners were out, he strewed copies of *The Necessity of
Atheism* on the counters and in the window displays. He
instructed the shop clerk to sell them quickly and
cheaply at six pence each.

Shelley made his escape, but he was foiled twenty
minutes later when a reverend strolled by, spotted the
pamphlet in the window, summoned the proprietors, and
had all copies burned in the shop's kitchen. Booksellers Munday and Slatter advised printers C. W. Philips
that if they continued to print such material, harm
might visit their machinery.

*Irving's self-publishing prowess influenced James
Fenimore Cooper to bring out* Pioneers *himself in 1823
following the success of* The Spy, *commercially published in 1821. Cooper's experiment failed because he refused to grant large enough discounts to booksellers.
His 3,500-copy printing sold out but was not reprinted.*

Shelley didn't quit. He brashly mailed his *Necessity* to bishops, his professors at Oxford, and heads of colleges. Even though he had published the tract anonymously, he made no secret of his opinions and was soon discovered to be the author. Shelley was expelled from Oxford for his self-publishing efforts.

About the same time that Shelley was shaking up Oxford, his companion in literary immortality, Lord Byron, son of "Mad Jack" Byron, was jolting the dons at Trinity College, Cambridge. Byron's behavior, rather than his publishing, was what irritated authorities. His tutor accused him of being a youth of "tumultuous passion"--perhaps because Byron brought a bear to campus and declared that it should sit for a fellowship.

The young lord rode horseback, shot with a pistol, boxed, swam, and traveled to resorts with a carriage, a pair of horses, a groom and valet, a bulldog, a Newfoundland dog, and a young girl dressed in boys' clothing whom Byron introduced as his "younger brother."

While not running up debts for boozing and gambling during his off-and-on stay at Cambridge, he somehow managed to develop an education in the composition of poetry. Byron hired a Newark printer to do his first collection, *Fugitive Pieces*, in 1806. When a clergyman friend objected to the license of one poem, Byron, unlike Shelley, obligingly ordered that the entire edition be destroyed. The next year he had printed another collection, *Poems on Various Occasions*, omitting the offensive verses. He sent review copies of this one-hundred-book edition to various critics and gained favorable notice. By 1812, Byron's reputation was strong enough that the London publisher, Murray, saw profit possibilities in *Childe Harold*. Overnight Byron became the Lion of London. Nobody knows what happened to the bear.

A self-publishing flop doesn't always remain a flop. Edgar Allen Poe was not yet twenty years old when he contracted with a Boston printer to do forty copies of *Tamerlane and Other Poems*. In 1827, Poe sunk most of his meager U.S. Army private's salary into the printing of this slim volume of 406 lines of poetry by "A Bostonian" and priced at twelve and a half cents.

Poe mailed review copies to all the proper sources

but his poems were totally unreviewed. Two magazines bothered to include the title in lists of recently published books. One hundred years later a single copy of *Tamerlane* offered in a New York auction brought over $11,000.

After attending public school, John Bartlett went to work in the University Book Store at Cambridge, Massachusetts. Later he bought the store and it became a meeting place for Harvard professors and students who admired Bartlett's knowledge of quotes, authors, and sources. Bartlett compiled a commonplace book of quotations, which evolved into the first *Familiar Quotations*, printed and self-published in 1855.

The first edition of Bartlett's *Familiar Quotations* contained 258 paperbound pages. Of the 169 sources quoted, Shakespeare and the Bible took up half the entries; the rest were quotes from English poets, principally Milton, Pope, Byron, and Wordsworth; only a few Americans were thought worthy of being quoted.

Bartlett continued to publish the book himself until 1863 when Little, Brown saw a good thing and brought out the fourth edition. Bartlett joined the firm, became a senior partner, and edited *Familiar Quotations* until his death in 1905.

Walt Whitman not only had some artistic know-how, he also knew how to wheel and deal. In 1855 he himself set the type for *Leaves of Grass* on the press of Andrew and James Rome in Brooklyn: ninety-five pages, twelve poems, somewhat under a thousand books. He got his review copies out and attracted some notice, but he wrote the best reviews himself.

Whitman's reviews appeared in the Brooklyn *Times*, the *American Phrenological Journal*, and *The United States And Democratic Review*. In one of these reviews, Whitman described himself as "of pure American breed, large and lusty, a naive, masculine, affectionate, contemplative, sensual, imperious person."

The copy he sent to Emerson brought a less prejudiced rave. Emerson's letter in reply stated, "I am not blind to the worth of the wonderful gift of *Leaves of Grass*. I find it the most extraordinary piece of wit and wisdom that America has yet contributed. I am very happy in reading it, as great power makes us happy...

I greet you at the beginning of a great career, which yet must have had a long foreground somewhere, for such a start."

Whitman himself was not blind to the value of the letter. Without Emerson's permission, Whitman splashed, "I greet you at the beginning of a great career--Emerson," in gold on the back of his next edition. This 1856 edition included Emerson's letter in full in an appendix devoted to reviews of the first edition, which Whitman bragged to Emerson had sold out.

This sales figure was not quite true. The 1855 edition had been placed in a bookstore, but when the bookseller bothered to read the poems, he judged them morally objectionable and ordered Whitman to get them off his shelves. Whitman took his books to a shop that specialized in volumes on phrenology, the watercure, and vegetarianism. This shop, Fowlers and Wells, found little market for the poems. Whitman gave away many copies and sold the rest for pennies each to a dealer in publisher's overstock.

The next edition, twenty-one poems longer, did no better. Reviewers were outraged by Whitman's sexual references. Fowlers and Wells were so frightened by the thunder of the moralists that they handed the entire edition back to Whitman. Emerson himself pleaded with Whitman to delete the more racy passages, but Whitman refused.

In 1860, Whitman found his first commercial publisher, Thayer and Eldridge of Boston. The firm sold four thousand copies of *Leaves of Grass* at $1.25 each and then went bankrupt.

Whitman's reputation was growing. In England, W. M. Rossetti published an unexpurgated, twenty-eight-page volume of Whitman poems in 1868, and other editions appeared on the continent. Meanwhile, Whitman self-published two more editions, losing money on both.

A stroke in 1873 left Whitman in failing health, but did little to effect his entrepreneurial spirits. He recuperated at his brother's Camden, New Jersey home and busied himself with writing and filling orders. He may have written the article in the *West Jersey Press* of January 26, 1876, that described him as "old, poor, and paralysed" and neglected by his ungrateful countrymen. No matter who wrote the article, Whitman sent it to Rossetti in England, and Rossetti began an international furor about the mistreatment of Whitman. Orders for *Leaves of Grass* flooded into the Camden house. With his full beard and his basket of books, Whitman became a familiar sight about town: poet, self-printer, self-publisher, and delivery boy.

In honor of the 100th birthday of the United States, Whitman self-published his sixth edition of *Leaves of Grass* in 1876, bound in half leather and selling for five dollars. Because of his promotional craft and determination, his books were selling well throughout the world.

Recognizing this sales record, the Boston firm of James R. Osgood decided to venture an edition. Osgood had sold 1,600 copies when the Boston Society for Suppression of Vice began to howl and threatened court action. Osgood asked Whitman to change a few words, received a flat refusal, and stopped publishing. He sent the plates to Whitman, but paid not a cent in royalties.

Whitman kept at it, self-publishing an autographed, three-hundred-copy edition in 1889 and a final volume in 1892, distributed by David McKay Co., as he lay on his deathbed.

Whitman's own words describe his lifelong, one-man publishing experience:

My foothold is tenoned and mortised in granite,
I laugh at what you call dissolution,
And I know the amplitude of time.

"Free translation" was Edward Fitzgerald's idea. He hoped to recreate the original effect of the classics he translated. But nobody was much interested in his concept until he self-published his version of the *Rubáiyát* by the Persian poet-astronomer Omar Khayyám.

Fitzgerald placed his paper-covered volume in a London bookstore in 1859, pricing it at five shillings. When few copies sold, he marked it down to a penny. However, a review copy reached the notice of Swinburne and others, and the *Rubáiyát* went through four editions in Fitzgerald's lifetime.

Mary Baker Eddy devoted nine years to writing and revising *Science and Health* only to discover that commercial publishers saw no market for her religious and metaphysical opinions. So she published it with help from her friends at the small Christian Science Home in Lynn, Massachusetts.

Although she was growing wealthy from "lessons" at $300 per student, Mrs. Eddy decided her pupils should underwrite the cost of her book. Two loyal students came up with $2,200 for a first printing of one thousand copies. This 1875 first edition of 476 pages was cheaply bound, crudely printed, full of typographical errors, poorly organized, contradictory, and contained numerous errors of grammar and composition. Today a copy is almost priceless.

The book was immediately pounced on by critics like Mark Twain. His gleeful, ironic attacks failed to stop Mrs. Eddy, her movement, or her book. She and her followers published a second edition in 1878 and a third in 1881.

With the sixteenth edition, Mrs. Eddy decided to bring in an editor, the Reverend Henry Wiggin, and the present edition, issued by the Christian Science Church, owes much of its polish to him.

With each edition Mrs. Eddy advised the faithful to keep up to date with the latest copy. By 1895 she was earning as much as $19,000 annually from the book. In 1900 the figure was $50,000 per year. When she died in 1910, she had sold more than 400,000 copies to her 100,000-member congregation and her estate was estimated at $2,500,000.

General Henry M. Robert, a West Point graduate, was known in his time as an expert military engineer, responsible for the defenses and improvement of most of the nation's ports. Today he is remembered for his *Rules of Order*.

When Robert was assigned to San Francisco in 1867, many people of various backgrounds and customs were tumultuously converging on the city with no idea of the proper procedures for organizing and running meetings. Robert wrote a book of rules "based in its general principles upon the rules and practice of Congress, and adapted, in its details, to the use of ordinary societies."

No commercial publisher wanted his *Pocket Manual of Rules of Order for Deliberative Assemblies*; they gave the usual excuse of no market. In 1876 he placed an order with a printer for four thousand copies of a first edition of 176 pages. He mailed a thousand review copies to business leaders and clergymen. About the same time, S. C. Griggs, a Chicago commercial publisher that had previously rejected the book, agreed to distribute and the edition was gone in a few months. To date more than two million copies have been sold. Robert would be remembered for his riches as well as his rules if he had continued to self-publish and kept the commercial people at bay.

Cheap shots sometimes make it big too. The reference books have forgotten about Thomas L. Haines and Levi Yaggy, but everyone knew about them a hundred years ago. They put together something dubbed *The Royal Path of Life or Aims and Aids to Success and Happiness*, a collection of sentimental essays on Life, Man and Woman, Mother, Children, Youth, Home, Family, Worship, Ambition, Avarice, Gambling, Fame--everything but Apple Pie. They dressed up their book with a half dozen steel engravings, knocked down the price to a mere $2.50, and sold a colossal 800,000 copies, a best seller for 1876.

For much of his early life, Henry George, a California journalist, knew poverty and near-starvation. He wrote a book about his solution to economic depression, *Progress and Poverty*, only to see it rejected by all publishers. With his slim finances, he and a printer-friend, William Hinton, produced four hundred copies in 1879, hoping to regain the cost of production.
Reception to his ideas was modest at first, but grew. The next year D. Appleton and Company took over publication, using George's plates. *Progress and Poverty* achieved a world sale of five million copies in ten languages. George was so well known for his economic views that he ran for mayor of New York, and lost.

One of the most popular children's-book authors, Kate Douglas Wiggin, self-published her first book, *The Story of Patsy*. The book helped raise money for San Francisco's Silver Street Kindergarten, the first free kindergarten west of the Rockies. *Patsy*'s entire three-thousand-copy edition was sold out on publication in 1882.

Kate Wiggin's best children's book, *Bird's Christmas Carol*, was privately published in 1887, but it remained for Houghton Mifflin's 1903 publication of *Rebecca of Sunnybrook Farm*, one of the most widely sold books of its day, to establish her reputation.

Mark Twain was hardly an underdog when he published *Huckleberry Finn* himself in 1885. His name was a household word. He expected to profit from the venture, but was only partly correct.

Twain formed a publishing company with his nephew, Charles L. Webster, and sold a creditable 40,000 copies of *Huckleberry Finn* by subscription in advance of publication. After pub date, Twain received an unexpected publicity break when the Concord, Massachusetts public library banned his novel. Twain exulted: "That will sell 25,000 copies of our book for sure!" Total sales reached over 500,000 copies.

Later he and his nephew published other books with varying success. His most important project was Grant's *Memoirs*, which sold 312,000 sets at nine dollars a set. Twain gave Grant's widow a whopping 70 per cent royalty.

Perhaps because of such generosity, Twain's self-publishing experiment ended in disaster in 1894. Twain labored four years on a world lecture circuit to pay off his debts.

"The most successful novels ever published," Archibald Clavering Gunter trumpeted about his books. *The Dictionary of American Biography* agreed, describing him as "the most sensational success in the history of American publishing."

Such raves seem unlikely for a London-born, California-raised former civil engineer, chemist, and stockbroker. His novels were just as unusual as he was. The first, *Mr. Barnes of New York*, featured a rich, clever, brash New York hero who found himself in the midst of Corsican intrigue and beat out the natives. After *Mr. Barnes* was rejected by all New York publishers, Gunter organized his Home Publishing Company with his wife in 1887 and sold a million copies of *Mr. Barnes* in the United States alone. The novel was pirated by *six* English publishers.

For the next decade, Gunter was the most popular

novelist in America. While his wife handled the bookkeeping and shipping, Gunter churned out thirty-nine
novels including such titles as *Mr. Potter of Texas,
Baron Montez of Panama,* and *Miss Nobody of Nowhere.*

William Morris, the 19th-Century English socialist,
mediaevalist, poet, painter, decorator, scribe, printer,
textile manufacturer, and translator became a publisher
through a love of finely made books. He founded his
Kelmscott Press in 1891 and printed his romance, *The
Story of the Glittering Plain,* the same year. Two hundred copies were manufactured on high-grade paper and
six on vellum. Morris used red and black ink in his
fine edition of his verse, *Poems By The Way,* published
the same year along with works by Ruskin, Shakespeare,
and excellent reprints of 15th-Century books.
At first Morris merely printed, assigning distribution to the London firm of Reeves and Turner. But
from 1892 until his death in 1896, he both printed and
published a total of fifty-three volumes. The triumph
of Kelmscott Press was a collection of Chaucer that required a year and a half just to print, included eighty-
seven pictures, and was bound in white pigskin with
silver clasps. A biography of Morris calls it "the
finest printed book ever produced."

Morris was a crucial influence on America's Elbert
Hubbard, who began printing and self-publishing his own
creations soon after a visit to Morris. Hubbard had
been a newspaper freelancer, an innovative advertising
and sales executive, and, at age thirty-nine, an undergraduate at Harvard. His trip to see Kelmscott Press
changed all that. He returned to start the Roycroft
Shop in East Aurora, a suburb of Buffalo. His shop was
named after the 17th-Century English printers, Thomas
and Samuel Roycroft.
In June 1895, Hubbard published an experimental
magazine, *The Philistine,* "a pocket-sized magazine of
protest." Hubbard mailed 2,500 sample copies to authors, publishers, and friends. Response to that issue
brought contributors, subscribers, and another issue
the next month. In 1899 after fifty-four issues, he announced he would write all future issues himself, including advertisements and testimonials for Roycroft
books. Circulation climbed to a peak of 225,000 copies.

At Hubbard's death in the sinking of the Lusitania, *The Philistine* was the longest established of the period's literary magazines, and his Roycroft shops, "The Roycrofters," employed over five hundred artists and artisans producing handmade books, furniture, wrought iron objects, music, paintings, and sculpture.

Commercial publishers concluded that Stephen Crane's *Maggie: A Girl of the Streets* was "too grim" and morally objectionable for 1892 readers. They saw no market for a realistic novel about Crane's neighbors living in poverty on New York's Bowery. So Crane borrowed $700 from his brother and hired an uneasy printer to manufacture several hundred paperback copies. The printer was so nervous that he refused to mention his name anywhere on the book. Crane, fearing the consequences for his job as a newspaper reporter, identified the author as "Johnston Smith."

The public ignored the event. *Maggie* sold one hundred copies. The rest of the edition went into the fire that warmed Crane's room through the winter of 1892. However, review copies reached the attention of Hamlin Garland and, through him, William Dean Howells, paving the way for wide acceptance of *The Red Badge of Courage* in 1895. After that success, commercial publishers were only too happy to reprint *Maggie*.

Propaganda proved to be as successful for William Hope Harvey in 1894 as for Thomas Paine a century earlier. Harvey, who adopted the pen name "Coin," started his career as a lawyer before becoming fascinated by economic theory. His first book of opinions about bimetalism, *Coin's Financial School*, was self-published in Chicago. Harvey found a ready market during an era when theories about the coining of money were heatedly disputed. His 156-page tract told the tale of a hero named Coin who conducted a school class for leaders of the period and craftily obliterated their gold standard arguments. "Coin's" story of Coin sold over one million copies, inspired the author to self-publish other books, and convinced him to run on the 1932 Liberal Ticket for Vice President, unsuccessfully.

About Edwin Arlington Robinson's self-publication of *The Torrent and The Night Before*, his biographer,

Hermann Hagedorn, says: "He did not ask acclaim. He knew well enough that all he could expect for years to come was a handful of intelligent and responsive readers, but he wanted those badly and was convinced that he deserved them. The obstacle, he was sure, lay not in the poems themselves, which he knew were valid and fresh. Slowly he came to see that so far as editors or publishers were concerned, these verses of his might as well be in the language of the Senegambians....Very well, if no publisher would bring out his book, he would bring it out himself."

An uncle arranged for the printing of three hundred copies of the paperback book, which contained forty poems. The bill came to fifty-two dollars. Robinson gave away the edition to a wide circle of literary figures, reviewers, relatives, friends, and former Harvard schoolmates. The relatives, friends, and schoolmates thought he was too gloomy. Most literary figures and reviewers were unappreciative, perhaps offended by Robinson's bitter introduction: "Printed for the author MDCCCXCVI. This book is dedicated to any man, woman, or critic who will cut the edges of it--I have done the bottom."

Early hack work by Upton Sinclair was accepted by commercial houses, but his first serious novel, *Springtime and Harvest*, was flatly rejected. So Sinclair wrote another potboiler, earned a few hundred dollars, borrowed two hundred dollars from his uncle, and published the novel himself in a 1,000-copy edition. Sinclair later labeled it "a cheap and unattractive looking little red volume" and termed the novel itself "pitiful." In 1901, however, he included a preface describing the novel as wonderful, bound the preface as a separate pamphlet, and mailed it to his friends and relatives' friends. Review copies went to all the New York papers, who chose to ignore it. Sales totaled two hundred. When Funk and Wagnalls reissued the same text as *King Midas*, Sinclair was amazed at the review attention the novel received.

Too much "blood and guts" a commercial house said when rejecting Sinclair's *The Jungle*. The author refused to compromise and, after five rejections, reported: "I was raging and determined to publish it myself."

Jack London contributed a manifesto calling on the

socialist movement in New York to rally to the novel, which he termed "an *Uncle Tom's Cabin* of wage slavery. It is alive and warm. It is brutal with life. It is written of sweat and blood, and groans and tears."

Sinclair ran a pre-publication subscription for *The Jungle* and, at $1.20 per copy, raised $4,000, more money than he had earned in his first five years of writing. The novel was in type, waiting for the press to roll, when Doubleday and Page happened along in 1906 and offered to publish a simultaneous edition.

Sinclair published many of his later novels by himself, notably *Upton Sinclair Presents William Fox*. In 1933 Fox, the great movie mogul, paid Sinclair $25,000 to write about him and then allegedly took the manuscript to New York and used it to threaten people who had deprived him of property. If they didn't return the property, he would have the book published and "tell all" about them.

When Sinclair heard of Fox's machinations, he angrily contacted a printing firm in Hammond, Indiana (which had printed other books for him, such as *The Brass Check* and *The Profits of Religion*). When the book was manufactured, he mailed review copies around the country, received orders at three dollars each, and sold fifty thousand copies. Fox was outraged, but could do nothing but ban the book from the Fox movie lot.

Sinclair didn't appreciate the reactionary ideas of Henry Ford. When Ford's plants were struck by the CIO in 1937 and Ford refused to bargain with the union, Sinclair reached an agreement with the union leaders and had his Hammond printers do 200,000 copies of his novel about Ford, *The Flivver King*. Soon striking Ford workers all over the world were carrying the green paperback novel in their back pockets, much to Ford's disgust.

Big noise and modern ballyhoo were first used extensively by a do-it-yourself publisher, Harold Bell Wright, and his Chicago mail-order bookseller friend, Elsberg W. Reynolds. Together they formed a potent publishing house dedicated to promoting Wright's novels about the corruption of church and society. After Wright's earlier self-published books—*That Printer of Udell's* (1903) and *The Shepherd of the Hills* (1907)— had sold well, Wright and Reynolds decided to push *The*

Calling of Dan Matthews in 1909 with a first printing
of 100,000 copies and a revolutionary advertising budget of $48,000--the first best seller to receive this
type of treatment.

A dentist named Zane Grey deserves brief mention
for his start in self-publishing. After moving to New
York from Zanesville, Ohio, and hanging out his shingle,
Dr. Grey found that tooth-drilling was too mundane a
chore for his imagination. Using journals of his ancestor and well known frontiersman, Col. Eb Zane, Grey
fashioned his first novel, *Betty Zane*. Nobody cared to
publish *Betty* so he did it himself in 1904, to little
success. Eight years later Harpers issued *Riders of
the Purple Sage*, and Dr. Grey forgot about the tooth
profession.

Carl Sandburg not only created his poems, he set
them into type, rolled the presses, hand-pulled the galley proofs, and bound the books. *In Reckless Ecstasy*,
Sandburg's first collection of poems, was manufactured
by Sandburg with the help of his professor, Philip
Green Wright, at Lombard College, Galesburg, Illinois,
in 1904. Sandburg described Wright as one of the major
influences in his life.
Wright, a poet himself, founded a club at Lombard,
The Poor Writer's Club, where Sandburg and a few other
students met weekly to read their own creations and
those of established authors. Wright also encouraged
his students with his Asgard Press imprint. The Asgard
edition of *In Reckless Ecstasy* was printed in the basement of Wright's home on a Gordon Press with Caslon
face type. The fifty-copy, fifty-page edition was
bound in cardboard and held together with ribbon. A
copy is now worth five hundred dollars.

While starving on a diet of potatoes, Ezra Pound
somehow managed to pay a printer and self-publish his
first collection of poems, *A Lume Spento*, in Venice in
1907. Pound priced his books at the equivalent of six
cents each, but unloaded most of his one-hundred-copy
edition free on reviewers and fellow poets. Yeats
found the poems "charming." Others, including William
Carlos Williams and Hilda Doolittle, were unimpressed.
Pound continued to encourage his friends to create

and publish their own works and was one of those chiefly responsible for the emergence of James Joyce's work.

Grammatical drill sergeant William Strunk, Jr., enjoyed a ready audience for his *Elements of Style*. After having the book printed by an Ithaca, New York printer in 1918, Strunk used it as a text for his Cornell English classes. Strunk drilled his pupils in the succinct commands of his forty-three-page opus: "Rule Six--Use the active voice....Rule Ten--Omit useless words," he demanded.
One of his pupils, E. B. White, fondly remembered Strunk and his attempts to cut the tangles of English rhetoric down to size and to write its rules and principles. In 1957, long after Strunk had died and wordier textbooks had replaced his "little book," White remembered Strunk in a *New Yorker* article. Soon afterward, Strunk's self-published *Elements* was republished by MacMillan with comments and additions by White. Today it remains in print as a pithy instructional classic.

Even Hogarth Press* couldn't bring out James Joyce's *Ulysses*. Leonard and Virginia Woolf were willing, but the commercial printers needed for such a long manuscript were too shocked by the novel to put it into type.
In Europe rather tame portions of *Ulysses* did appear in the little magazine *Egoist*. However, in the United States, twenty-three installments that were published in various issues of *Little Review* resulted in confiscation of some issues by the post office and the fining of the editors. *The New York Times* editorialized that *Ulysses* was incomprehensible and dull but not immoral, though the use of certain "realistic" words was deplorable and deserved punishment.
The American publisher B. W. Heubsch, who had issued Joyce's *Portrait of the Artist as A Young Man* in 1916 and *Exiles* and *Chamber Music* in 1918, intended to publish *Ulysses* but because of the fate of the *Little Review* editors, he requested that Joyce censor certain passages. Joyce refused. On April 5, 1921, Heubsch rejected the manuscript. In Paris a despairing Joyce

See Leonard Woolf's chapter later in the book.

is reported to have said to Ezra Pound, "No country outside of Africa will print it."

Joyce went to see Sylvia Beach, owner of the Shakespeare and Company bookshop and complained, "My book will never come out now."

"Would you let Shakespeare and Company have the honor of bringing out your *Ulysses*?" she asked.

Joyce gladly agreed. He and Sylvia Beach contacted a French printer, Adrienne Monnier, for a first edition of a thousand copies: one hundred on Holland paper, signed by the author and selling for 350 francs; the rest of the edition on less expensive paper and priced from 250 to 150 francs. Joyce's royalty was a generous 66 per cent.

Joyce and his friends assembled a pre-publication subscriber list. Harriet Weaver, editor of *Egoist*, contributed the names of people who had been interested in her magazine's installments. Sylvia Beach drew up her own list.

A four-page prospectus was mailed to several hundred people with partial success. George Bernard Shaw grouched that he had read parts of the novel and thought them "a repulsive but accurate picture of Ireland." Hemingway subscribed enthusiastically, as did Ezra Pound, who brought along the subscription of Yeats. André Gide arrived at the bookshop in person to subscribe.

On December 7, 1921, a party was held at Shakespeare and Company attended by more than 250 persons who heard praises for *Ulysses* and requests for subscriptions.

Troubles plagued *Ulysses*. Joyce was constantly rewriting on his galley proofs, much to the printer's torment. While a woman was typing a portion of the manuscript, her husband read it and threw it into the fire. She managed to smuggle most of the manuscript back to Joyce, and photostatic reproductions of the burned pages were rushed from New York.

On the day before pub date, the printer dispatched two copies of *Ulysses* on the Dijon-Paris express. Sylvia Beach met the train at 7 A.M. on February 2, and taxied the first copy to Joyce's apartment. The other copy went on display at Shakespeare and Company during the day, to be followed by Joyce's combination 40th-birthday/pub-day dinner party that evening.

Much hard work and trouble remained. Joyce helped in the mailing and packaging of his book. He also dunned critics, sending them copies, asking for opinions, suggesting that they write reviews, even composing phrases and indicating where the reviews should appear. His demands that Sylvia Beach do more for his novel strained their friendship.

Success was not immediate. Paul Claudel returned his inscribed copy. André Gide gossiped that it was "a sham masterpiece." T. S. Eliot's efforts to get it reviewed in the *Times Literary Supplement* failed.

Although the first edition sold out in a month, subsequent editions were intercepted by customs authorities: 499 copies were seized by English customs; hundreds were burned in New York. Not until Judge Woolsey's landmark 1933 decision was *Ulysses* legally published in the United States.

Accusations of obscenity crippled the printing and publication--and typing--of D. H. Lawrence's *Lady Chatterly's Lover*. The first typist stopped after five pages with a red face and rocketed the manuscript back to Lawrence. Finally Lawrence persuaded Catherine Carswell and Maria Huxley, wife of Aldous Huxley, to share in the typing job.

No publisher would have anything to do with the typescript. Neither would any English printer. So in 1928,* Lawrence went to a printer in Italy who wasn't bothered by the novel because he didn't know what the words meant. *Lady Chatterly's Lover* was self-published in Florence in a limited edition of two hundred copies and was immediately pirated elsewhere for prices up to fifty dollars a copy. Like *Women In Love*, which Lawrence self-published through subscription in New York in 1920, *Lady Chatterly* became both a critical and a financial bonanza for commercial publishers after Lawrence's death in 1930.

Quick mention belongs to Edgar Rice Burroughs, who, like Mark Twain, decided to self-publish after he became a household word. McClurg did Burroughs' initial

A notable year for do-it-yourself publishing. In this year, on a handmade press, Stephen Spender set into type the first volume of poems by W. H. Auden.

successes starting in 1914, *Tarzan of the Apes* and *The Return of Tarzan*. By 1931, Burroughs saw the profit in publish-it-yourself and established Edgar Rice Burroughs, Inc. of Tarzana, California. When his output ceased in 1942, his company reported fifty-three titles published by itself and previous houses and a world sale for *Tarzan of the Apes* of five million copies.

Anaïs Nin arrived in New York in the winter of 1939. Her novel *Winter of Artifice* was published in Paris by Obelisk but, because of the war, received no distribution or reviews. When American publishers refused the book, she decided to do it herself with the help of a friend, Gonzalo More.*

With loans from friends, they bought a second-hand press and rented an inexpensive skylit studio at 144 Macdougal Street in Greenwich Village. In her diary she describes the start of the press: "The creation of an individual world, an act of independence, such as the work at the press, is a marvelous cure for anger and frustration. The insults of the publishers, the rejections, the ignorance, all are forgotten."

She recalls working and sleeping at the press with ink in her food, hair, and nails. Finally *Winter of Artifice* was printed and made public at the Gotham Book Mart in May, 1941.

More and Nin then published other works they admired, but the press was constantly threatened by financial problems. Sustained by friends such as novelist Richard Wright, who termed the press "courageous," and by the praise of book designers, she continued the effort and in 1943 published *Under A Glass Bell*, a collection of her short stories. A key review of this volume by Edmund Wilson in the *New Yorker* of April 1, 1944, brought her to the notice of publishers, who contacted her only to request that she write in "a more saleable manner." She refused.

Certainly not every do-it-yourself published book brought adulation or cash to the author. Many books are unknown because the author lacked writing talent or had insufficient enthusiasm and endurance in proclaiming his work to the public.

See Anaïs Nin's chapter for more information.

Publishing-it-yourself is in the individualistic tradition of the American Dream. Although some writers may claim that the tradition is dead, that it is impossible to gain attention in competition with today's giant commercial publishers, they are wrong. The underground-press movement of the 1960's has spawned important associations, directories, and distributors. Publishing has been and remains one of our most democratic institutions.

Today, as always, if a talented author remains unpublished and unnoticed, the fault is the author's.

B. H.
Yonkers, New York

THE STORY OF MY
PRINTING PRESS
by Anaïs Nin

ANAÏS NIN's *printing and publishing experiences have inspired self-publishers and small-press people for years. More about her contribution to the publish-it-yourself literary tradition may be found in the Introduction to this book and in* The Diary of Anaïs Nin, Volume Three 1939-1944 *and* Volume Four 1944-1947. *Her chapter concerns the publication of her novel,* Winter of Artifice, *and the collection of her short stories,* Under A Glass Bell. *She currently lives in New York and Los Angeles.*

In the 1940's, two of my books, *Winter of Artifice* and *Under a Glass Bell*, were rejected by American publishers. *Winter of Artifice* had been published in France, in English, and had been praised by Rebecca West, Henry Miller, Lawrence Durrell, Kay Boyle and Stuart Gilbert. Both books were considered uncommercial. I want writers to know where they stand in relation to such verdicts from commercial publishers, and to offer a solution which is still effective today. I am thinking of writers who are the equivalent of researchers in science, whose appeal does not elicit immediate gain.

I did not accept the verdict and decided to print my own books. For seventy-five dollars I bought a second-hand press. It was foot powered like the old sewing machines, and one had to press the treadle very hard to develop sufficient power to turn the wheel.

Frances Steloff, who owned the Gotham Book Mart in New York, loaned me one hundred dollars for the enterprise, and Thurema Sokol loaned me another hundred. I bought type for a hundred dollars, orange crates for shelves and paper remnants, which is like buying remnants of materials to make a dress. Some of this paper was quite beautiful, left over from de luxe editions. A friend, Gonzalo More, helped me. He had a gift for designing books. I learned to set type, and he ran the machine. We learned printing from library books which gave rise to comical accidents. For example, the book said: "oil the rollers," so we oiled the entire rollers including the rubber part, and wondered why we could not print for a week.

James Cooney, of *Phoenix* magazine, gave us helpful technical advice. Our lack of technical knowledge of printed English also led to such comic errors as my own (now famous) word separation in *Winter of Artifice*: "LO - VE." But more important than anything else, setting each letter by hand taught me economy of style. After living with a page for a whole day, I could detect the superfluous words. At the end of each line I thought: "Is this word, is this phrase absolutely necessary?"

It was hard work. Patient work, to typeset prose, to lock the tray, to carry the heavy lead tray to the machine, to run the machine itself, which had to be inked by hand. Setting the copper plates (for the illustrations) on inch-thick wood supports in order to print them. Printing copper plates meant inking each plate separately, cleaning it after one printing, and starting the process over again. It took me months to typeset *Under a Glass Bell* and *Winter of Artifice*. Then there were the printed pages to be placed between blotters and later cut, put together for the binder and gathered into signatures. Then the type had to be redistributed in the boxes.

We had problems finding a bookbinder willing to take on such small editions and to accept the unconventional shape of the books.

Frances Steloff agreed to distribute them and gave me an autograph party at the Gotham Book Mart. The completed books were beautiful and have now become collector's items.

The first printing of *Winter of Artifice* was three hundred copies, and one publisher I met at a party exclaimed: "I don't know how you managed to become so well known with only three hundred books."

Under a Glass Bell was given to Edmund Wilson by Frances Steloff. He reviewed it favorably in *The New Yorker*, and immediately all the publishers were ready to reprint both books in commercial editions.

We did not use the word *underground* then, but this tiny press and word of mouth enabled my writing to be discovered. The only handicap was that newspapers and magazines took no notice of books by small presses, and it was almost impossible to obtain a review. Edmund Wilson's review was an exception. It launched me. I owe him that and am only sorry that his acceptance did not extend to the rest of my work.

I had to reprint both books with a loan from

Samuel Goldberg, the lawyer.

Someone thought I should send the story of the press to the *Reader's Digest*. The *Digest*'s response was that if I had to print the books myself, they must be bad. Many people still believe that, and for many years there was a suspicion that my difficulties with publishers indicated a doubtful quality in my work. A year before the publication of the *Diary*, a Harvard student wrote in *The Harvard Advocate* that the silence of critics and the indifference of commercial publishers must necessarily mean the work was flawed.

A three-hundred-copy edition of *Winter of Artifice*, press, type and bookbinding cost four hundred dollars. The books sold for three dollars. I printed announcements and circularized friends and acquaintances. The entire edition of both books was sold out.

But the physical work was so overwhelming that it interfered with my writing. This is the only reason I accepted the offer of a commercial publisher and surrendered the press. Otherwise I would have liked to continue with my own press, controlling both the content and design of the books.

I regretted giving up the press, for with the commercial publishers my troubles began. Then, as today, they wanted quick and large returns. This gamble for quick returns has nothing whatever to do with the deeper needs of the public, nor can a publisher's selection of a book be considered as representative of the people's choice. The impetus starts with the belief of the publisher, who backs his choice with advertising disguised as literary judgement. Thus books are imposed on the public like any other commercial product. In my case the illogical attitude of publishers was clear. They took me on as a prestige writer, but a prestige writer does not rate publicity, and therefore sales were modest. Five thousand copies of commercially published *Ladders to Fire* was not enough.

The universal quality in good writing which publishers claim to recognize is impossible to define. My books, which were not supposed to have this universal quality, were nevertheless bought and read by all kinds of people.

Today, instead of feeling embittered by the opposition of publishers, I am happy they opposed me, for the press had given me independence and confidence. I felt

in direct contact with my public, and it was enough to
sustain me through the following years. My early dealings with commercial publishers ended in disaster.
They were not satisfied with the immediate sales, and
neither the publishers nor the bookstores were interested in long-range sales. But fortunately, I found
Alan Swallow in Denver, Colorado, a self-made and independent publisher who had started with a press in his
garage. He adopted what he called his "maverick writers." He kept all my books in print, was content with
simply earning a living, and our common struggles created a strong bond. He had the same problems with distribution and reviewing I had known, and we helped each
other. He lived long enough to see the beginning of
my popularity, the success of the diaries, to see the
books he kept alive taught in universities. I am writing his story in volume five of the diaries.

   What this story implies is that commercial publishers, being large corporate establishments, should sustain explorative and experimental writers, just as business sustains researchers, and not expect hugh immediate
gains from them. They herald new attitudes, new consciousness, new evolutions in the taste and minds of
people. They are the researchers who sustain the industry. Today my work is in harmony with the new values,
the new search and state of mind of the young. This
synchronicity is one nobody could have foreseen, except
by remaining open minded to innovation and pioneering.

ON VANITY

PUBLISHING

by Martin J. Baron

MARTIN J. BARON was formerly an editor in a vanity publishing house.

Scattered among the back pages of journals of opinion, literary magazines, and book-review media, the small display or classified ads announce, "Publisher seeks manuscripts." For most readers, the fleeting glance that these ads draw is likely to be their only contact with the world of vanity publishing. A few will send for the brochure proffered in the ad and a handful-- the unluckiest of all--will eventually sign contracts with vanity publishers. This essay is written to the end that their numbers might not increase.

Vanity publishing is to legitimate publishing as loansharking is to banking. A grasp of the legitimate function is a prerequisite for the understanding of its bogus opposite number. Publishing is a time-consuming, expensive craft. First, there are the ongoing expenses of operating a business. Second, once the decision has been made to publish a book, the author will frequently receive an advance against future royalties which the publisher may or may not recoup from sales. The manuscript must be edited and the book designed; composition, paper, printing, binding, and jacketing must be paid for; and distribution, promotion, and advertising must be looked to before a cent can be recovered by the publisher through sales. These are the economic facts of life in publishing.

They lead to certain consequences. Before investing the substantial sums required to turn a manuscript into a book, the publisher must have a reasonable prospect of recovering costs--and hopefully a profit as well--from sales. The economics of publishing, that is, force the publisher to ask: Will this book sell at least enough to recover costs? If this question cannot be answered in the affirmative, the publisher will not as a rule accept the manuscript.

There are exceptions. A publisher may on occasion accept a manuscript of whose merit he is convinced even though he knows it will lose money. The reasons for such altruism are varied: a desire to win critical recognition for a new author and eventually a profitable readership for his subsequent books; a feeling of obligation to literary merit; or the conviction that a book makes an important contribution to public discussion. But these exceptions aside, a publisher will not ordinarily accept a manuscript without the prospect of sufficient sales to recover the initial investment.

Beyond this consideration, standards vary enormously, of course. Some publishers are exceptionally scrupulous and will decline manuscripts of dubious quality whose profitability is not in doubt. Other publishers are much less scrupulous.

The publisher who will accept a manuscript lacking both merit and commercial appeal has not yet been invented. Or rather, he has been invented. The invention goes under the name of vanity publishing, or, as its practitioners prefer to call it, "subsidy publishing."

The whole mystery and art of vanity publishing is a consequence of but one fact: the author pays. Once this fact is understood, the logic of vanity publishing is immediately comprehensible. Since the author pays for the publication of his work, the vanity publisher will accept *any* manuscript--libelous and obscene manuscripts excepted--no matter how worthless and no matter how remote are the chances of selling the book. To the vanity publisher, it is all the same: what the author will pay for, he will publish. Because the author pays, the vanity publisher takes no risk. The vanity publisher, as a result, is wholly oblivious to considerations of literary merit and sales potential, which are the tests the risk--as opposed to the vanity--publisher must apply to any project inasmuch as the risk publisher, as explained previously, invests his own money, not the author's, to turn the manuscript into a published book. Vanity publishing, therefore, is a species of fraud perpetrated with the willing cooperation of the author-victim.

No doubt some of the authors who sign contracts with a vanity publisher are at least dimly aware that something is out of kilter; others must be more or

less ignorant. But virtually none grasp the full implications of vanity publishing before the contract is
signed. A step-by-step account of what happens in vanity publishing may, therefore, be helpful.

The vanity publisher, without exception, advertis-
es for manuscripts; the risk publisher does not. Since
the vanity publisher is a huckster, the deception begins with these ads. The ad typically says, "Publisher seeks manuscripts." But as should be clear by now,
the manuscript is quite irrelevant. What the publisher
does want, though concealed by the language of the ad,
is the author's money, usually several thousand dollars
worth. The manuscript, so eagerly sought by the publisher, is simply a pretext.

The deception that has begun with the ad continues
once the eagerly sought manuscript arrives in the office of the vanity publisher. The manuscript is given
a cursory reading--since quality is irrelevant, a thorough reading is, from the vanity publisher's point of
view, a waste of time and money. The reading of the
manuscript is designed to rule out libelous and obscene
manuscripts, and in addition provides the vanity publisher with the minimum amount of information about
the manuscript required to correspond knowingly with
the author.

Though the editorial reading is superficial, the
attention to the financial details is thorough. A very
precise estimate is made of publication costs. This
figure is determined by the length of the manuscript,
by the presence or absence of footnotes, illustrations,
bibliography, and any additional features the author
may have requested, all of which increase the cost of
publication. To this estimate is added the publisher's
profit. It follows that, should the author sign the
contract and return it with the first payment, the publisher has no incentive whatever to sell the book once
it is published, since the publisher's profit is guar-
anteed in advance--by the author. (Of course there
are additional reasons that dissuade the vanity publisher from any serious attempt to sell the books that
he publishes. The vanity publisher is well aware that
most of his titles are little, if at all, better than
rubbish and that they cannot be sold even if an attempt
were made to do so. A further important reason will
appear shortly.)

The vanity publisher is now prepared to send the author a contract. The contract divides the amount that the author must pay: one third when the contract is signed and returned, one third when the galleys are sent to the author, and one third upon publication. There is much else of interest in the contract. Clause after clause is devoted to the matter of subsequent printings and subsidiary and foreign rights, though the possibility that a vanity book will ever, for example, be sold to the movies is, to say the least, exceedingly remote. But the author, no doubt, is impressed, and then there is a clause, surely among the most informative in the entire contract if one only knows how to read it properly, which deals with royalties. It is by no means unusual for a vanity publisher to offer the author royalties as high as 30 to 40 per cent of the retail price on the first printing of a book. The comparable figure for a risk publisher is as low as 10 per cent. The discrepancy is easily explained.

The bookseller commonly receives 40 per cent of the retail price of each copy sold. The vanity publisher promises to pay the author an additional 40 per cent in the form of royalties. Eighty per cent of the retail price of each copy of the book has already been spoken for. Subtract from the remaining 20 per cent the publisher's overhead and taxes and his profit must very shortly reach the vanishing point. (This, incidentally, means that there is no incentive for the vanity publisher to sell vanity-published books. The author's royalties are so high that the publisher doesn't stand to make much of a profit even if he does promote and sell the book.) Logic might seem to dictate that the vanity publisher pay the author a royalty more nearly resembling that of the risk publisher. But while logic might seem to do so, huckstering dictates otherwise. The large royalty paid by the vanity publisher allows him to contrast his generosity with the niggardliness of the risk publisher. It also allows the vanity publisher to intimate that the author may well recover the contract price if the first printing should sell out. The vanity publisher fails to mention, however, that a vanity book rarely if ever sells at all. It is by no means unusual, for example, that a volume of poetry published by a vanity press will fail to sell a *single* copy. The typical vanity book sells fewer than one hundred copies. A sale of even as many as several hundred copies is unusual. Since the vanity publisher knows that the book won't sell, he is perfectly free to offer large royalties. The publisher won't have to pay them. The few hundred copies that may be sold are easily covered by the first printing, which, because paid for by the author, costs the publisher nothing. In a word, the vanity publisher's profit is independent of sales. It is figured into the contract. The author's ability to recover his investment, however, is dependent on sales, sales which will rarely if ever materialize.

This also explains why the vanity-press contract provides that in the event the first printing sells out, subsequent printings are entirely at the publisher's expense. This eventuality is so unlikely that the provision is purely hypothetical. But, again, the author is no doubt impressed.

There are other interesting clauses in a vanity contract. The author is promised a first printing of as many as two or three thousand copies, all of which remain the property of the publisher, whether they sell or not. (If, as is usually the case, they don't sell, the publisher can always remainder them at a nickel or dime per copy or better yet sell them to the author for his personal use at much more than a dime a copy, in which case the author ends up paying for his own book twice.) What the author does not realize, however, is that the publisher frequently has no intention of printing, much less binding, two or three thousand copies of a book that is simply going to clutter his stockroom. In the absence of an advance order for a substantial number of copies--almost unheard of for a vanity book-- the vanity publisher may well place a minimum print order for 1,200 sheets of which as few as 400 copies will be bound and even these few probably won't sell. The vanity publisher protects himself with the claim, true enough in the case of most vanity books, that he has shipped all copies for which orders were received.

There are still other aspects of vanity publishing which can best be observed as the manuscript is turned into a book.

Once the author has signed the contract and returned it with his first payment, the editorial work begins. This is of the most superficial kind. Good

editing can improve a sound manuscript, but the vanity
publisher knows that the manuscripts he has signed are
beyond salvaging as a rule, and editing costs money.
As a result, the vanity publisher tells his editors to
confine themselves to the correction of the grosser
errors of spelling and syntax and no rewriting, please.
The editorial work is soon enough finished. The
manuscript is now prepared for the press. The composition, paper, presswork, binding, and jacketing of a
vanity book are frequently substandard, the cheapest
materials being used to enhance the publisher's profit.
Lacking a practiced eye, the novice vanity author can
rarely tell the difference.

It is at this point, just as the book is about to
be published, that the author's interest in its fate is
at its most intense. Authors are keenly interested in
the promotion and distribution of their books, and vanity authors especially so. It is the vanity author's
only chance of recovering the thousands of dollars he
has paid the publisher, and it is just here, when for
the first time the circle broadens to include others
in addition to the author and publisher, that the fraud
of vanity publishing becomes the more obvious. It is
not now the author who must be convinced, but the reviewers, booksellers, and the reading public.

The vanity contract, though it carefully refrains
from guaranteeing sales, makes elaborate provisions
for sending out review copies, advertising, and promo-
tion--most of them largely bogus.

Take the matter of review copies. As the vanity
publisher is well aware, a review copy of one of his
publications sent to the editors of book-review media
is commonly consigned to the wastebasket. The vanity-
press imprint, obscure to the general public, but well
enough known in the publishing world, stigmatizes the
book and effectively consigns it to oblivion the moment it is published. The only review which the author
may be lucky enough to obtain is that furnished merely
as a matter of courtesy in a local newspaper or two.
Anything more is passing rare.

Next, advertising. The vanity publisher's ad in
The New York Times Book Review takes the form of what
is known in the trade as a "tombstone"--a narrow, tomb-
stonelike column in which numerous titles are advertised with a miniscule amount of space devoted to each.

To the practiced eye of a bookseller or librarian, the vanity-press stigma is instantly discernible. A larger, more conspicuous ad might be of some slight help in a few cases, but the vanity publisher is reluctant to spend money advertising books whose potential is, as a rule, so limited. And in any case, as previously indicated, his profit margin is too small to make advertising pay even if it were effective in selling the books he publishes. The tombstone is worthless, but it does allow the vanity publisher to claim that he has fulfilled the contractual obligation to the author to "advertise" his book.

Finally, bookstore distribution. This can be dealt with shortly. For a vanity-press book, there isn't any. Bookstores as a matter of course refuse to stock, much less display, vanity books. There just isn't any reason for them to do so. The demand for vanity books isn't large enough to justify the waste of storage and display space. Every vanity publisher, therefore, runs a mail-order operation. Only a vanity publisher sells vanity books. The rare exception is accounted for by the bookseller who accommodates a local author as a matter of courtesy.

Risk publishers do make mistakes. The history of publishing is replete with authors whose work at first has been rejected unjustly and who have eventually won a critical hearing or a large readership, and sometimes both. An alternative to risk publishing should certainly exist. Vanity publishing, rather than offering such an alternative, is a formula for lining the pockets of a few unscrupulous publishers. Authors beware!

CANTO y GRITO MI LIBERACIÓN

(y lloro mis desmadrazgos ...)

PENSAMIENTOS, GRITOS,
ANGUSTIAS, ORGULLOS,
PENUMBRAS POÉTICAS,
ENSAYOS, HISTORIETAS,
HECHIZOS ALMALES DEL
SON DE MI EXISTENCIA ...

by Ricardo Sánchez

ILLUSTRATED BY
MANUEL G. ACOSTA

Typography and art from Ricardo Sánchez's *Canto y Grito Mi Liberación*, first published by the author and his friends. Reprinted by permission of Anchor Books from the title page of Anchor's 1973 edition.

MÍCTLA: A CHICANO'S

LONG ROAD HOME

by Ricardo Sánchez

*RICARDO SÁNCHEZ of El Paso came to writing and publish-
ing through the long, tortuous path described in this
chapter.* He has been director of several programs for
Chicanos, is an associate of La Academia de Nueva Raza,
and has published extensively in such periodicals as
Afro-American, Magazín, El Grito, Nosotros, and Car-
bunkle Review. *His self-published* Canto Y Grito Mi
Liberación *is an eloquent, angry collection of autobiographical essays and poems.* Doubleday Anchor recently
brought out a paperback edition with sixteen black and
white drawings by Manuel Acosta.

Life in the east-side barrios of El Paso demands much.
It is a life-style that permeates one's being with hunger and awesome need. A need, on one hand, to touch
the concrete ground and, on the other, to pluck a star.
The near-anomie and hunger, coupled with crushing mortality, generate forces that compel one to indite, imprint, and neonize one's spectral reality on the horizon. But being Chicano, being dispossessed, and having
to fight every inch of the way to survival become obstacles that deflect will and complusion. After being
crushed and societally defeated, the average Chicano
potential writer/artist finds resignation in oblivion.
He vents his futility by writing his name and con/safos
on countless walls. Within a myriad of graffitied es-
capades he establishes a comic wispy imprint that mo-
mentarily stabs passersby with a flighty realization
that somewhere in that anonymous barrio there exists a
latent Cervantes or Octavio Paz. But it is only a potential voice.
    I am a Chicano. A Chicano who has struggled con-
stantly for the right to publish, for the right to
raise his voice beyond crap-house walls, and for the
way to simply project his perceptions not only to his
people but to all peoples. My history is similar to
that of most of the other Chicano writers in my milieu.
    My life began in the tragic-comic setting of *El
Barrio del Diablo*, "The Devil's Ward" in El Paso. A
ward that had more than physical boundaries. It was a
haven full of laughter, yet it was also what its name
implied: a horrendous assault on my sense of humanity.
Hope in that barrio was mirrored in my parents' eyes
when they spoke of school, but little did they know
that school was just another horrible, killing tenacle
of the barrio, for it was in school that I first

learned that one's soul/mind can be murdered, if only one step at a time.

Like all small children, I was amazed that whole universes existed in words and books, and being inquisitively adventurous, I too wanted to devour those words--and in two languages, not just one. Ironically enough, my mother enrolled me in a Catholic school at first. After a turbulent year of prayers, mindless castigations, spiritual dehydration, and being terrified for the future of my soul (their stories of hell were imprinted on my mind), my mother had a fight with the head nun over my getting sick due to their forcing me to eat when I was not hungry. Presto, my mother plucked me out of their clutches and sentenced me to another institution: Zavala Elementary School, the El Paso Public Schools' deformatory. Here there were no prayers, just a bunch of preying mentors who satiated themselves on the wishes, hopes, and aspirations of their pupils, only to eventually destroy their futures. Zavala was probably no different from the other schools in El Paso, it is only that Zavala was the first school to bluntly put me in my so-called place.

It was in the fifth grade that my will to write first emerged, and during this time I felt the first major blow on my sense of self. It was at this time that I wrote my first poem--a child's welcome to Christmas and Santa Claus. With trembling hands and hopeful mind I presented it to my "tee-chur," and with scornful perversity she gave it back. Sometime later she asked the class what they wanted to be upon growing up. Responses ranged from policeman to nurse to teacher to fireman. I quaveringly said, "I want to write." "In Spanish," she responded mockingly. It was a statement, not a question. And when I said in both languages, she told me bluntly that I should aspire to something within my means, for Mexicans should live the way they were meant to. Her suggestions ranged from my becoming a cop to a janitor or something useful. What followed that episode were years of longing and secretive writing.

Thomas Jefferson High School was but an extension of the same callous attitude. After applying to the journalism department that I might be on the *Branding Iron* staff, I was told that there were already too many freshmen on the staff and I should wait my turn. My

yearning for writing and getting published consumed
every moment, but all doors seemed to be closed. More
years followed--years of rebellion that was interpreted
as symptomatic of a bad streak. High school was a disaster, and I became another pushed-out statistic. The
Army supposedly offered a way out, but it was still the
same. Its regimentation got to me. In between sips of
beer at the P-X, I would write poems on napkins. Other
times, being stationed at the Presidio in San Francisco,
I would trip on to North Beach and just rap.

It was at those rap sessions in North Beach and
Sausalito that I once again seriously started to write.
It was beautiful to just talk with people who shared
the same drives to write, to explosively encapsulate
on paper the levels of death, life, love, and desperation coursing through the mind. Some of my poems were
first printed then--in small, short-lived journals. It
was good--more than merely good--to see my writings
printed, but that too was to end. I was transferred to
Fort McArthur and then to the Magic Mountains in the
Los Angeles Forest as a radar operator, and then all
hell broke loose. Personal tragedy struck: two brothers
died one month apart in accidents, and I was shortly in-
dicted in Los Angeles on serious felony charges.

Tried, found guilty. Sentenced at nineteen to a
term of not less than one nor more than twenty-five
years and remanded to the California Department of Corrections, Chino Reception-Guidance Center (C-RGC). All
forms of death awaited me. The heady, endless shuffle
of prison-garbed automatons cynically purveying a sor-
did world; the steel-beady eyes of counselors and
guards; and the regulations.

Assigned to the library, I read and read and read.
My mental horizon elongated, expanded; my physical
world contracted. Amid riots and turbulence, hatred
and viciousness, hope and dejected desperation, and
need for love and realization, I wrote. Poem after
poem flowed out of my mind/soul. Poems and love songs,
protests and questions. But seemingly to no avail, for
I was not able to send any writings out. Soledad offi-
cials arbitrarily confiscated most of my writings.
More years of yearning passed.

After being paroled from Soledad, I returned home
to the desolate streets of El Paso. The woman who had
promised fidelity was now promising fidelity to others.

Things were different, and I now ran with another kind of friend . Writing hopes turned to hustling needs. I got to know Juarez frenzy and pimping, robbing and conniving. It is ironic that at this juncture I met members of the El Paso Writers' League--but their writings did nothing for me, as life to me was more serious than the hopes they projected. I wrote and submitted some manuscripts, but Chicanismo was as invisible as the thoughts in my mind, and nobody wanted to read about Chicanos. I wrote of social brutalization and hurt, of the barrio venting expletives, of the many ironies of the barrio. No one listened, and my impatience led me once more to pick up a gun. In between hustling, scuffling, I had met my wife, María Teresa Silva. We fell in love and got married.

I tried to settle down and work--to become, in short, a good citizen and accept social regimentation. The need for writing and publishing still burned within and nothing could cauterize the burning tissues of desire and need. Teresa shared my needs and asked nothing in return. We attended writers' league meetings, yet I became more dejected for I could not--and would not--write the things these people advised me to write in order to get published. Mine was a socio-political need; theirs, it seemed, was an exercise in sweet-nice poetry and fanciful essays. My writing was on the level of developing a tertiary approach to life--for I had begun to formulate an awareness of my being mestizo: the trinity-pyramidial person, i.e., the intellectualization of my being. Indio/Español merging to create the third person: MESTIZO. It was more than a passing whim; I was on the level of the colored-becoming-Negro-becoming-Black. I was defining and redefining my own parameters as a human being becoming appreciative of his own uniqueness: Spanish/American-Mexican/American-CHICANO. Unlike the Black man, I did not have a popular/politicized movement to sustain and nurture my onrushing awareness, nor to find publication in. It was still basically a question of my becoming less and less my reality and accepting the mostly unspoken mandates of a WASP (gringo)-oriented society.

Aside from my philosophical/spiritual quandaries, I still had to survive a world that looked down on ex-cons. Being on parole, married, and about to become a father, I learned to grovel and beg for jobs--any job would do, just as long as I could survive to feed and maintain my family. But it was mostly, "Don't call us, Mr. Sánchez, we'll call you," at interviews. When I did land a job, there was always a parole officer making it his business to notify employers that I was a dangerous man and not to be trusted, and my job would, of course, vaporize. I would then be harassed for my being unable to maintain proper employment. Underneath, where no one could tamper with my ideas, I continued burning with the desire to publish. It was a paradox, a phantasmagoric contradiction: I started speaking about creating a humanistic society while plotting ways to get money to support my family. Survival on a social level became paramount, even if it meant risking body and soul; so just before my son was born I once again picked up a gun--a thirty-eight police special, Smith & Wesson--and held up people.

Again did I go to prison--this time in Texas--and I learned the bitterest of lessons: A CONVICT, especially a Chicano convict, IN TEXAS EXISTS ONLY TO WORK LIKE A BEAST. The cotton fields, the constant whippings, the mad sojourns to and from isolation, the pisser, and all the other manic forms of dehumanization now demanded that I go deeper and deeper into the why of my existence. Each letter sent home was a labor of literary definition, definition of the topsy-turvy world that strove to obliterate convicts. Thoughts of publication ran through my mind, as if they were demons that demanded to be printed and distributed.

Game playing became the most important ingredient in my surviving the system. I learned to swerve and jive, to project a smiling countenance, for it became imperative that I get out soon. My son was growing fast and I yearned to know him; my father had recently died and I felt the emptiness of realization hit--I WOULD NEVER AGAIN TALK WITH MY OLD MAN--plus I still burned with the need to write and hurl out the feelings running their hectic course twixt blood and flesh. It was opportune that there were some extension-college courses offered to the inmates, so I became a model inmate. I also was reassigned from the cotton fields to the education department and for the next two years began to absorb a world of books and expression. The wildness of a new world assailed me with the pungent words of Camus, Gibran, Goethe, Paz. The old anomie

began to fade as I started to realize my own liberation
as a human being, a Chicano proud of his heritage, for
I read of the Nahuas and the Españoles merging. More
than ever before I felt the need to write and publish,
but all was almost in vain. The months stretched out,
each one filled with a lonely hurt, with a mounting
anxiety, with a heady turbulence, until I finally got
paroled, March 13, 1969. In all the years spent behind bars, I had only had one bilingual poem published.

Leaving the Huntsville Unit, I analyzed the past
four years. Much had gone through my mind from the El
Paso County Jail sojourn to the mad inhumanity of the
Texas Department of Corrections' Ramsey I Prison Farm.
I mandated myself to write and to publish.

El Paso awaited me. Being jobless, I sought out
"gainful employment." The same token sayings were
salivated out, and then through the intervention of
friends, I was awarded a Frederick Douglass Fellowship
in Journalism in Richmond, Virginia. Flying to the
South was a weird, gelatinous experience. I was the
only Chicano in the program. The rest were Black, but
I saw them as fellow travelers who shared the same
societal conditions, comrades also in need of a place
in the sun.

The streets of Richmond reeked with the same racism that Texas is noted for. There were demonstra-
tions to cover, police-court buffoonery to report on,
and racism to uncover. All the time spent there, writing for the *Richmond Afro-American* Newspaper and the
Richmond Chronicle (underground paper), made me aware
of the need for our own publishing industries. Now
I had expanded on the willy-nilly dreams dreamt in
Soledad,Ramsey , and Huntsville. I terminated my fellowship by contracting one year into six months, and
I went to work at the School of Education, University
of Massachusetts, Amherst, as a staff writer in January, 1970. That milieu gave me a broader, more mean-
ingful overview of the world. The fears which the barrio had gestated in my soul now crumbled, and I realized the awesome power of self-awareness and determination.

During my Amherst venture I spoke with several
editors from big publishing houses, but they could not
yet see the need for Chicano publications: WE WERE NOT
CHARISMATIC ENOUGH, for as yet there had not been a

Watts nor a Newark in the Chicano Movement. My anger
mounted, and more than ever I determined that the world
would yet get to savor the Chicano reality, that our
literature would flood desiccated minds and create pan-
oramas that would flower out in a dual linguistic pattern.

Six months was all I could take of Amherst. Its
placid and verdant beauty did not move me like the
rapid eternities of the Southwest. I hungered for
earth that is bronze and burnt by a vibrant, loving
sun.

We moved back. Back to Aztlán. Denver, where my
compadre, Abelardo B. Delgado, was trying to put together a publishing house--Barrio Press. In between
directing the Itinerant Migrant Health Project for the
Colorado Migrant Council, I found the time to compile
and edit a short anthology: *Los Cuatro*. Four of us
had contributed writings and money to create and project Barrio Press. There we were: Magdaleno Avila,
Abelardo Delgado, Reymundo "Tigre" Perez, and myself--
four gorilla-sized, piano-moving-type Chicano poets.
We lost money on the book, but we loved the response
we had gotten, and somehow we managed to gain more
faith and hope.

I soon began to get my poetry and articles published in many movement journals and papers, but the lure
of El Paso's burning sun beckoned me. Along with an
atavistic streak and a desire to return, there were
the adamant demands and cajolery of friends and family.
I could not really resist, for El Paso is steeped deeply in my mind/soul. Dr. Reymundo Angel Gardea kept
persisting that I self-publish, even though I was then
being asked by publishers for a book. He demanded that
he be the one to finance my first book, and perhaps in
the process we could set up a publishing house in El
Paso. Abelardo wanted to do his thing in Colorado, but
his soul also cried out for the aridness of El Paso to
cascade over him.

I sought out people to embark on the project of
a publishing house in El Paso. One night, while sip-
ping beer with Dr. Gardea, it was decided that I would
return to El Paso and that we would harness the resources needed. It was August, 1970.

In September and early October, I met with the
carnales (brothers) at Colegio Jacinto Treviño. They

too wanted to start their own publishing house. We
agreed to further each other's goals and somehow link
resources. I made contacts with groups all over the
country. Part of my plan was to seek out promotional
avenues and to establish a name. I chose the name,
Míctla Publications, for its poetic allure and its
strong implications. Míctla is the ninth level of
death. The publishing house would help put to death
once and for all the comic stereotyping of my people.
In killing the enslaving myths of Hollywood and the
mass media, we would create a truer image of ourselves,
that our children might develop positive identities,
that their socially-imposed complexes might at last be
buried.

I spoke with Bradford Chambers. He was putting
together some articles on minority publishing. Abelardo and I met with him. Bradford wanted an interview;
we denied him such, but did agree to write him two articles right then and there on Chicano publishing needs
and horizons. Within the space of forty minutes we
wrote them, Abelardo at one typewriter and I at the
other. The articles were published March 15, 1971, in
Publishers Weekly.

I was back in El Paso. It was a perilous moment,
for my parole officer wanted arbitrarily to revoke my
parole. He disagreed violently with my coming back
home--and more so with my involvement in the Movement
and with my writings. I bobbed and weaved, and for
sketches of time saw prison just around the corner.

Meanwhile I finished my manuscript, *Canto Y Grito
Mi Liberación*, a collection of autobiographical essays
and poems, and gave it to Manuel G. Acosta, undoubtedly
one of America's artistic giants. He read it and drew
illustrations for it.

A printer was sought out; so was a binder. Manuscript and illustrations were submitted for printing
and binding. But that was merely the beginning, the
difficult part was still ahead.

I began going to the University to scout out re-
cruits for Míctla. I met with numerous students and
community people. Out of many tumultuous encounters,
three young people came up to me and Míctla was on the
way. José Antonio Parra, a young intelligent *carnal*
from San Elizario; Eduardo Rubén Ochoa, a young printer from El Paso; and Mrs. Patricia Roybal Sutton.

Along with Dr. Gardea, we began formulating the philosophy of Míctla. We delineated the responsibilities
of each and set to work developing distribution and
promotion.

As Míctla began to take form, we started the in-
corporation process. We did not necessarily want to
be funded, for the special conditions of funding agencies would restrict us. We decided to set up a profit-
making corporation that would eventually seed out funds
to other areas of need in our community. It was--and
continues to be--our hope to build up economic power
that can be used for the development of cultural centers, etc. The printing cost of my book, *Canto Y Grito
Mi Liberación*, was taken care of by Dr. Gardea. We
managed to get the binding done on a sixty-ninety re-
newable note, and we paid the binding out of the first
sales.

Canto Y Grito Mi Liberación, we had decided, would
be hardbound with brown ink on quality bronze paper,
and include some four-color reproductions. We wanted
to establish a hallmark for Chicano publishing. It became our stated goal to strive for aesthetic service-
ability.

Our hopes were high and our expectations unlimited,
but the realities that continually assailed us were
brutal. We--the four of us (Dr. Gardea was too busy
with medicine to do more than back our efforts)--had
little or no business experience. Antonio (Tony) Parra
was our business manager, but he lacked expertise; Patricia was in charge of public relations, but her classes
were too demanding of her time; and I was busy trying
to eke out a living to support my family. Eduardo, as
our production manager, was kept waiting for something
to produce. We mostly ran around trying to drum up
business--yet we could not seem to link up with promotional outlets.

Patricia, already overburdened with awesome commitments, decided to quit Míctla. The slack was taken up
partly by Tony and me, and then we began to bring in
other people who had more time to develop the things
that have had to be developed. Míctla is at last able
to begin hiring some staff. Among our projections at
Míctla are such things as a series of Chicano perspectives entitled *Míctla: The Ninth Level of Death*, the
first one being a monograph, *Voces De La Gente* by J.

63

Olvera; *Fury at Noon: The Story of Rubén Salazar* by
Dr. P. Ortego; a teacher's manual, *Teaching English or
Spanish as Second Languages* by Carlos Rivera; a quarterly magazine, *Bronce: Chicano Literary Review*; and
other works.

Doubleday Anchor Books has picked up the paperback
rights to my first book, *Canto Y Grito Mi Liberación*.
We permitted it for the resources we hope it will generate for Míctla. Aside from the money (as author of
the book I have assigned a percentage of the royalties
to Míctla), the publicity will give us the boost we
need.

All the monies that have come in from the first
edition of my book have gone totally to support Míctla
Publications, Inc. The book retails for $8.50, and it
is expected that this book will give Míctla a means to
implant itself. Still, the realities of minority publishing demand that we continually seek out resources--
from manpower to money--to support the many dreams we
have.

It has been a trying year. The road home: home
to where I, as a Chicano writer, can feel more alive
than ever before. In developing the idea of Míctla and
in seeking out others to help it come true, I further
defined the parameters of my own existence. The inter-
action with Tony, Dr. Gardea, Eddie, and countless others imbued me with a sense of liberation that is projected in the title of my first real book: *Canto Y
Grito Mi Liberación*. To sing out and shout my liberation is the ultimate message in my mind, for in singing
it, shouting it, crying it, caressing it, loving it,
spurting it, and adamantly affirming it, one affirms
one's human existence on a spiritual, emotional, intellectual, and sensual level. Self-publishing was the
impetus to my liberation as a Chicano human being; it
was the affirmation of my sense of self through others,
and I realize that I exist only within the bronze context of my people.

I have slept with Míctla, eaten with Míctla, dreamt
Míctla, thought Míctla, loved and hated Míctla, needed
Míctla, enslaved Míctla, and now liberated Míctla. It
is with mixed feelings that I have turned the helm over
to Tony, for in the period of eight months, Míctla has
had two presidents--I was the first. And now in the
spirit of a youthful movement, it is deeply touching to

see Tony becoming another decisive *carnal* creating out of the muck and mire surrounding us his own version of Míctla.

Our formula was basic enough: sense a need that went beyond our own needs, couple them, and then seek out people and resources. We were not afraid to tackle areas of expertise that always had been closed to us-- we bluntly and brashly crashed in and thus developed Míctla...it feels good to be home...home at last.

Home, but in the type of home that a wandering mind can only inhabit for brief sketches of time, for the lust for total expression is dominant, and it demands a continuous involvement in all that is happening around me.

As a Chicano writer, I find that my first priority is in being a Chicano involved in the movement, and if there is time afterward, then I find that it is as a part-time writer that I must exist. It is galling having to wait for interludes ladened with brevity to write the things that demand to be written, so much so that inspiration becomes a demonic thing that spontaneously explodes/implodes, but time is usually not opportune. Even this very moment is stolen--frankly, brutally stolen from a program I am currently working for as a counseling supervisor. Brief moments in which to write, and my senses complicate my very life-style, for I view many different worlds and time-frames. Affected by emotional valuations of barrio life and imprisonment, moved by illogical probability, and galvanized by time's mutability, I sit when possible to encapsulate a bilingual/bicultural world and let it all surge out:

> *con fuerza*
> *cuando la vida*
> culminates in moments
> burning anguish
> deeper into *mente/alma;*
> prodigious feelings
> flutter *locamente*
> *por mi ser,*
> it is never enough
> just spurting out
> one's quixoticness,
> *uno debe de actuar*

                    resolutely,
                  writing is escape
                  into reality,

and it can be hectic feeling oneself imposing on oneself, but its beauty is that the hectic, turbulent, and
wanton thoughts prevailing in my mind force me to live
on a schizophrenic level, whereby I continuously rede-
fine existence.

    It is not academic, it is not pragmatic, it is
not structure--though those things are vital in their
own way--it is ultimate acceptance of vital processes
and then dealing as passionately with them as possible.
Life for the artist is awareness of infinite possibilities and interacting as completely as one can with por-
tentous events so that protagonists and antagonists
merge into oceanic humanity. Thus I can only supply
mental resources to the writer-bitch/devil residing in
my gut/soul. What flows out is complexity mixed with
idiocy, a panoramic view as clown, victim, oppressor,
and deracinator. Pedantry belongs in archives, not in
the blood and soul of writers--and writers have no
justification for the madness they indite. There are
no bounds, just the infinity of language, the nuances
of words, and the vexations of sounds that commingle
with all senses. It is loving sensuously and abysmally,
it is soaring and exploding, and not even drugs can
compare with the awesome high of creating out of sun-
dry, everyday life moments that transport the total
self.

    Because experience can only be lived, no one can
create parameters for it...irrespective of treatises
and papers on the dynamics of poetry. An academician
cannot hope to capture the elusiveness of art in his
constricting formats, and the artist cannot stop to e-
valuate his art form before he creates it. It is universal to take human struggle and focus it artistical-
ly--and man's condition is predicated on struggle.

    As a writer I am the realizer of mine own insecu-
rity, for life is flux lived by bits and pieces of in-
teraction, and a lifetime can range from less than a
second to more than a hundred years. Coming to grips
with my mortality has afforded me the luxury of writing
about it; realizing my limitations has paved the way
toward making decisions about setting up a publishing

vehicle; becoming aware of my ability with language
has given me the courage to dare to publish; and loving
life and humanity has filled my being with a sense of
worth.

The writer without a place to publish must generate his own courage--it will be adversity that will
keep him going. Patrons (in the old sense) and grants
will not determine the validity of his expression nor
facilitate it. The only determinant will be his own
psychic/philosophical approach to his life. As a writer, I welcome adversity, I welcome causes that compel
me to go beyond myself. Because of the fact that I
have a people; the fact that our very survival is in-
cumbent on the whims of an out-there, dominant society;
the fact that the death of my culture and language
threatens us in many different, leering ways; and the
fact that as a human being I must record history and
struggle, I must write and write and write.

Because our social reality is prohibitive, Chicanos must either kowtow to circumstance or create circumstance, and within the movement we go beyond the
moment. We, in fact, are creating moments that stretch
out, as if eternalizing our existence.

Like other Chicano writers, I seek ways and means
to change social conditions. My primary concern is to
develop linkages to communications resources and to but-
tress the spirit of my people, in hopes that our children will grow up with a world that shall afford them
the opportunity to live humanly.

It is important that the writer write about his
experience and knowledge; it is doubly important that
he write with feeling and spirit--for writing is an art
that must express the inner man and his dealings with
the social environment. It is important that the writer view language as a highly flexible tool--that he
understand that all words are usable. Language must
be communicative and aesthetic; it must have all the
ranges of man's mind/soul--from mountain peaks to val-
leys and plains; it must be choppy like the sea, gur-
gling like a brook, rippling like the air, tintinnabu-
lating like cathedral bells, explosive like cannon,
soothing like symphonic overtures. It is not run to
your dictionaries, but rather listen to the speech patterns of humanity and read all you can with an ear for
language.

The self-published writer must have more than just
hope, he must have a new world view to offer a sated
reading public. He must be creative, for he does not
have publicity avenues nor distribution mechanisms to
sell his works. He has only the validity of his ideas
and views and the beauty of his linguistic expression.
   Most self-published Chicanos have a dual-language
process to offer the reader, a way of merging different
cultures and linguistic perceptions to project the tertiary reality of a people heretofore socially invisible.
The Chicano writer is developing a new literature, and
thus his writings are new, explosive, and exploratory
for the reader. Chicano creativity, by its very existence, creates new parameters and dimensions. The mono-
lingual writer must likewise create new visages--he
must go deeper into his existence and out of that wel-
ter of mixed feelings come up with new perspectives.
He also must write for a cause--a cause that existenti-
ally transcends each moment and adds to the quality of
life. A writer cannot afford to be afraid of languages
--he must not prefer certain words, but must find con-
ciliation to language and all its dynamics. There are
no twenty-five-cent words--there are words and words,
and all can be used to exemplify and further define the
life process. Language exists to serve man, and man
must experiment constantly with language to better define his humanity. All shades of humanity are valid
and worthy of expression and definition. It is not
difficult to write and/or self-publish, all it takes
is determination and self-generating will.
   What one gets from self-publication and from selling one's work to a public that wants to read one's
outpouring is gratification that cannot come from being
an author for an established company. After self-publication, I knew the beauty of total creation of a
book. I shall never forget the awesome sense of creativity when *Canto Y Grito Mi Liberación* first came off
the press and then was bound. I had been involved in
every stage of production in one way or another and
thus felt this book to be very much an extension of my
reality. Time and opportunity no longer coincide, and
my following books shall be fully produced, aside from
the writing of them, by others. Still the enrichment
of having been an instrument for the setting up of a
Chicano publishing house and having had to coordinate

the necessary resources to publish my book did give me
ways to better understand my human proportions in relation to my people and other people.
   I began with fear of failure and ended up with the
realization that one can only live as much as possible
and make the most out of one's celerity through life.

        it begins
        fleetingly flighty--
        it terrifies,
           boggles the mind,
           yet, it demands so much
           and
           one cannot afford the luxury of fear;

        days and nights, weeks on end,
        spent
              bent and almost crushed,
        waiting for final proofs and copy
              to mixed-feelingly correct...

        then, one day, the final proof is done,
          the printing starts
                          and then the binding
          and then the running around
          taking orders for the book;

        the word gets around,
        coming and going you feel good,
        orders from all over
        and you are home,
              you are home...for good.

    I am home: not to El Paso nor with any publishing
house, but home as a writer regarded for his art/craft.
Míctla is also home--not to me, but to itself--and
Míctla can now make it on its own. We both were instru-
ments for one another.

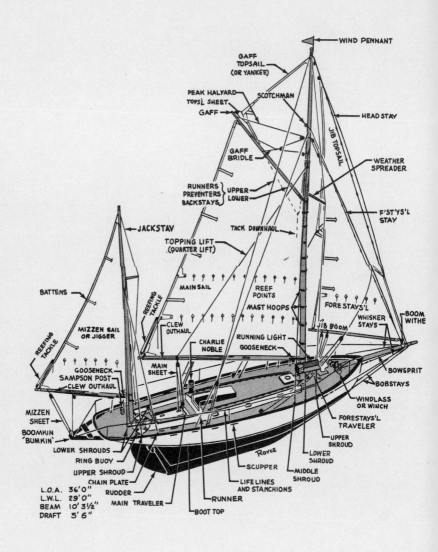

WIND PENNANT

GAFF TOPSAIL (OR YANKEE)

SCOTCHMAN

HEAD STAY

PEAK HALYARD

TOPS'L SHEET

GAFF

JIB TOPSAIL

WEATHER SPREADER

GAFF BRIDLE

UPPER LOWER

F'ST'YS'L STAY

RUNNERS PREVENTERS BACKSTAYS

JACKSTAY

TACK DOWNHAUL

TOPPING LIFT (QUARTER LIFT)

BATTENS

MAIN SAIL

REEF POINTS

MAST HOOPS

FORE STAYS'L

WHISKER STAYS

BOOM WITHE

REEFING TACKLE

MIZZEN SAIL OR JIGGER

CLEW OUTHAUL

JIB BOOM

REEFING TACKLE

CHARLIE NOBLE

RUNNING LIGHT

GOOSENECK

GOOSENECK

SAMPSON POST

CLEW OUTHAUL

MAIN SHEET

BOWSPRIT

BOBSTAYS

MIZZEN SHEET

WINDLASS OR WINCH

BOOMKIN 'BUMKIN'

FORESTAYS'L TRAVELER

LOWER SHROUDS

RING BUOY

UPPER SHROUD

CHAIN PLATE

RUDDER

MAIN TRAVELER

SCUPPER

LIFE LINES AND STANCHIONS

RUNNER

BOOT TOP

UPPER SHROUD

LOWER SHROUD

MIDDLE SHROUD

Royce

L.O.A. 36' 0"
L.W.L. 29' 0"
BEAM 10' 3½"
DRAFT 5' 6"

An illustration of an older yawl from the fifth edition
of *Royce's Sailing Illustrated*. Drawn by Pat Royce.
Copyright © 1971 by Patrick M. Royce.

ROYCE'S

SAILING ILLUSTRATED

by Patrick M. Royce

PAT ROYCE was a commercial artist until he took up sailing as a hobby. From that hobby came his first book, **Sailing Illustrated**, self-published in 1956 and now in its fifth edition. It was followed by **Trailer-Boating Illustrated**, for portable power boats, now undergoing a major revision for its third edition. This was followed by **Junior Sailing Illustrated** and courses in sailing and trailer boat operation. His headquarters is the West Coast boating center, Newport Beach, California.

The phone rang. A university student was contacting successful businessmen to discover how they had started their businesses. For the purposes of her term paper success was defined as the necessity to employ at least six persons. My wife laughed replying, "Sorry, we can't help because we aren't 'successful.' We've been in business sixteen years, but we've avoided hiring that first employee."

After a long pause, the confused student hung up the phone. My wife looked up mischievously from behind her desk piled high with orders, needling me with one of her favorite lines, "Just when did you say you were going to put me on the payroll?"

Our first book, *Sailing Illustrated*, published in 1956, opened a new, wonderful world beyond our expectations. We had been working on the book in our spare time for about five years while learning to sail. We found that sailing books in stores and libraries did not provide information we could apply. Those available tried to describe the complex sport of sailing in a foreign *written* language we couldn't understand, producing endless snafus.

After a major foul-up which left me overboard twenty minutes one stormy night in the Atlantic Ocean off Staten Island, the first mate gave me a dirty grin as she quipped, "Why don't you *draw* the book on sailing you are looking for?"

At the time I was a technical and advertising artist trying to break out of the regimented art mills into the magazine illustration business in my spare time. My wife's remark prompted me to put away the paint brushes and begin recording our sailing mistakes in the international language of illustrations. The size of the book was of major importance because it had to be carried in my pocket for quick reference on the boat or dock.

We finally found a publisher interested in our developing book, but this contact fortunately proved a disaster. The publisher wanted to completely rewrite our book himself after which misguided effort he could no longer afford to let us own the copyright. Because of this involvement, other publishers wouldn't touch it either. The answer: publish the book ourselves without having to compromise with the whims of other publishers. Our hobby became our business.

The total cost of publishing our first two thousand books was $2,000, leaving a couple of dollars still in our bank account. This cost included renting an IBM typewriter, renting a post-office box, purchasing a business license, and printing the books. On weekends we made the rounds of book and marine stores hoping to make maximum profit by selling directly to dealers--our first major mistake. Some of their bills weren't paid for two years. We needed distributors who would earn their percentage by handling deliveries, keeping records, and making collections.

We started with a couple of well-known book distributors who did a poor job with slow collections. Soon we began to receive letters from readers in a variety of businesses asking to sell or distribute our products. While we have over thirty distributors at present, they represent such a wide variety of organizations that we still don't know how we could find them in any other way if we had to start from the beginning again. Although we receive considerable publicity from distributors showing our products in their catalogs, our best distributors are small, hardworking outfits with minimum overhead who found us; we did not find them.

We bought some ads in the beginning, yet they didn't pay for themselves in spite of my advertising background. What launched our book sales besides person-to-person recommendations was book reviews. Over eighty orders resulted from the first review in *Sea and Pacific Motor Boat* magazine, with additional orders coming from farther outposts throughout the Pacific which the magazine reached at a later date. Five months later orders finally started coming from Australia due to this one review.

A major lesson we learned from reviews is to push the ideas others have about our books, since readers have considerable faith in reviews from their favorite magazines, instead of pushing what the publisher himself may feel is important. If you have an outstanding service product that can withstand the criticism of experts in that field, many excellent ways are open to start selling your book which are far superior to just buying advertising space.

Our sales curve has gone continually upward, dipping only in 1964. Sailing has taught us the lesson of 180° thinking, which is also applicable to publishing. If standard methods or your present idea doesn't seem to be working out, consider the opposite approach. You may suddenly realize that what was successful in one situation is wrong in another. For example, instead of buying advertising like our competitors, we have continually invested our time, effort, and money into improving our sailing books through the years.

We are a practical team: my wife takes care of our distributors and individual orders, leaving me to research new ideas, teach sailing, answer correspondence, and work on our boating books and courses. From 1960 to 1971, when time permitted we offered full-day, year-around private sailing lessons to know the needs of the new sailors. This continuous exposure to the new sailor gave us the edge to keep ahead of other sailing authors, as many East Coast writers have a short boating season without a continuous exposure to the new sailor's problems.

Advantages of being a nonconforming self-publisher are many. After what seemed endless years working in offices on both coasts, I prefer to keep oddball hours and to work at home. A normal office routine is good for mechanical operations, but is only marginally creative, because ideas and inventions have yet to learn to arrive in the eight-to-five pattern. We try to break our patterns in various ways such as studying ideas or problems sometimes at our home office, sometimes on our boat at anchor or underway, and sometimes in our mobile office with mountain, ocean, or desert panorama in the background. We vary our sleeping patterns, sleeping late and working late one day, then waking up at 2 or 3 A.M. another day, especially when facing a difficult problem or situation. For example, part of this chapter was written in Mexico in our mobile office, and much of the rest on our boat in San Pedro harbor while we were also studying the operations of large vessels for a future publication. I typed the final copy in our home office wearing my favorite working clothes, swim trunks.

The change of hours and scenery, plus spirited discussions with experts in the field, gives a considerable edge on conformist competitors. As we found the hard way, even simple ideas for our boating publications may prove elusive under the best office conditions. One of the toughest ideas for our *Junior Sailing Illustrated* continually eluded us. I was working at it too hard, developing twenty-twenty tunnel vision. Something was wrong but we couldn't find the answer. Saying to ourselves, "To heck with sailing, let's forget the whole idea," we headed for the desert in our mobile office. Five days afterwards, when I was sitting on a sand dune with an empty mind, the ideas suddenly began to flow so rapidly that the typewriter and recorder could hardly keep pace. The problem was a basic concept we had been following in this book which had common acceptance in similar sailing books. No one seemed to have taken the time to fully analyze the idea before. That vacation paid for itself handsomely, but I shudder to think how I would have resolved the problem in a New York office.

We have found that a self-publisher should have enough practical art *and* printing knowledge to recognize the capabilities and limitations of printing methods. It is essential to know how to turn out a good quality book with minimum cost. Instead of having type set, we type our pages on a 1957-vintage IBM typewriter. The uneven right margin, called a ragged right in printing, seems to relax readers, especially in technical publications. We have a printer reproduce our typed pages and illustrations by photo offset.

The ability to make simple, accurate line illustrations to demonstrate concepts is a major advantage in publications such as ours. Most of my art school training seemed unproductive, wasteful, and often far from reality. I really learned during my art-agency apprenticeship and during employment at various advertising and technical agencies, where I developed, tasted, and acquired practical methods to turn out quality line illustrations in minimum time with minimum effort. Quite a few of the sailboats we detail in our books take a month or two each to complete.

While the self-publisher pays the bills and takes the risks, he is just a member of his team, which includes the copyright office, the printer, the post office, and his certified accountant.

Our copyright, secured through the Copyright Office in Washington, D.C., is our best friend. We have a sample copyright which we have carefully filled out and which we use for reference when filling out a copyright form. It is too easy to overlook a seemingly minor detail that may disastrously cancel out a copyright, our only protection.

Our angel is a printing salesman who has had our account since 1956. He analyzes the job, provides price quotations, makes recommendations when asked, and is directly responsible for our job. Book printing operations are much more complex than most people realize, and snafus must be expected by both you and the printer. At that time a highly trained, competent printing salesman who is the middleman between us and the printer has to come up with answers. For example, we once received a full printing of the wrong edition as the printer used the wrong negatives, which was not our responsibility.

The post office is our partner. We explain our new products to the postmaster, let him have a sample of each book, then follow his recommendations as closely as possible. Since postal employees see enough sour faces during the day, the value of a smile and an easy-going attitude with postal employees cannot be over-stressed.

We expect shipping damage but find that it can be minimized with good planning. Maximum book weight per box should be under thirty pounds. The books should be packaged snugly in a strong cardboard box wrapped both ways using three-inch, nylon-cord-reinforced adhesive tape. We put an address label on the top of the box and another on the side in case either label is damaged. We use self-adhesive address labels which can't be removed.

While books sent to the South Pole, North Pole, Vietnam, and Kuwait arrive in a couple of days, book-rate packages to Hawaii, even without shipping strikes, can take up to four months. We usually send single orders to Hawaii by air mail as a matter of goodwill, absorbing the extra postage cost ourselves. Canadian orders of any size are a pain in the neck since both Canada and the United States seem to require endless customs forms.

We have found that the self-publisher should choose his certified public accountant carefully, then have him set up bookkeeping procedures and process income tax to avoid that first mistake, which may seem small to everyone but the tax collector.

We constantly analyze the quality of our output. Many authors are happy to be continually on a treadmill producing many volumes sometimes under various names, sometimes compromising quality. We have chosen to do the opposite: we publish a few volumes of the best quality we can produce. Our first book, *Sailing Illustrated*, required five years part time to research; our next book, *TrailerBoating Illustrated*, took three years full time. While a few pages are retyped three to four times, most are redone at least ten times to put our ideas across accurately in our limited space. My creative working period is limited from November through May, with the rest of the year devoted to developing new ideas by research, testing, and our sailing lessons. While magazine writers may be prolific turning out endless articles with a short life span, the book author usually needs considerable thinking time to produce a book of worthwhile importance for a limited or long period of time.

Finally, what did we expect from publishing our own books? In the beginning we wanted a small, simple operation so we could be independent and masters of our own decisions. We started on a part-time basis, paying for our books with the salary from my full-time job. After a couple of years, sales were sufficient for us to begin working full time on our publications. Financially we want a comfortable life in which we can meet our responsibilities and pay our bills, and have the time and money to do a lot of sailing and power boating, which in turn will improve our publications. Our dealers, distributors, and especially our readers make this kind of life possible. Though we've had several offers from other publishers, we see little

point in merging or expanding for I feel all that can
result is more overhead with no sufficiently improved
service for our boating readers...who haven't given
us a bad check since we first started our business.
    Our public relations effort is minimal. We don't
belong to the Elks, Rotary, yacht clubs, or follow the
society cocktail circuit. We do contribute columns to
boating magazines and tabloids without consideration
of payment. We study our competition big and small,
try to know their operations, objectives, and problems.
    We have had booths at the yearly Long Beach Sail-
boat Show to hear from our readers. New approaches develop, a couple of mistakes we hadn't realized were
brought to our attention, and we ended up with some
new dealers and distributors. The self-publisher whose
book is about a hobby, sport, or similar subject may
accomplish more for his investment at a show than he
will by buying advertising space in magazines and newspapers.
    In addition to our publications, we've taken on
some pretty hot political causes to help the boating
public without interest in personal gain. Basically
these battles deal with local, state, and national gov-
ernment organizations, often in the charge of non-boat-
ing-oriented people trying to save us at their profit
and our expense as they often blunder through. Our
stand has given others confidence to battle big brother
from time to time. We feel that other self-publishers
who are experts in their field have similar responsibilities. Yet instead of expecting thanks be thankful
if not too many bricks are heaved your way afterwards.
For example, we recently produced and paid out of pocket for a twenty-four-page booklet in answer to show
why the U.S. Coast Guard demands for licensing were
not only impractical, but how in the past fifteen years
the Guard has shown minimum interest in boating safety
for the public, which was its primary responsibility.
    A major frustration till now was that we didn't
have the means to pass along such self-publishing information as we wished we could have had when we first
started business. Self-publishing may not be the solution for every writer trying to get his work to the
public, but it has a much better place in the publishing field than is presently realized.
    Distributors have observed with justification

that we operate our business like a country store. Yet its foundation of honesty and craftsmanship seems a much more important factor. The self-publisher expecting instant overnight success may instead expect a disaster. For the plodding, curious, nonconforming perfectionist rankled by stifling confines, one-upmanship, and battles of nerves of the eight-to-five office routine, self-publishing may be another matter.

If you know your subject or learn it thoroughly and feel you can do a better job than the competition, then take the time and effort to produce a superior product... Self-publishing is a humbling, wonderful way of life with fringe benefits far beyond the dreams of the person satisfied with menial office routine.

WHY ASSEMBLING

by Richard Kostelanetz

RICHARD KOSTELANETZ *is the co-inspiration (with Henry James Korn) behind* Assembling, *an annual journal of "otherwise unpublishable creative work." Residing in New York, where he was born in 1940, he is a poet, critic, and cultural historian, who is the author of several books and the editor of over a dozen more. In addition to* Assembling *(Box 1967, Brooklyn, N.Y. 11202), he self-published a collection of his poetry,* Visual Language, *in 1970.*

For Henry James Korn and Michael Metz

> *As an unreconstructed anarchist, I still must
> consider the solution of this issue [proprie-
> tary control of the media by the tribe of in-
> termediary bureaucrats] easy, easy in theory,
> easy in practice; if we do not apply it, it is
> for moral reasons, sluggishness, timidity,
> getting involved in what is not one's business,
> etc. The way to get rid of dummy intermedi-
> aries is by direct action.*
>
> --Paul Goodman,
> "The Chance for Popular Culture" (1949).

Assembling grew out of an oppressive crisis in avant-
garde literary communication; for while experiments in
writing seemed both possible and necessary, genuinely
innovative manuscripts found increasing resistance
from both book and periodical publishers. *Assembling*
was established in 1970 by Henry James Korn and myself,
two young writers who had known each other since childhood. (His older sister and my younger sister were
best friends in high school.) Five years older than
Korn, I was already a full-time freelance, hyperactive
mostly as an essayist and anthologist. I discovered
that, in contrast to my expository prose, my visual
poetry and comparably eccentric fiction encountered
considerably more difficulty in getting published.
Even the best of these pieces seemed to take at least
two years to get into any sort of public print (at
which point, curiously, a few would be anthologized
with remarkable speed); and I had good reason to suspect that, as often as not, the periodical editors accepting them were implicitly honoring, or flattering,
my critical-anthological activities. The problem was

scarcely personal, however, because other work in such
veins, including much that I critically regarded as
excellent, was similarly blocked. Korn, on the other
hand, had produced some remarkably witty and inventive
fictions, only one of which had ever been publicly
published; and his work as a museum administrator made
him aware of grave problems in cultural communication.
I suppose that my own anthological experience also
gave me a compiler's passion for making available a
goodly amount of avant-garde literary material that
might otherwise be lost.

    It also became clear, at the onset of U.S. pub-
lishing's most severe recent depression, that commercial houses were less and less inclined to take risks
with any kind of counterconventional work and/or unes-
tablished authors. Among the principal reasons are
not only editorial ignorance and opacity but a gross
rise in the costs of book production and the increasing
profit-hunger of even the more "enlightened" publishing
firms. The best seller has become their all-engrossing
ideal, while interest in commercially more modest work,
such as anything avant-garde or unknown, had declined
dangerously. Only one one-man collection of visual
poetry, for instance, has ever been commerically published in the United States, even though "concrete" is
reportedly "faddish"; and since that single book, N. H.
Pritchard's *The Matrix* (1970), was neither reviewed nor
touted, it seemed unlikely that any others would ever
appear--another example of how the rule of precedent
in literary commerce produces de facto censorship. Established literary periodicals, on the other hand, were
dying or retrenching, while few of the new ones were
open to experimental work. For several reasons, therefore, the future of avant-garde writing seemed increas-
ingly doubtful.

    In the preface to our initial issue, I noted:

> *As young writers of stylistically "different"*
> *poetry and prose, we faced not only the in-*
> *evitable objections to our youth, but also*
> *the equally inevitable resistances to our way-*
> *ward literary purposes. And so we wanted an*
> *institution that would publish alternative*
> *work by imaginative artists who genuinely be-*
> *lieved in what they did. Since rejections*

often came with the excuse, particularly from those editors pretending to sympathy, that "our printer can't handle this," it seemed best to overcome this obstacle by direct action--by becoming one's own publisher, which is more practicable in this era of photographic reproduction processes; for the oldest truth is that, when other demands are more pressing, the writer must do more than just write.

Somewhat influenced by a beautiful German book called *Omnibus* (1969), we hit upon what we think is the most appropriate structure for a cooperative self-publishing channel. In brief, *Assembling* invites writers and artists whom we know to be doing unusual work, which we broadly characterize as "otherwise unpublishable," to contribute a thousand copies of up to four 8.5- by 11-inch pages of whatever they want to include. Since each contributor is responsible for arranging, by whatever means and funds available, for the production of his own work, he becomes his own sub-self-publisher, so to speak. There is no doubt that writers should usually be paid for what they do; but just as serious poets often give much of their work away gratis, so there are times when every artist feels it worth a few dollars and/or a little effort to put into public print a work that he likes but could not otherwise place. (Indeed, self-publication at such modest cost could stand as an ultimate test of creative seriousness--not just in Russia but in the United States too.) In practice, self-printing turns out to be less forbidding than it initially seems, for not only do academics have access to xerox machines (and did one writer call upon a family printing business), but recently developed offset and Itek processes can commercially reproduce one side into a thousand sheets for less than ten dollars and both sides for less than fifteen. We advised our invited collaborators to put their names on their work, as we ran no table of contents, and to center their contributions toward the right, leaving at least an inch on the left-hand margin, because *Assembling* promised to collate the contents alphabetically and then return three bound books to each contributor. The remaining copies would ide-

ally be sold through bookstores and the mails, hopefully defraying the costs of binding, mailing, etc.
Since all copyrights, which are the literary form of
"property," were returned to the contributors, *Assembling* could make no money from subsequent reprints; and
once the thousand copies were gone, it would be impossible to "reprint" the entire issue.

Since both Korn and I were inclined to transcend
the boundaries of writing, we opened the book to artists of all sorts. Our form letter invited "poetry,
fiction, graphic art, designs, architectural proposals,
or any other ideas adaptable to print." As we were also trying to abolish the restricting prerogatives of
editorial authority, we agreed to accept everything
contributed by those invited. (Our invitation mentioned our "reserving the right to exclude a contribution
for reasons unforeseen or in case of libel." I was
thinking of egregious slander when I wrote that, but it
remains an option we have never considered exercising.)
We abrogated editorial authority not because we were
lazy but because we wanted a structural contrast to the
"restrictive, self-serving nature of traditional editorial processes." Since we are collators rather than
true publishers, we customarily refuse requests to
handle the printing, for necessity demands that counterconventional writers learn some essential points a-
bout reproduction, such as discovering the method(s)
most conducive to their particular work. As a result,
each entry ideally represents the best that each contributor can do untouched (or unretouched) by grubby
editorial hands. As "compilers" rather than true publishers, we also avoided the editorial pains (or plea-
sures) of rejecting anything, along with the anxiety
of needing to fulfill a predetermined concept; and given the elasticity of our production methods, we never
faced the predicament of accepting more material than
could be "accommodated by our precious space."

The only editorial control left to us was the invitation itself, so that just as unfamiliar would-be
collaborators were asked to contribute examples of
their work (before receiving an invitation), so a few
contributors to one *Assembling* were not invited to the
next. The almost paradoxical reason was not that we
thought their work "no good," whatever that might be,
or that we wanted to impose a particular style or

taste, but that we were obliged, in principle, to keep
the medium committed to alternate, otherwise unpublishable imaginative work--a domain that was, to be sure,
elastically defined. (None of these unreinvited people ever asked to contribute again, perhaps because of
awe or disgust with the rest of the book; and none, to
my knowledge, have founded their own collaborative periodicals.) "Don't hesitate to send material that has
made the editorial rounds," our initial invitation
said, "but remember that there's a difference between
manuscripts that are just too freaky to get published
elsewhere and those that are simply not one's own best
work." It continued: "The long-range goal of *Assembling* is opening the editorial/industrial complex to
alternatives and possibilities. The short-range goal
is providing the means for unpublished and unpublishable work to see print light, partly to see what kin-
dred spirits and spooks are doing." We also promised
to type and print, at house expense, biographical
notes, in part to introduce the contributors to each
other.

   Large cartons poured into our homes and post-office box during the summer, as our one hundred fifty
invitations produced forty responses. Late in August,
two months after our announced deadline, Korn and I
rented a small panel truck and lugged a half ton of
paper to a commercial collator (whose services cost us
three hundred dollars). The bound books came back a
few weeks later, and contributors' copies were immediately put into the mail. (The post office remains an
innocent collaborator in the development of experimental writing, for it is largely by posted print that
most of its creators know each other's work.) We sent
possible reviewers a query, since available copies
were so few; and though we honored all requests received, only four reviews appeared, three of them pos-
itive--in a Belgian new-poetry journal, a New York undergraduate newspaper, and a Detroit rock magazine.
(The single negative notice rather dumbly criticised
the absence of editorial authority!)

   Our copyright line read: "© 1970 for automatic
assignment with the printing of this notice to the individual contributors." However, we subsequently discovered that this was invalid. Since copyrights must
be connected to a particular name, it should have

said: "©1970 by Assembling Press. All rights reassigned to their respective authors upon request." We
also made the mistake of incorporating (which cost us
another hundred), in part to protect against personal
liabilities; but we later discovered that this precau-
tion was unnecessary, as long as we published an editorial disclaimer (for "the views expressed herein")
on the title page. Indeed, since we eschewed editorial
authority, responsibility for all material definitely
belonged to the individual sub-publishers. We dis-in-
corporated simply by letting Gnilbmessa, Inc., which is
assembling spelled backwards, die of bankruptcy. We
also opened a checking account, which was both need-
lessly expensive and, in practice, rarely used.

The results of such self-publishing licence not
only confirmed our initial polemical point--both *Assembling* itself and most of its contents were unlike anything seen before--but the book also showed the possibilities and productivity available to society if artists were granted absolute creative freedom. Some
pieces were poetry or fiction, while others were visual
graphics or words mixed with pictures. Some contributors resorted to commercial reproductive processes (of
varying quality), while a few used handpresses. Scott
Hyde contributed an especially elegant multicolored
photograph. One contribution must have been individually hand-stained, as the shape of each brown blot was
different. The well-known rock critic Richard Meltzer
sent us, as he explained, "a thousand pages of all different shit (including the only copy of the only novel
I ever wrote) so each one-page thing is gonna be a
whole different show-stopper." Some contributors exploited such anti-editorial opportunity to surpass
their earlier work, such as the novelist Nancy Weber,
whose handwritten story, "Dear Mother and Dad," was
subsequently anthologized. Others, like the poet David
Ignatow, introduced work (an excerpt from his journals)
that would later appear in a book. The stipulated page
size became an inadvertent constraint, as one writer
offered a thousand artistically doctored baseball
cards, "each with a literary move." We were embarrassed to tell him that the available collating machines
could not handle such work.

What was most impressive about *Assembling* was the
sheer variety of counterconventional alternatives, as

individual contributions could be roughly characterized
as visual poetry, verbal poetry, abstract photography,
playlets, minimal poetry, verbal collage, stream-of-
consciousness narrative, representational graphics,
picture-accompanied words, scenarios for happenings,
sculptural documentation, personal journal, esthetic
manifesto, etc.; for the hundred flowers blooming here
were really different. A few pieces could best be termed "other"; and the only signature on one poem, its
face suspiciously turned backwards, read "Richard M.
Nixon." The overall constraint of alphabetical order
generated some peculiar juxtapositions that, in turn,
made the whole book resemble a loony collage. It
struck me afterwards that very few contributors por-
trayed sexual experience, partly because the liberties
that artists now want to take and that are blocked by
established channels, deal not with content but concept and form.

The contributions were uneven, to be sure, in both
artistry and technology (printing quality), but such
discrepancies epitomize *Assembling*'s characteristic
style and integrity, as well as perhaps its charm. "If
you don't turn on to something," one contributor noted,
"all you have to do is turn the page." Such blatant
chaos marked *Assembling* as a counterbook or anti-book
(though *not* a "nonbook") which nonetheless gains its
cohering definition (which is approximately repeatable)
from its unprecedented diversity. In my admittedly
biased opinion, more than half of the material has
been uncommonly interesting, while a few contributions
are awesomely extraordinary. It is more important to
judge that very few pieces, if any, would have otherwise gotten beyond private musing into public print.
(Korn and I also awarded, in total secrecy, a booby
prize to "that contribution most likely to have appeared elsewhere" and thus needing *Assembling* least--a
rather fine story by a sometime contributor to the
slicks.) Collaborators in the first *Assembling* included such eminences as the painters Edward Ruscha and
Arakawa; the poets Robert Lax, Keith and Rosemarie
Waldrop, Vito Acconci, and Bernadette Mayer; the play-
wright Lee Baxandall; the novelists Marvin Cohen,
George Chambers, Arno Karlen, and Raymond Federman; the
composer Arthur Layzer; the polyartists Liam O'Galla-
gher, Dan Graham, and Alan Sondheim; along with a few

artist-writers making their initial public appearances.
Most of the contributors were pleased, not only
with the collaborative concept but with individual
works, so that we decided to do the book again in 1971.
Second Assembling, as we called it, materialized out
of nothing in response, like its predecessor, to a
summer's correspondence. Many of the same artists and
writers joined us a second time--Elizabeth Ginsberg,
Tom Ahern, Gay Beste, Jan Herman, Rosalie Frank, and
Roni Hoffman; but more than half of the fifty-two contributors were new, including such eminences as the
film-maker Stan VanDer-Beek (who neglected, however,
to send enough copies); the poets Robin Magowan, C. P.
Graham, Tom Ockerse, and Ruth Krauss; the fictionists
Russell Edson and M. D. Elevitch; and the polyartists
Ken Friedman and Bern Porter. Michael Metz, a process-
documenting artist who contributed to the first book,
took charge of production for the second, not only designing a stunning cover (which, this time, wrapped
around the spine), but also joining Korn and me as a
"co-compiler."
And its preface became yet more assertive, if not
strident, in part because the closure crisis had become more severe, but also because I had spent most of
the previous year drafting *The End of Intelligent Writing* (1973). In the second preface, I said:

> *Anyone who gets [experimental] writing fre-
> quently into print is bombarded with requests
> for advice: Where can one publish? Who?
> Why not? And while one could give specific
> suggestions before [in the sixties], now the
> answer is invariably "nowhere," accompanied
> by a brief and inevitably bitter analysis of
> the current predicament....The terrible point
> is not that "one can't get published," but
> that nobody is publishing anymore. The fresh
> fruits we bear are turning into sour grapes,
> while the only money falling from those trees
> of dollar bills is counterfeit and/or con-
> federate; and terror of a kind rules the
> roost. As writers largely lead isolated
> lives and have excessively sensitive egos,
> they tend to take rejections as strictly per-
> sonal; but when nearly everything in certain*

*veins is kept unpublished, the problems are
not individual but collective--and, thus,
amenable to political, or more specifically
literary-political, solutions. Since it
would be naive to solicit help from elsewhere, the initiative in introducing any
New Art to the reading public must first of
all come from the artists themselves. Our
guiding rule in an acclimating task comparable to that confronting Ezra Pound and his
allies sixty years ago must be this: WHAT-
EVER NEEDS TO BE DONE, WE, AS WRITERS, SHALL
PROBABLY HAVE TO DO OURSELVES.*

After years of courting established publishers on
behalf of experimental writing--not only my own but
that by others--I am reluctantly coming to the conclusion that more than half of the consequential literature produced in this country today remains unpublished. The more closely one examines the situation, the
clearer it becomes that only temporary idiosyncracy or
lapse can explain the commercial release of such genuinely innovative works as Pritchard's *The Matrix* and
Eecchhooeess (1971), Richard Horn's *Encyclopedia* (1969),
Madeline Gins' *Word Rain* (1969), Kenneth Gangemi's *Olt*
(1969), Raymond Federman's *Double or Nothing* (1971), or
G. S. Gravenson's *The Sweetmeat Saga* (1971). Indicatively, most of those consequential novels cited above
came from smaller commercial publishers. But it is a
more telling fact that some of the past decade's most
important American avant-garde texts were self-published: Edward Ruscha's widely admired picture books (especially *Thirty-Four Parking Lots* [1967]), Dick Higgins'
Jefferson's Birthday/Postface (1964) and *Foew&ombwhnw*
(1969), Russell Edson's *The Brain Kitchen* (1965), John
Giorno's *Raspberry* (1967), Charles Henri Ford's *Spare
Parts* (1968), Dan Graham's *End Moments* (1969), Wally
Depew's *Once* (1971), Vito Acconci's *Book Four* (1968),
among others.
"Ahead of us, especially if the censorship presently implicit in the editorial/industrial complex
becomes complete," my second preface concludes, " is a
writing situation comparable to that current in Soviet
Russia, where nearly everything consequential is *Samizdat*, which means 'self-published,' and circulated from

hand to hand. The practice of experimental writing
in America is thus coming to resemble private research,
like that in science, where new discoveries are first
announced on stapled xeroxes mailed to one's professional friends rather than trying to generate a demand
for his product." We did a *Third Assembling* in 1972
with over ninety contributors, most of whom, once a-
gain, had not contributed before; and we expect to do
a fourth in 1973.

Assembling has set an initial stone in the implicit edifice of International Cooperative Self-Publish-
ing--a growing, unorganized, artistic movement that
includes Dana Atchley's comparably pioneering *Space
Atlas* (1970, 1971, Box 361, Crested Butte, Colo.
81224), which was done with the help of art students
at the University of Victoria, British Columbia; Ely
Raman's *8 x 10 Art Portfolio* (Box 363, New York, N.Y.
10013), which began in lower Manhattan in 1971; and
Jerry Bowles' *Art Work, No Commercial Value* (Grossman,
1972). Notwithstanding similar concepts in editorial-
production, these media differ in several crucial res-
pects. Atchley collates his hundred-plus contributions into two hundred fifty loose-leaf clipbooks and
sends two apiece back to the contributors, thus having
nothing left to sell; and he has recently taken to
traveling the country, collecting spare work in one
place (usually academic) and then, like Johnny Apple-
seed, distributing it gratis elsewhere. This extraordinary service implicitly extends his earlier aim of
open-ended, unfettered artist-to-artist communication
with a different kind of inseminating activity.

Raman's periodical, which appears sporadically,
asks for only two hundred copies of one's text, returning two cardboard folders apiece to the thirty-or-
so contributors and then selling off the rest to subscribers, who are asked to pay what they can. Bowles'
one-shot resembles Raman's and Atchley's in favoring
graphics over literary (or post-literary) work, and
its large loose-leaf binding was issued, to much publicity and after a gallery-sponsored collating party,
by a commercial publisher that, even though it mini-
mally reimbursed its paper-producing contributors, expected to make a profit. Thus, *Assembling* has three
clear distinctions: its literary emphasis (in response to an initially literary predicament); its

ideological underpinnings (elaborated in the prefaces--
a feature indicatively lacking in the others); and its
stapled binding, which we feel creates the sense of a
fortuitous community united in process, though disparate in style.

What is most important about all these media, in
spite of difference, is their common anti-authoritarian
structure--quite literally, a participatory democracy
that successfully redistributes both initiative and
responsibility. In addition to epitomizing the human-
ist theme of ultimate self-determination, this collaborative concept represents, in my opinion, an important development in literary communication, precisely
because it transcends "dummy intermediaries," and it
has the further advantage of easy imitation. (Its com-
mercialization also signals a certain, perhaps dubious
success that probably explains why Bowles' enterprise
rejected a duly submitted contribution, albeit an out-
rageous one, that went instead into *Third Assembling*.)
In the mail recently came *Clone*, which is comparably
produced by students at the Rhode Island School of Design, and another pile of unbound pages from British
art students, along with independent invitations to
send self-published packets to Holland, Germany, and
Italy.

Unless the crisis in literary communications is
radically solved, it seems likely that self-publishing,
both individually and collaboratively, will continue
to be necessary and respectable, and xerography paper
may at times become more honorific than letterpress
printing. Especially since the means of production
have become more accessible, the pressing problem now,
for all alternative publishing, is how to distribute
the results beyond one's immediate acquaintances (or
mailing list). The best solution is so obvious it remains visionary: a national network of art-conscious
wholesalers and retailers capable of handling small,
probably slow-moving quantities. It should be mentioned that we still have for sale, at $2.50 apiece,
the first two issues of *Assembling* (Box 1967, Brooklyn,
N.Y. 11202); the third issue, which is larger, costs
$2.95. At last count, the enterprise has cost us sev-
eral hundred dollars that we can theoretically recoup.

We were pleased to discover that *Assembling* has
been read, not only by fellow contributors (who com-

prise a most ideal audience) but by its purchasers,
and even those who browse in literary bookstores. The
last tell me that they were intrigued by a subtitle
that reads, "A Collection of Otherwise Unpublishable
Creative Work," and they quickly discovered that the
book's contents are, at minimum, clearly unlike anything they had read/seen before. There are good reasons to believe, as I wrote elsewhere, "that the magazine's distinctiveness caused it to be enthusiastically
possessed, if not securely lodged within the imaginative memories of many readers; for as the anthropolo-
gist Edmund Carpenter observed, 'It is one of the cu-
riosities of a new medium, a new format, that at the
moment it first appears, it's never valued; but it is
believed.'" Most important, in our judgment, is *Assembling*'s realization, simply by existing, of our initial
threefold commitment to individual opportunity, unhin-
dered communication, and creative adventurousness, for
both the contents and its structure finally reflect
values intended by, and hopefully intrinsic to, the
process. Behind such a cordial gathering of genuine
idiosyncracy is a freedom and anarchy I personally find
exemplary. "Assembled we stand," runs our reiterated
motto, "disassembled we fall," and for the *Third Assembling* I added: *"POWER TO THE PEOPLE WHO DO THE WORK."*

POETRY &

A ONE-WOMAN PRESS

by Daisy Aldan

DAISY ALDAN *has received a DeWitt American Lyric Poetry Award, a National Foundation of the Arts poetry prize, and first prize for poetry at the Rochester Festival of Religious Arts. She is an experienced translator, a lecturer and critic, and has served as a member of the Executive Board of the Poetry Society of America. A native of New York, Dr. Aldan teaches creative writing and speech at the High School of Art and Design. Her most recent books are* Love Poems of Daisy Aldan *published by Barlenmir House Press, New York, and* Breakthrough, Poems in a New Idiom, *published by Folder Editions, New York.*

Shall not each individual have the right to attempt,
weak or strong as the attempt will be in proportion to
the particular gifts involved, to give his work the
kind of definition that is bestowed by presentation in
a book? Time and the world will prove the book's value,
for I am convinced that in mysterious ways, intangible
forces sift the good from the bad, and the worthy will
become known. In years to come, if the work merits a
place in mankind's artistic heritage, what will it matter who published it? How unworthy are those "friends"
who, impressed with name publishers, demean a self-
published work in spite of its inherent merit.

Poet friends and even I often tried to disguise
the fact that we were publishing our own work, because
of the onus of the label *self-published*. We fabrica-
ted names of nonexistent presses, or I was asked to
lend the name of my press to a friend's book to hide
the fact that it was self-published. In time, I came
to realize the folly and false vanity of such acts and
to recognize the merit of such publication and the joy
involved. Now I proudly list my own books under the
title of my own press, Folder Editions, which has a-
chieved a reputation among collectors and libraries
for fine poetry books.

A poet, like every writer, must respect himself
and his work. Is it not a greater rather than a less
self-respect to refuse to accept the kind of treatment
name publishers in many instances accord to a manuscript, especially to a manuscript of poems? Abuses
like holding a manuscript for years without a decision;
a positive decision followed by a change of heart after
the poet has been wined and dined; an editorial altera-
tion of structure, placement, and content; and so on!
Let's face it! Commercial publishers are in business

to make money from wide distribution. Poetry book buyers are few. A publisher once wrote me:
"Your poems are dynamic, beautiful, of high universal quality, breathtaking. We here all enjoyed reading them, but we regret we are unable to publish them because they are not political and do not reflect the current American scene."
Commercial publishers often publish only one volume of serious poetry a year or one every two years, in a small edition, as a prestige item which is a tax-deductible loss. Considering the number of poetry manuscripts publishers receive, the possibility of acceptance is small indeed. I have friends, excellent poets, who have borne the cost of publication even by name publishers. Once in print, a minimum is done by commercial houses to publicize volumes of serious poetry, and this is understandable. Why waste time and the huge cost of advertising on books one can predict will be a financial loss?
If the goal of the self-publishing poet is financial gain, he is living in a world of illusion. Since comparatively few people possess the ability to read good poetry with pleasure and understanding, the poetry field never has been and never will be a lucrative one. Joy in the work and a sense of creative achievement should reign. If sheer unrestrained ambition to see oneself in print is the motivation, then one should think twice before adding to the mountains of dead written matter which clutter homes and libraries. The question must be asked, "Will my work, in even a small way, enrich lives?"
In my teaching, I have tried to encourage students to use an imagination that works through the living hand in their creation of poems and poetry books, because for him who has a sensibility for such matters, a special essence emanates from a work that the hand has fashioned. More and more, IBM machines are being used to produce mass quantities of books at high speed, and I for one can always recognize when an IBM machine has set the type. The book whose paper was felt and chosen with care, whose pages of type may have been set by hand or written in calligraphy, whose illustrations grew out of inspiration and were reproduced with personal supervision, whose binding was scrupulously chosen to fit the individual quality of the poems,

such a book projects a quality born of love and pre-
serves for the world its fast disappearing handcrafts.
In my small way, I am striving to help preserve
this quality in book production. For many years now,
I have been involved in designing, publishing, and distributing my own books and the books of poet friends.
Publishing for me has been a sideline (I am a poet, a
teacher, and for a time, I was an actress). I am a
one-woman publisher, and it is amazing what one person
can accomplish. There have been helpful friends, of
course, ready to contribute their artistic skills, and
I am grateful to them.
I learned the art of book production as the need
arose. I never took a course in graphic design or book
production. My first acquaintance with such matters
was as a sixteen-year-old editor of the Hunter College
literary magazine, *Echo*. The seed planted then began
to sprout in 1946 when, as a young teacher-poet, I decided to publish a modest collection of my poems. One
friend composed them in calligraphy while another did
a pencil portrait of me. I stapled the pages together,
bound them in laundry cardboards covered with wall paper, made a small woodcut for the cover design, and gave
copies as gifts to friends. Shyly bringing some to a
few established literary bookshops, I was surprised and
encouraged when they were accepted for sale. William
Rose Benét, who saw a copy somewhere, wrote me a treasured letter. Not long ago, at a book party to celebrate the publication of my anthology, *Poems From India*,
published by the Thomas Y. Crowell Company, a copy of
that booklet, *Poems by Daisy Aldan*, made its appearance
and was sold for fifteen dollars. Recently, two separate dealers contacted me, seeking copies for two individuals who were collecting everything written and published by Daisy Aldan and willing to pay high prices
for them. I stole my mother's copy and lamented the
instructions I had given to a friend shortly before to
burn the remaining two hundred copies that I, many years
ago, had left in a box in her attic.
I did not return to publishing until 1953 when,
writing my doctoral thesis on French surrealism, I met
young and older poets whose work was daring, experimental, and who, because of this, were unable to find acceptance in the largely academic literary magazines of
the period. At that time, there were only about forty

so-called "little" magazines in America, whereas today the number is legion. I decided to publish the only magazine for avant-garde writing. (*View*, an excellent periodical, had been forced to suspend publication before that time.) I was teaching and salaries were low, so in my innocence, I dreamed of using school drawing paper and stapling the pages. However, when I started work I renounced this plan. I became and remain convinced that the visual is an important aspect of the total poem experience. There is the heard poem and there is the written poem, and they are different experiences. The written poem is heard with the inner ear, and what is thus heard often is determined by the design of the poem on the page. Too many self-publishers ignore this.

When finally I started examining paper samples, I chose one of the most expensive laid papers available because it felt so fine, looked so beautiful, and had a quality of endurance. Then I went in search of an inexpensive neighborhood printer. I had not reckoned with union rates of $350 a week even for young apprentices. A professional print job was obviously out, so I decided to purchase a handpress which I had seen in a printer's catalogue, listed for ninety dollars. A handpress without type is useless. Next I began to read books of type. Because my magazine was meant to be avant-garde, I chose Vogue, a sans serif modern type, and ordered a case. When it arrived, I began the ludicrous task of setting forty pages of poems and stories by hand, letter by letter. The state of my apartment can be imagined: piles of paper, smears of black printer's ink on everything in sight, wooden and metal space indicators scattered everywhere.

I had to decide on the form of my magazine, and suddenly the idea of stapling that exquisite paper seemed too mean. Discovering that binding is the most expensive item of any book, I attempted to design a kind of folder into which unbound folios might be placed. The use of a folder had the additional appeal of permitting the allocation of four pages to every writer, and it made possible the inclusion of drawings, original serigraphs, photographs, and music sheets. Two friends, Richard Miller and Floriano Vecchi, were assisting me, and we spent days with ruler and razor blade, cutting five hundred covers, one by one, into shape. I did not

realize that any shape could be cut to any size in any
number of copies from a mold in a matter of minutes.
I chose the title *Folder* for my magazine, changing it
from the more pretentious first choice inspired by my
Dada research, *Any Minit Now Somebody's Going To Do It!*
When the pages were finally printed, I laid them
out. Poets and painters, who were unknown at the time
but who now would form a Who's Who in the artistic
world, laughing with enthusiasm, delighted to see their
work in print, walked around the table collating the
pages as if for a literary smorgasbord. In the group
were Frank O'Hara, John Ashbery, Kenneth Koch, Jane
Freilicher, among others. Thus *Folder 1* came into being. The abstract-expressionist painter, Grace Harti-
gan--called George Hartigan in those pre-Women's-Liber-
ation days, because as Grace she had difficulty obtain-
ing exhibitions--had made three serigraphs on screens
we fashioned from wooden frames, and these won a Museum
of Modern Art prize for graphic arts. Our leftover copies of her serigraphs were selling at the Museum for
fifteen dollars each, while I was having difficulty
selling *Folder 1*, which contained those three serigraphs
plus forty pages of poems and stories, for one dollar.
At present, this rare issue is listed in dealer catalogues for sixty-five dollars and is difficult to come
by at that price.
When time came to publish *Folder 2*, I knew that
to set it letter by letter was unthinkable. I discovered linotype. One could have whole lines of type composed and still be in control of design through spacing
and placement of those lines within the chase. I remember being told that if the printers' union discovered
I was setting type as a nonunion member, I would be
fined. I also believe I was the only woman typesetter
at that time. By then, *Folder 1* had been given an excellent review in *The New York Times Book Review* by
Stuart Preston and *Arts International* had somehow heard
about it and reviewed it. In *Folder 2*, I included
translations from Haitian, Spanish, and French poets;
our featured artist was Alfred Leslie; there were photographs by Walter Silver, a masque in nine tableaux by
Eugene Walter, a short surreal play by Jimmy Schuyler
and poetry by Arthur Gregor, Kenward Elmslie, Harriet
Zinnes, M. C. Richards, Donald Windham, and others.
By the time *Folder 3* appeared, the *Folder* poets

were becoming known. The abstract-expressionist painters we were associated with--Joan Mitchell, Mike Goldberg, Larry Rivers, Helen Frankenthaler--were also
gaining recognition. The Princess Caetani and Caresse
Crosby, who with their own presses, Botteghe Oscure in
Rome and Black Sun Press in Paris, had been influential
in publishing the works of Dylan Thomas, André Breton,
Tristan Tzara, and René Char, communicated with me and
encouraged me in my work. These two remarkable women,
who remain little known benefactresses of the literary
world, inspired me greatly. About this time, I met
Anaïs Nin, that unique writer who also had had her own
press, and who in fact wrote to ask if I had bought up
her type, which by coincidence had been Vogue. The cover of *Folder 3* was an exquisite serigraph by Grace Hartigan, who shortly afterward became famous. The contents included a group of Greek poets in translation,
with one of the early appearances of the later Nobel
Prize winner, George Seferis, one of the first translations of the poetry of Pier Paolo Pasolini, and drawings by Michael Lekakis and Jane Freilicher.

Folder 4 contained my translation of a twenty-two-
page poem by Stéphane Mallarmé, *Un Coup de Dés* ("A
Throw of the Dice"), which critics called a perfect
poem and André Gide in the early 1900's characterized
as "the most untranslatable poem in any language." *Un
Coup de Dés*, which is essential to an evaluation of
Mallarmé's lifework, is constructed in an unusual form
which commercial publishers found too expensive to have
typeset. Even *Cosmopolis*, the first French periodical
to publish the poem, did not reproduce the form, thereby distorting the poem's meaning, of which the innovative structure is an integral part.

By handsetting the poem, I was able to fulfill
Mallarmé's wish to have it appear on music sheets because of its affinity to a four-part symphony. As in
an intriguing word game, I measured, counted letters
and spaces, moved words hither and yon. When doing this
work, I never asked myself, "How large will its audience
be?" For I knew that it would be limited, but I had
faith in the work as an important contribution to the
English-speaking literary world. Now when I travel to
distant universities and even as far as India, I am a-
mazed that my translation is known to students and
scholars.

By the time *Folder 4* was issued, the number of literary magazines in America had grown to about four thousand, and I felt that my mission as a publisher of the
avant-garde was over. I decided to wind up my *Folder*
activities with a book which was to include the work of
forty-six poets and thirty-two painters, about half
that number to be women, and to call this anthology *A
New Folder: Americans: Poems and Drawings*. I had become sophisticated about book production: I had the
names of paper houses at my fingertips, I knew about
layouts, pasteups, linotype, and printing techniques.
Bookstores had often complained that *Folder* had to be
kept off the shelves because "bookstore readers" would
mix up and drop the pages, so I decided to bind the anthology. I discovered that there were paper, cloth,
and board bindings; that pages could be stapled, glued,
or sewn. Choice often depends on available funds: the
most expensive, lasting, and beautiful books are sewn.
I had the majority of the copies of the anthology bound
in boards. Boards means that cover, title, and illustration are printed on sheets of paper which, when cut
to size, are pasted on thick cardboards. I had returned full circle on a new level to my first publication:
it was the same principle I had intuitively followed
with my laundry cardboards and wall paper. I had a limited number bound in cloth with titles in gold lettering, signed and numbered. By now, collectors were interested in Folder Editions.
      For this book, I also learned a great deal about
photography because the drawings had to be photographed
for reproduction. A young photographer, Marlis Schwei-
ger, set up cameras, lights, and ladders in my apartment, which was crowded with paintings and drawings by
artists who are now considered to be among the most distinguished in America: Pollock, Kline, DeKooning,
Motherwell, Stamos, Frankenthaler, Kiesler, Glasco,
Blaine, among others. The poetry represented every section of America where poets were active. Wallace Fowlie
wrote a fine introduction. One historical midnight, I
organized a reading of eighteen poets and I projected
slides of the drawings on a huge screen behind them at
the Living Theatre. The audience crowded in, a distinguished representation of the New York world of art
and literature, and in a champagne intermission, the
listeners met the poets. That was a time when poetry

readings were rare. *Mademoiselle* did a two-page spread
of the *Folder* poets, photographed at the Brasserie.
The book received excellent reviews and has since been
reprinted by Krauss Reprint Company, New York.

A couple of years later, I was urged to publish a
paperback of the anthology, and I added new names and
photographs of poets and painters. I love this edition
with photographs of young painters and poets, some of
whom are already dead: Kline, Pollock, O'Hara, Maas,
Kerouac, Olsen, Yorke.

My friends were saying, "It's time you had a book
of your own poems. Being published in magazines is not
enough. You are not being recognized as a poet but as
an editor and critic." I had become American editor
of *Two Cities*, a bilingual magazine published in Paris,
and Jean Fanchette, the Paris editor, agreed to colla-
borate with me on the publication of my book, *The Destruction of Cathedrals*. I designed it and included illustrations by DeKooning, Kline, Pollock, Hartigan,
Blaine, and Kirkpatrick, and the cover drawing was by
Leon Hecht. Once again shy about my own book, I was
startled when it received excellent reviews from respected critics in *Poetry* (Chicago), *The New York Times
Book Review* (which also listed it among the hundred
outstanding books published in 1964), and in the *Poetry
Society of America Bulletin*. When Sylvia Spencer gave
a party for me to celebrate the publication, I feared
that no one would show up, and I was deeply touched
when several hundred writers, actors, dancers, painters,
and photographers came to share this occasion with me.
Remember, all you readers, that this was for a self-
published book. Orders arrived from universities, bookstores, and individuals, and readings in America,
France, England, and India enhanced its popularity.
Other reviews followed. Now in its second printing,
The Destruction of Cathedrals continues to be cited as
one of my best collections of poems.

During special studies in Switzerland, I was introduced to the work of Albert Steffen, a Swiss poet, dra-
matist, essayist, and philosopher. His work made a
profound impression on me. I felt that Steffen, with
over seventy volumes to his credit, was one of the major literary figures of the 20th Century. He was almost unknown in the English-speaking world. In collaboration with Ili Hackländer, a connoisseur of his work

who spoke German and English fluently, I translated
selected poems and with Elly Simons, a poet who wrote
in German and in English, I translated his five-act
play in verse, *The Death Experience of Manes*. With the
authorization of the Albert Steffen Foundation, I published them in America. The P.E.N. Club honored the
appearance of the play. Subsequent work with students,
readings to interested audiences and on FM stations, and
letters I received showed me the validity of my conviction that Steffen's poetry contains a healing for the
ills of the present world. How long might I have waited for acceptance of these translations by a name publisher in America?

Two commercial publishers were interested in bringing out my next collection, *Breakthrough, Poems in a
New Idiom*. I withdrew the manuscript from both because
each wished to print it in a cheap paperback edition,
which would not permit generous spaces around words and
groups of words as the poems required. After two years,
I decided to renounce my search for a publisher and to
do it myself. When I look at this book with its screen-
ed cover, Glastonbury laid paper, and generous page
space, I love it and I am convinced that readers would
not react as they do to the poems if they saw them
cramped on tiny paperback pages.

When I was in India, I had the good fortune to meet
Stella Snead, a painter-photographer who lived and worked there. During a journey by automobile through Rajis-
tan, we conceived a book of poems and photographs. The
delicacy of her photographic patterns lent itself
to the kind of poetry I was writing at the time. Because I had complete control of the production, our
book, *Seven:Seven*, was designed in an unusual size.
It received fine reviews in America, England, and India,
and sold out in a very short time.

A couple of years ago, I wrote a twelve-page poem
in the same form as the poems in *Breakthrough*, called
Journey. Only one or two words appear on many pages
and the placement of the words in a special consonantal
rhyme structure is complicated. Experience had taught
me that no commercial publisher would undertake the publication of *Journey*, which was too long for the literary magazines which publish my work. I decided to have
it composed in calligraphy and to present copies as
gifts to friends. Poet friends who saw it asked me to

consider publishing their poems in such small pamphlets. I grew enthusiastic because of the beautiful appearance of the hand-done calligraphy. In a few months, I did a series of eight booklets with illustrations by artist friends. These booklets are already collectors' items.

Another painter friend, Seymour Leibowitz, who does etchings in the Blake tradition, asked me if he might do some etchings for poems of mine, and thus my collection, *Or Learn To Walk On Water*, came into being. In collaboration with his own press, the Shaw-Leibowitz Press, we did a limited edition on handmade paper in folder form. I learned thereby to understand another graphic-arts process of rare book production.

I am presently publishing a collection of poems by Alexandra Grilikhes, and with the experience of years, I expect this to be one of the finest of Folder Editions.

When I look at the pile of books I have published, I hardly believe my eyes. Self-publishing gave me the opportunity to experiment in new forms, structures, designs, and printing methods. For whatever encouragement it may be to readers, my closets are not filled with unsold copies, nor have I ever had to bring copies to remainder bookstores. On the contrary, the University of Texas recently purchased several manuscripts, galleys, and first editions from me, so that even financially my contributions (I refuse to call them "investments") were returned. Of course the years of hours of dedicated work have their own reward in creative fulfillment, attested by letters which speak of how a destiny has been changed somewhere because someone picked up a book of mine and experienced it. There is a mystery in this before which one stands in awe.

Finally, let me warn would-be self-publishing poets to avoid those parasitical presses who prey on the ambitions and frustrations of unpublished writers-- the so-called Vanity Presses. Give yourself the pleasure of attempting to carry out the whole process yourself. Let me summarize what steps you will have to take. Organize your manuscript in an attractive arrangement. Decide whether you want a paperback edition, cloth binding, or a pamphlet, and equate your wishes with the size of your purse. Decide whether offset, calligraphy, letterpress, or plain handwriting would be

suitable for your poems. Ask paper houses to send you
sample booklets. Choose and order paper cut to the
size of the book you foresee. Ask artist friends about
possible illustrations or photographs. Make a *dummy*,
which is a sample copy of the arrangement of your manuscript which a printer may follow; it need not be elaborate. Give this and the finished manuscript to a
small neighborhood printer, discussing with him your
choice of reproduction. You will receive *galleys*, a
printer's first copies, arranged on special sheets and
awaiting your corrections. You can find professional
correction symbols in the back of any good dictionary.
Return corrected copies to the printer. When you receive the corrected galleys, paste up the pages as you
wish to see them in the book. If you cannot paste accurately, ask for help from a friend who can. When you
return these pages to the printer, he can proceed to
print on the paper you ordered. Find a binder, who will
show you binding samples. Make your choice of binding
and wait for the finished book to arrive. Make room
in a closet or attic and prepare for the most difficult
step of all: distribution! If your book is poetry, do
not expect to find a distributor.

   If you are not content to give and sell copies to
friends alone, if you have decided objectively that
your work can stand with that of admired poets, *and* if
you are prepared to devote time to the promotion of your
book, here are some of the activities you will have to
pursue. Send announcements to university libraries,
bookstores, and poetry readers. You can find lists of
addresses in R. R. Bowker's publications in your public
library or you can buy mailing labels from R. R. Bowker
in New York. Carry copies to literary bookshops for
sale, send a few copies to well-selected periodicals for
review, and make yourself available for poetry readings.
These activities will lead you to others which will be
effective in bringing your work to the attention of
the world.

   If all this promotion is not to your taste, then
simply make one or several copies of your poems in calligraphy or written by hand on fine paper, and using
your creative ingenuity, bind the pages yourself. You
will have a gem you can present to special friends or
keep for yourself as a work of completed art, a work
of creative definition.

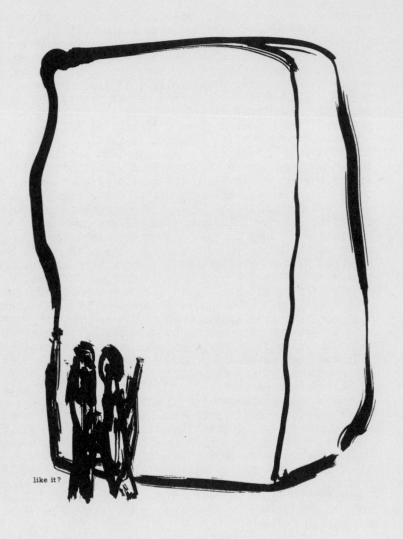

like it?

A drawing by Ray Barrio in *Art: Seen*, which the author describes on the title page verso as "Being A Kind of Graphic Compendium of Loose Sketches, Compromising Ideas, Irrelevant Commentaries, Irrelevant Coincidences, Wry Observatorios, & Prehensile Pretensions." Copyright © 1968 by Ray Barrio. Self-published.

PLUM, A NOVEL ABOUT

CALIFORNIA FARM

WORKERS

by Raymond Barrio

RAYMOND BARRIO's The Plum Plum Pickers *is a novel a-bout Chicano agricultural workers and their exploiters, the growers. An artist and teacher, Barrio published his novel under his Ventura Press imprint, until Harper and Row took over distribution. About his self-pub experiences he comments, "All this has done wonders for my pride, my confidence, my integrity, my ideals, and--ironically enough--for my faith in the American Dream." Barrio, with his wife and children, lives in Santa Clara County, California.*

Have you ever tried to publish yourself? I have. It's fine, it's fun, and it costs. As the author of eight books (WHAT? You've never heard of me???)--six of them self-published--it's also frustrating. But it's nowhere as frustrating as being the author of X number of unpublished books. So now, finally, I'm the author of several books, all selling. I've cut out a little niche of the universe for myself, doing my own hoeing, reaping my own rewards.

Is it literature? I hope so. I mean it to be so. But I couldn't care less for the judgment of others. It's the fun I'm after. After all, I'm my own editor, copier, vice president, publisher, distributor, creator, salesman, producer, writer, and general overseer of my own all-star productions.

As an independent (euphemistically, freelance) writer, I've contributed to many presses, big and little, for many years. At the same time, my manuscripts have also been rejected a huge hunger of times.

So I invented my own Ventura Press. All it is is a P.O. Box in Sunnyvale, California. The first book I did, in 1966, was a small, one-dollar how-to paperback called *The Big Picture*. I sold all 1,500 copies of it in three months. Hey! Subsequently, Sterling of N.Y.C. (after thirty-four other publishers refused it) turned it into a nice $5.95 hardback and now it is called *Experiments in Modern Art* with color plates.

Next, I self-published four little art-oriented booklets. These are still puttering along.

Then I risked the biggest gamble of all. My novel, *The Plum Plum Pickers*, went into its fourth printing within a year.

I'm hopping mad over having spent a good part of my mature ambitions trying to politely find out what

the heck a writer has to do to get his stuff published.
I've seen a lot of stupid, rotten trash published.
Haven't you? As I've done. For years and years. Polite. Hat in hand. A stinking beggar. Polite and intelligent. Indigent and intellectual. Ill-educated
and part-time teacher. Waiting my stupid turn to turn
in. Those pearly gates. Then I stopped to think: I
thought: what the hell. How could a man write a book,
a poem, a story, and NOT get it published?
       So I woke up--and published it, them myself.
       By this time, you see, I'd written my sixth (un-
published) novel, *The Plum Plum Pickers*. *Plum* was a
monster that welled up out of my guts, my depth, my
ideals my California conceit, my concern, and my hatred
of, my deep hatred of greed. I wrote it because I had
to. I hated seeing millions of fellow Americans of Mexican descent being crushed by big bankers, bookkeepers,
and growers. I've seen first hand the exquisite subtle-
ty of how it's done here in the prone prune country of
Santa Clara County.
       In all this dark tunnel of hope and desperate prep-
aration, only one professional voice gave me any encouragement at all: and this was Earl Conrad, author of
Jim Crow America. He not only gave me a beautiful tes-
timonial, but he also permitted me to use it as my
foreword.
       I wrote, revised, polished, rewrote, edited, and
set the type myself. I got loans from a couple of
friendly finance companies. A printer in San Jose ran
off a thousand copies. They were delivered June 23,
1969, liberation day. I was able to tell it like it
is. Nobody breathed over my shoulder. The only certain prospect I faced was that of utter ruination,
while the books rotted there in my drafty garage.
       How did I make the book sell? I had launched my-
self as a one-man publishing venture. I had no organization, no outlets, no contacts, no sales force, no
advertising department, no faith in the publishing
world, and no know-how as to how to go about it. I
started completely cold, like Henry Miller, and ran my
family's comfort straight into the cold, cold ground.
I embarked on five different routes: (1) mailing fliers;
(2) mailing copies to book reviewers; (3) going to local bookstores; (4) sending multiple queries to New York
publishers; (5) locating a book distributor. The sixth

route, approaching college instructors, had simply not occurred to me, and yet this was to be the route that made *Plum* come to life as a readable, circulating, distributable book.

For the first route, before the book was printed, I put together a single-sheet brochure, a flier describing *Plum*, and included Earl Conrad's excellent foreword. I mailed out 1,300 fliers announcing *Plum* locally and all over the country. Each flier cost ten cents and the total mailing cost $130, which isn't peanuts, not to mention the expenditure of time in folding,stamping, etc. As far as I can tell, that mailing did not result in a single order for a single book, and I had mailed the flier to what I thought were important people, U.S. Senators, social workers, and the like. Later, when the book started moving, brochures were more helpful. But not at the start.

When the thousand copies of *Plum* were delivered to me from my San Jose printer, I immediately mailed out more than a hundred copies to book reviewers, mostly in California, but also around the country. From this enormous mailing, I received three favorable *local* reviews--and was ignored elsewhere. Again, this was very little return from such an enormous exertion.

Next I approached a couple of local bookstores, whose owners or managers I knew personally, and they agreed to try out a limited order averaging five copies each. Bookstore managers have to be very selective in the titles they choose to carry because their space for book display is limited. A trial order by the manager of the San Jose State College Bookstore turned up unexpected interest. For soon after an order for a hundred copies arrived at my P.O. Box. A Chicano instructor there, Mario Garcia, who taught Mexican-American studies, saw my book, read it, and immediately incorporated it into his course. Several other instructors did likewise, and I began to look into this interest. But I was still after bookstores, and I went to Berkeley and up the San Francisco Peninsula, and managed to place average orders of five copies at most of the twenty bookstores I visited. The large, well-known bookstores in San Francisco would have nothing to do with me, presumably because I was an unknown publisher peddling an unknown book by an unknown author--me.

Because of the effort and expense and difficulty

in placing orders, I do not consider this a very fruit-
ful investment of one's energies. Book salesmen suc-
ceed in making a living because they represent a large,
well known firm or firms and have a large list of books
to offer.

In the meantime I was also mailing out queries to
all New York publishers, inviting them to take over
Plum from me. No takers, only nibbles. For the next
year and a half I logged what I claim to be the top
reject rate of any American novel. Total reject. E-
ven Harper and Row, who eventually took it and who now
have a handsome Canfield Press edition out both in paper and hardcover, turned it down initially.

I was totally unsuccessful in interesting any book
distributor. I couldn't even get to see the managers.
I made a special trip to San Francisco. I walked
round the warehouse of one distributor and asked the
truck drivers and loaders but they either didn't know
or wouldn't say where the boss was. Most distributors
are big business operators who have no use for a single
title. Another heartless operation, which added to my
hatred of bigness.

Finally I started catching on that if college instructors took an interest in *Plum*, multiple orders
might ensue. So I started sending out other mailings
of fliers, and soon I started getting spot orders from
colleges throughout California.

I used up my initial printing order of a thousand
copies. It cost $1,800. I listed *Plum* at $1.75 retail
as a paperback. I gave a 40 per cent discount. I
blithely kept filling orders, selling the books for
$1.05 wholesale, after paying over $1.80 for each copy
to the printer. Every book I sold thus sent me seventy-
five cents deeper into debt, or $750 for the first one
thousand copies. How long can anybody other than How-
ard Hughes keep that up? I was subsidizing myself,
taking loans out from banks and finance companies on
my good credit, getting deeper and deeper into debt.
The book was beginning to move at last, but, as my dear
wife pointed out, how much longer could we afford to
keep digging ourselves deeper into the mire?

I sold five thousand copies in three printings
that way. On the fourth printing of two thousand, I
finally dared to raise the list price to $2.75. The
books kept right on selling and from that point on

managed to keep the project solvent, though I haven't
yet recovered the initial losses. Thus I went through
a total of ten thousand copies in five printings in
less than two years, when Harper picked it up, offering
me an advance of a thousand dollars and putting me on a
royalty contract. Which, of course, was what I devout-
ly wished to consummate from the very start.

Time magazine's impressive book section of June 29,
1970, discussed the statistics of that year's 130 first
novels, saying in part: "...even when properly handled,
the best guess at an average sale is 3,500 copies, with
more than half coming from public libraries..." Now my
Plum sold more than 5,000 copies the first year. So I
sent my flier to the eighty editors listed on the *Time*
masthead, matching their statistics against *Plum*'s record. In their smugness and bigness, my clearly excep-
tional experiences were not worth a damn, not even the
courtesy of one single reply from those highly-placed
gentry. Why should they condescend to answer me? I
was merely a blustering, belligerent nut. Yet total
sales in the past three years are now approaching 20,000
copies.

In addition, sections from *Plum* have been incorporated into at least twelve new high school and college
anthologies--some have yet to appear--a record that I
doubt any other contemporary novel can match. I would
blush at inviting any comparison to Horatio Alger, but
I did land on the moon, by myself, without any help
from the huge, well-trained army of intelligent publishing experts. Not that I don't need them--I obviously
must learn to live with everyone's right to ignore anything he wishes--but the lesson, the smart lesson, the
well hidden lesson to the serious writer should be perfectly clear.

I mean, where facts are concerned, are facts facts?
Or not? How is the judging done? Have I made an honest breach of their pompous stand, or not? Isn't this
merely another case of bigness and bigotry, big hooks,
bigwigs, big names, big sales, and big shots rubbing
each others' asses? Or not?

Would I do it again? If I had the dough, yeah.
Dough is king, yeah. But I'm still paying off past
debts.

Would I recommend anyone else doing it? If you
have the dough, yeah. A vanity press can't do more

than you can. If you can do it yourself, you can accomplish quite a bit of your own promotion yourself.

You must be prepared to face the mathematical fact of life that the odds for your book, any book, will not justify going beyond the initial printing of a thousand copies. So what if you turn out to be wrong? Or if the world won't recognize your genius? You'll at least have the satisfaction of getting your thoughts out. If you can live with that and can afford the gaff without causing your progeny undue anguish, I say go to it.

HOGARTH PRESS

by Leonard Woolf

LEONARD WOOLF, *critic and writer on economics, founded Hogarth Press in 1917 with his wife, Virginia, the novelist. Their dining-room-press experience has inspired many of the contributors to this book. Hogarth continues to flourish although Woolf died recently. This chapter is a section from* Beginning Again © *1963, 1964 by Leonard Woolf. Reprinted by permission of Harcourt Brace Jovanovich, Inc.*

And now I come to the fortuitous way in which we started the Hogarth Press and became publishers. In the
last two years of the war Virginia's health became
gradually more stable. She was writing again strenuously and regularly. She was at work on *Night and Day*
and finished it at the end of 1918, and she also from
time to time wrote short pieces like the *Mark on the
Wall*. In 1917 and 1918 there was not a single month
in which she did not have reviews in *The Times Literary Supplement*; many of these were reprinted in *The
Common Reader* in 1925. She earned from these reviews
95 pounds.9s.6d. in 1917 and 104 pounds.5s.6d. in 1918.
The routine of our life became pretty regular. We
worked strenuously during the week. In addition to my
political activities I was writing *Empire and Commerce
in Africa*. Over the weekend we usually went for what
we called a treat. It was a mild "treat," a bus to
somewhere up the river and a walk and tea in Hampton
Court or Kingston perhaps. In those days--forty or
fifty years ago--Richmond and Richmond Park, Ham, Kingston, Hampton Court were still very beautiful, and even
on Saturdays and Sundays the beauty of trees and grass
and river and willows was not yet obscured by hundreds
of cars and thousands of people crawling like queues
of blackbeetles and ants every week out of London in
the morning, and having scattered their paper bags,
ice-cream cartons, and beer bottles over the landscape,
back again into London in the evening. Socially it
was the prehistoric era in which one still had servants
living in one's house. We had almost inherited from
Roger Fry two: Nellie the cook, and Lottie the house-
parlourmaid, who stayed with us for years. In 1917
they cost us in wages 76 pounds.1s.8d. Though we had
two servants and two houses our expenditure in 1917

was under 700 pounds. And we saw and entertained a good many people. They came out to lunch or dinner with us at Richmond and often stayed the night.

I have never known anyone work with more intense, more indefatigable concentration than Virginia. This was particularly the case when she was writing a novel. The novel became part of her and she herself was absorbed into the novel. She wrote only in the morning from 10 to 1 and usually she typed out in the afternoon what she had written by hand in the morning, but all day long, when she was walking through London streets or on the Sussex downs or over the watermeadows or along the river Ouse, the book would be moving subconsciously in her mind or she herself would be moving in a dreamlike way through the book. It was this intense absorption which made writing so exhausting mentally for her, and all through her life she tried to keep two kinds of writing going simultaneously, fiction and criticism. After some weeks on a novel she would switch to criticism as a relief or rest, because, though she devoted great care and concentration to even a comparatively unimportant review, the part of her mind which she used for criticism or even biography was different from that which she used for her novels. The relief or relaxation which she obtained from this change in the angle of her mental vision was of the same kind as that obtained by a man whose work entails hard, concentrated thinking and who finds refreshment and relaxation for his mind in a hard, serious game of chess, because in the game he is using a different part of his mind and for a different purpose from what was required for his work.

As I have explained more than once in my autobiography, such wisdom as I possess is largely derived from the saws and sayings of my nurse who came from Somersetshire. One of the great truths which I learned from her was that all work and no play did irreparable harm to all humanity whom she and I recognized in a boy called Jack. The difficulty with Virginia was to find any play sufficiently absorbing to take her mind off her work. We were both interested in printing and had from time to time in a casual way talked about the possibility of learning to print. It struck me that it would be a good thing if Virginia had a manual occupation of this kind which, in say the afternoons, would

take her mind completely off her work. Towards the end
of 1916 we definitely decided that we would learn the
art of printing. But that proved to be not at all an
easy thing to do. The individual finds that very few
actions are easy or simple for him, entangled as he is
in the complicated machinery of life which, with him
in it, is turned round and round and round by the colos-
sal anonymous engine of 20th-Century society. When we
went to the St. Bride's school of printing down Bride
Lane, Fleet Street, we learned that the social engine
and machinery made it impossible to teach the art of
printing to two middle-aged, middle-class persons.
Printing could only be taught to trade union apprenti-
ces, the number of whom was strictly limited.

This seemed to end our career as printers before
it could begin. But on March 23, 1917, we were walking
one afternoon up Farringdon Street from Fleet Street to
Holborn Viaduct when we passed the Excelsior Printing
Supply Co. It was not a very large firm, but it sold
every kind of printing machine and material, from a
handpress and type to a composing stick. Nearly all
the implements of printing are materially attractive
and we stared through the window at them rather like
two hungry children gazing at buns and cakes in a baker
shop window. I do not know which of us first suggested
that we should go inside and see whether we could buy
a machine and type and teach ourselves. We went in and
explained our desire and dilemma to a very sympathetic
man in a brown overall. He was extremely encouraging.
He could not only sell us a printing machine, type,
chases, cases, and all the necessary implements, but
also a sixteen-page pamphlet which would infallibly
teach us how to print. There was no need to go to a
school of printing or to become an apprentice; if we
read his pamphlet and followed the instructions, we
should soon find that we were competent printers. Before we left the shop we had bought a small handpress,
some Old Face type, and all the necessary implements
and materials for a sum of 19 pounds.5s.5d. The machine was small enough to stand on a kitchen table; it
was an ordinary platen design; you worked it by pulling
down the handle which brought the platen and paper up
against the type in its chase. You could print one
demy octavo page on it, and, I think, you could just
squeeze in two crown octavo pages.

When the stuff was delivered to us in Richmond, we set it all up in the dining room and started to teach ourselves to print. The Excelsior man proved to be right; by following the directions in the pamphlet we found that we could pretty soon set the type, lock it up in the chase, ink the rollers, and machine a fairly legible printed page. After a month we thought we had become sufficiently proficient to print a page of a book or pamphlet. We decided to print a paper-covered pamphlet containing a story by each of us and to try to sell it by subscription to a limited number of people whom we would circularize. Our idea was that, if this succeeded, we might go on to print and publish in the same way poems or other short works which the commercial publisher would not look at.

We set to work and printed a thirty-two-page pamphlet, demy octavo, with the following title page:

Publication No. I.

TWO STORIES
WRITTEN AND PRINTED
BY
VIRGINIA WOOLF
AND
L. S. WOOLF

HOGARTH PRESS
RICHMOND
1917

Virginia's story was *The Mark on the Wall* and mine was *Three Jews*. We even had the temerity to print four woodcuts by Carrington. I must say, looking at a copy of this curious publication today, that the printing is rather creditable for two persons who had taught themselves for a month in a dining room. The setting, inking, impression are really not bad. What is quite wrong is the backing, for I had not yet realized that a page on one side of the sheet must be printed so that it falls exactly on the back of the page on the other side of the sheet.

We began to print *Two Stories* on May 3 in an

edition of about 150 copies. We bound it ourselves by
stitching it into paper covers. We took a good deal
of trouble to find some rather unusual, gay Japanese
paper for the covers. For many years we gave much time
and care to finding beautiful, uncommon, and sometimes
cheerful paper for binding our books, and, as the first
publishers to do this, I think we started a fashion
which many of the regular, old established publishers
followed. We got papers from all over the place, including some brilliantly patterned from Czechoslovakia,
and we also had some marbled covers made for us by
Roger Fry's daughter in Paris. I bought a small quantity of Caslon Old Face Titling type and used it for
printing the covers.

We printed a circular offering Publication No. 1
for 1s.6d. net and explaining that we in The Hogarth
Press proposed to print and publish in the same way
from time to time paper-covered pamphlets or small
books, printed entirely by our two selves, which would
have little or no chance of being published by ordinary
publishers. We invited people to become subscribers to
the publications of The Hogarth Press, either A subscribers to whom all publications would automatically
be sent, or B subscribers who would be notified of each
publication as it appeared. We sent this notice to
people whom we knew or who, we thought, might be interested in our publications. I do not know how many
people we circularized, but we published in July and
by the end of the month we had practically sold out the
edition for we had sold 124 copies. (The total number
finally sold was 134.) I still have a list of the 87
people who bought the 134 copies and all but five or
six of them were friends or acquaintances. There are
some rather unexpected names among them, e.g., Charles
Trevelyan, M.P., Arthur Ponsonby, M.P., Mrs. Sidney
Webb, and Mrs. Bernard Shaw. The total cost of production was 3 pounds.7s.0d., which included the noble sum
of 15s. to Carrington for the woodcuts, 12s.6d. for paper, and 10s. for the cover paper. The two authors
were not paid any royalty. The total receipts were 10
pounds.8s.0d., so that the net profit was 7 pounds.1s.
0d. Eventually forty-five people became A subscribers
and forty-three B subscribers. Among the A subscribers
was one bookseller, James Bain of what was then King
William Street, Strand, and except for him every copy

of our first publications was sold to private persons at the full published price. By 1923 the Press had developed to such an extent that we had become more or less ordinary publishers, selling our books mainly to booksellers at the usual discount, and we therefore gave up the subscriber system altogether.

We so much enjoyed producing *Two Stories* and its sale had been so successful (134 copies!) that we were induced to go on to something more ambitious. Katherine Mansfield and Murry were extremely interested in what we were doing, and Katherine offered us for Publication No. 2 a long short story which she had written, *Prelude*. When I look at my copy of *Prelude* today, I am astonished at our courage and energy in attempting it and producing it only a year after we had started to teach ourselves to print. For we printed only in the afternoon and even so not every afternoon; it is a sixty-eight-page book and we printed and bound it entirely with our own hands. The edition must have consisted of nearly 300 copies for, when it went out of print, we had sold 257 copies. Virginia did most of the setting and I did all the machining, though I did set when there was nothing to machine.

I did not machine *Prelude* on our small handpress; in fact, it would have taken much too long to do it page by page. I machined it on a large platen machine which printed four crown octavo pages at a time and which belonged to a jobbing printer called McDermott. McDermott had a small jobbing printing business in a street near The Green in Richmond. I got to know him in a curious way and we became great friends. While printing *Two Stories*, I one afternoon, when I took a proof of a page, found that there was something wrong with it which I could not get right and could not understand. None of the letters printed completely black, there were tiny white dots everywhere. My pamphlet gave me no help. I had noticed McDermott's printing business; it was called The Prompt Press. (When I got to know McDermott, I sometimes thought that he had called it The Prompt Press on the principle of "lucus a non lucendo.") After struggling with my page for hours, I took a proof, walked down to McDermott's shop, and boldly--and rather tremulously--went in. I explained to McDermott that I was trying to teach myself to print and that I had got into an inexplicable difficulty. I showed him my speckled proof and asked him whether he could tell me what was wrong. "Wrong?" he said; "it isn't on its feet, that's all; it isn't on its feet." He explained to me that, in locking up type in the chase, you might get the whole page infinitesimally not flat on the imposing surface--it would be "off its feet" and would not print evenly.

This was the beginning of a friendship which lasted as long as we were in Richmond. McDermott had for years been a compositor in a very large London firm of printers. They had printed *The Spectator* and McDermott was never tired of telling me stories of the editor, St. Loe Strachey, Lytton's cousin, and what a fuss he made about the "colour"--i.e., the inking--of the paper; it had to be very black indeed, too black for McDermott's liking. He had always had a longing for independence, for a small jobbing business of his own; he saved up for years, and late in life bought the business in the street near The Green. He began with an old-fashioned Albion press, on which he printed posters, and two large platen machines, one worked by power and the other by treadle. Just before I got to know him he had bought and installed a very large rotary machine.

He was an extremely nice man and he was very much interested in our--to him--rather eccentric and amusing printing antics. He came and looked at our outfit and at what we were doing, and said that I could, if I liked, borrow the chases for his big treadle platen machine, lock up four pages of *Prelude* at a time, carry them down to The Prompt Press, and machine them myself on his machine. This I did, a pretty laborious business, but not quite as laborious as it would have been to print the sixty-eight pages one by one. In the process I got to know McDermott and his business better and better. His large rotary press was really a white elephant; it was too large to be economical for the size of his business. It was continually going wrong; partly, I always suspected, because, having been a compositor all his life, he did not really understand machining and the kind of machine he had purchased. The result was that quite often, when I went down to print my own pages, I found him covered with oil and ink, pouring sweat, and pouring a stream of the most hair-raising language over his bloody machine. When that happened, instead of machining *Prelude* I spent the next few hours helping him to tinker at his bloody machine until I too was covered with oil and ink and pouring with sweat.

McDermott, I am sorry to say, produced one of the worst printed books ever published, certainly the worst ever published by The Hogarth Press. By 1919 we had become very friendly and he was eager that I should let him print a book for us. I had my doubts about this, because, though he was, of course, a first-class compositor, he was a terribly impatient, slapdash worker, and in the other branches of printing was almost as much an amateur as I was. However, Virginia and I had discussed bringing out a book of her short stories and sketches, but had felt that it would be too much for us to print ourselves--and so, with considerable hesitation and certainly foolishly, I gave it to McDermott to print. It was bound in paper over boards with a woodcut design by Vanessa on the cover, and there were four woodcuts by her in the text. My greatest mistake was to allow him to provide the paper. He produced a nasty spongy antique wove and, ignorant as I was in those days about paper and printing, I had my doubts about it from the first. I went down and helped him to print the beastly thing. I have never seen a more desperate, ludicrous--but for me at the time tragic--scene than McDermott printing *Monday or Tuesday*. He insisted upon printing the woodcuts with the letterpress. The consequence was that, in order to get the right "colour" for the illustrations, he had to get four or five times more ink on his rollers than was right for the type. His type was soon clogged with ink; but even that was not the worst: he got so much ink on the blocks and his paper was so soft and spongy that little fluffy bits of paper were torn off with the ink and stuck to the blocks and then to the rollers and finally to the type. We had to stop every few minutes and clean everything, but even so the pages were an appalling sight. We machined a thousand copies, and at the end we sank down exhausted and speechless on the floor by the side of the machine, where we sat and silently drank beer until I was sufficiently revived to crawl battered and broken back to Hogarth House.

By having *Monday or Tuesday* printed for us by a commercial printer, we were, of course, abandoning the original idea of the Press, which was to print small

books ourselves. In fact we had been already in 1919
forced fortuitously to take a similar step, the first
step on the path which was to end in our becoming regular and professional publishers. In 1918 we printed
two small books: *Poems* by T. S. Eliot and *Kew Gardens*
by Virginia. Of Tom's *Poems* we printed rather fewer
than 250 copies. We published it in May, 1919, price
2s.6d. and it went out of print in the middle of 1920.
Of *Kew Gardens* we printed about 170 copies (the total
sold of the first edition was 148). We published it
on May 12, 1919, at 2s. When we started printing and
publishing with our Publication No. 1, we did not send
out any review copies, but in the case of *Prelude*, Tom's
Poems, and *Kew Gardens* we sent review copies to *The
Times Literary Supplement*. By May 31 we had sold 49
copies of *Kew Gardens*. On Tuesday, May 27, we went to
Asham and stayed there for a week, returning to Richmond on June 3rd. In the previous week a review of
Kew Gardens had appeared in the *Literary Supplement*
giving it tremendous praise. When we opened the front
door of Hogarth House, we found the hall covered with
envelopes and postcards containing orders from booksellers all over the country. It was impossible for us
to start printing enough copies to meet these orders,
so we went to a printer, Richard Madley, and got him
to print a second edition of 500 copies, which cost us
8 pounds.9s.6d. It was sold out by the end of 1920 and
we did not reprint.

The expansion of the Press into something which we
had never intended or originally envisaged can be seen
in the following list of books published by us in the
first four years of its existence:

1917. L. and V. Woolf. *Two Stories*. Printed and bound
          by us.
1918. K. Mansfield. *Prelude*. Printed and bound by us.
1919. V. Woolf. *Kew Gardens*. 1st ed. printed and
          bound by us.
          T. S. Eliot. *Poems*. Printed and bound by us.
          J. Middleton Murry. *Critic in Judgment*. Print-
          ed for us.
1920. E. M. Forster. *Story of the Siren*. Printed and
          bound by us.
          Hope Mirrlees. *Paris*. Printed and bound by us.
          L. Pearsall Smith. *Stories from the Old Testa-*

ment. Printed for us.
Gorky. *Reminiscences of Tolstoi.* Printed for us.

The publication of T. S. Eliot's *Poems* must be marked as a red-letter day for the Press and for us, although at the time when I began to set the lines

> *The broad-backed hippopotamus*
> *Rests on his belly in the mud;*
> *Although he seems so firm to us*
> *He is merely flesh and blood.*

I could not, of course, foresee the remarkable future of the author or the exact course of our long friendship with him. I do not remember exactly how or when we first met Tom, but it must, I think, have been in 1917, or even 1916. I bought a copy of *Prufrock* when it was published by The Egoist Ltd. in 1917, and it has the following inscription written on the cover:

> Inscribed for Leonard Woolf (my
> next ⎫
> second ⎭ publisher
> with gratitude and affection
> T. S. Eliot

Tom showed us some of the poems which he had just written and we printed seven of them and published them in the slim paper-covered book. It included three remarkable poems which are still, I think, vintage Eliot: "Sweeney among the Nightingales," "Mr. Eliot's Sunday Morning Service," and "Whispers of Immortality." Professional compositors, indeed all professional printers, do not attend to the sense of anything which they print--or so I was told by McDermott, who also one day said to me that of all the millions of lines which he had set in his time he doubted whether more than a few hundred were worth reading. But as an amateur printer and also the publisher of what I was printing, I found it impossible not to attend to the sense, and usually after setting a line and then seeing it appear again and again as I took it off the machine, I got terribly irritated by it. But I never tired and still do not tire of those lines which were a new note in poetry and came from the heart of the Eliot of those days (and sounded with even greater depth and volume in the next work of his which we published, the poem which had greater influence upon English poetry, indeed upon English literature, than any other in the 20th Century, *The Waste Land*):

> The host with someone indistinct
> Converses at the door apart,
> The nightingales are singing near
> The Convent of the Sacred Heart,
>
> And sang within the bloody wood
> When Agamemnon cried aloud,
> And let their liquid siftings fall
> To stain the stiff dishonoured shroud.

When we first got to know Tom, we liked him very much, but we were both a little afraid of him. He was very precise, formal, cautious or even inhibited. One can feel this in the language of one of the first letters which he wrote to Virginia--in 1918--particularly in the first sentence:

Dear Mrs. Woolf,

Please pardon me for not having responded to your note immediately--on Mondays I never have a moment up till late at night. And I was not furthermore quite sure of being able to come, as I thought my wife might be arranging to return on Friday morning, but I now hear that she is coming tomorrow.
I shall look forward to Friday with great pleasure.

Sincerely yours
T. S. Eliot

Rather nervously after the war we asked Tom to come for a weekend to Monks House, and this broke the ice. The reserve, even the language thawed, and by 1922 it was Dear Virginia and Dear Leonard instead of Dear Mrs. Woolf and Dear Woolf. And the following is his letter accepting an invitation to tea, new style:

Be sure that Possums can't refuse
A tea with Mrs. Woolf on Tues.
And eagerly if still alive,
I'll come to Tea with you at five.
I'd like to come at half past four,
But have a business lunch before,
And feel responsibility
To do some work before my Tea.
But please don't let the kettle wait
And keep for me a cup and plate,
And keep the water on the bile,
A chair, and (as I hope) a Smile.

Or this in 1937:

Thank you, Virginia, I will come to Tea on Tuesday the 4th May at 4.30 and I hope that Leonard will perhaps be in before I leave; anyway, it seems the only possibility between now and the end of May. But I don't see why you should be broadcasting without pay, unless you are appealing for a Good Cause (which is hard work at that): I should say that there was quite enough unpaid work to be had without adding broadcasting to it. To go to the Opera in a box is the only endurable way of going to the Opera: I have not been under such conditions for many a long year. Perhaps I shall go to Vienna and see if they have any cheap Opera there. I wish I might see you oftener, because as things are I seem to be degenerating into an Old Buffer. All my sports are getting to be Old Buffers' sports-- e.g. I went to Wisbech last weekend, by way of the high table of Magdalene, to drink Port, and I have taken to the vice of Dining Clubs. It would not surprise me if I ended as a member of the Wine Committee of something or other; and this June I am to deliver the Prize Day Speech at Kingswood (Methodist) School. A respected citizen. And I have gone to live in Emperor's Gate. O dear. Am I a humbug? I envy you having finished an opus so recently as not to be expected to be working on a new one. I am trying to write a play, but it is very difficult, irritating when interrupted and tedious when not interrupted. O dear.

                              Your faithful   Tom

It was not until the end of 1922 that Tom gave us
The Waste Land to read; we agreed to publish it; printed it ourselves and published it on September 12, 1923.
That does not belong to this volume, but Tom was responsible for an interesting episode in our history as
publishers which took place before the end of the war.
He told us at the end of 1917 or the beginning of 1918
that Miss Harriet Weaver of *The Egoist*, which had pub-
lished his *Prufrock*, was much concerned about a MS. by
James Joyce which she had. Both she and he thought it
was a remarkable work, but it was indecent and there
were grave doubts whether it was publishable in England.
He asked us whether we could perhaps consider it for
The Hogarth Press or at any rate have a talk with Miss
Weaver about it. This we agreed to do and on Sunday,
April 14, 1918, Miss Weaver came to tea, bringing with
her a large brown paper parcel containing the MS. of
Ulysses by James Joyce--though not the whole of *Ulysses*
because Joyce was still writing it. She left the MS.
with us and we put this remarkable piece of dynamite
into the top drawer of a cabinet in the sitting room,
telling her that we would read it and, if we thought
well of it, see if we could get a printer to print it
for us. The entry in my diary for the day is:

Miss Weaver to tea about Joyce's book and the
Egoist, a very mild blueeyed advanced spinster.

And this is Virginia's entry:

But almost instantly Harriet Weaver appeared.
Here our predictions were entirely at fault. I did
my best to make her reveal herself in spite of her
appearance, all that the editress of the Egoist
ought to be, but she remained unalterably modest,
judicious and decorous. Her neat mauve suit fitted
both soul and body; her grey gloves laid straight
by her plate symbolised domestic rectitude; her
table manners were those of a well bred hen. We
could get no talk to go. Possibly the poor woman
was impeded by her sense that what she had in the
brown paper parcel was quite out of keeping with
her own contents. But then how did she ever come
in contact with Joyce and the rest? Why does their
filth seek exit from her mouth? Heaven knows. She

131

is incompetent from the business point of view and
was uncertain what arrangements to make. We both
looked at the MS. which seems an attempt to push
the bounds of expression further on, but still all
in the same direction. And so she went.

We read the MS. and decided that we would publish
it if we could find a printer to print it. I showed it
to William Maxwell of R. & R. Clark, Edinburgh, and to
Clay, both very respectable printers of the highest
rank. Neither of them would touch it and both of them
said that no respectable printer would have anything
to do with it, for the publisher and printer of it would
certainly be prosecuted. All this took some time and
it must have been in 1919 that we finally had to return
the MS. to Miss Weaver.

The publication of Maxim Gorky's *Reminiscences of
Leo Nicolayevitch Tolstoi* in 1920 was also another mile
stone on the road of the Press towards ordinary, commercial publishing. I do not remember how we first came
to know S. S. Koteliansky, always known as Kot, but I
think that it must have been through Katherine Mansfield
and Murry. In 1919 he came to us with a copy of the
Reminiscences, just published in Moscow, which Gorky
had sent to him, giving him the English translation
rights. Kot suggested that he and I should translate
it and The Hogarth Press publish it. We agreed to do
this and thus began a collaboration between Kot and Virginia and me in translating Russian books. Our actual
procedure in translating was that Kot did the first
draft in handwriting, with generous space between the
lines, and we then turned his extremely queer version
into English. In order to make this easier and more
accurate, we started to learn Russian and at one moment
I had learned enough to stumble through a newspaper or
even Aksakov.

Gorky's book was a great success. We published it
in July and had to reprint it almost immediately, and
in the first year we sold about 1,700 copies. It was
reprinted many times and is still selling forty years
after publication. We serialized some of it in *The London Mercury*, and sold the American rights, so that at
the end of 1920 Kot received nearly 50 pounds which both
he and we in those early days thought extremely satisfactory.

Kot was a fine translator from the Russian, and
Lawrence and Katherine also at one time or another col-
laborated with him in translating. The translation of
Bunin's *Gentleman from San Francisco*, a masterpiece or
near-masterpiece, which he did with Lawrence and which
we published in 1922, is magnificent. Gorky's *Reminiscences* is, I think, indisputably a miniature masterpiece of the purest water. Kot's English, which I had
to turn into my English, was usually very strange, but
it was also so vivid and individual that I was often
tempted to leave it untouched. For instance, he wrote:
"She came into the room carrying in her arms a peeled-
off little dog," and on another occasion: "she wore a
haggish look." If he was in doubt about a word, he
sometimes looked it up in his dictionary and put all
the variants into his translation, occasionally with
curious results, e.g., "he looked in the glass at his
mug, dial, face." One learned to the full Kot's iron
integrity and intensity only by collaborating with him
in a Russian translation. After I had turned his English into my English, we went through it sentence by
sentence. Kot had a sensitive understanding of and
feeling for language and literature, and also a strong
subtle mind. He would pass no sentence until he was
completely convinced that it gave the exact shade of
meaning and feeling of the original, and we would sometimes be a quarter of an hour arguing over a single
word....
     It is perhaps worth while recording the finances
of The Hogarth Press in the first four years of its existence, during which we published the nine books listed on pages 127 and 128. By the end of 1920 the total
capital expenditure was 38 pounds.8s.3d., on the printing machine, type, accessories, and a paper cutting machine. The following shows the net profit on each of
the eight books:

	p.	s.	d.
Two Stories	7	1	0
Prelude	7	11	8
Kew Gardens	14	10	0
Eliot's *Poems*	9	6	10
Murry's *Critic in Judgment*	2	7	0
Forster's *Story of the Siren*	4	3	7
Mirrlees' *Paris*	8	2	9

Stories from the Old Testament	11	4	5
Gorky's *Reminiscences*	26	10	9

In the first four years, therefore, the total net profit was 90 pounds, but this was without any charge for
rent and overheads. We usually paid the author 25 per
cent of the gross profits, and, where we printed the
books ourselves, nothing was charged for printing and
binding.
  When the war ended, though the MS. of *Ulysses* was
in the cabinet in the drawing room and I was on the
point of buying McDermott's large platen printing machine from him for 70 pounds, we still had no idea of
turning ourselves into an ordinary, commercial publishing business. But by 1924, if not indeed by 1922, we
had, without realizing it, done so. For in 1922 we
published Bunin's *Gentleman from San Francisco*, Dosto-
evsky's *Stavrogin's Confession*, Virginia's *Jacob's Room*,
The Autobiography of Countess Tolstoy; in 1923 *Tolstoy's
Love Letters*, Goldenweiser's *Talks with Tolstoy*, Roger
Fry's *Sampler of Castile*, Stephen Reynolds' *Letters*,
Forster's *Pharos & Pharillon*; in 1924 Freud's *Collected
Papers* and the beginning of the Psycho-analytical Library, *Kenya* by Norman Leys, *The Rector's Daughter* by F.
M. Mayor, Living Painters: *Duncan Grant*, *Seducers in
Ecuador* by V. Sackville-West, *Early Impressions* by Leslie Stephen.
  Ten years after we started printing *Two Stories*
The Hogarth Press was a successful commercial publishing business. It remained for Virginia and me, and has
always remained for me, a half-time occupation. I have
little doubt that, if I had made it my full-time occupation, it would have become a bigger, fatter, and rich-
er business. I have often heard it said by professional
publishers and other people who know the book producing
and book selling industry far better than I do that it
would be quite impossible today to do what we did in
1917 to 1927, i.e., build up a successful publishing
business from zero with no capital. Costs of production have increased to such an extent and publishing
is so geared to large scale, best seller industry that
today there is no place for the kind of books with which
we began and which floated The Hogarth Press into pros-
perity. I see the added difficulties, but I am not convinced that the thing would not be possible in 1963.

First, one would have to have, of course, the kind of luck which we had--to know or find a few writers, unknown but potentially of the first class. Secondly, one would have to start it, as we did, as a very part-time occupation, making one's living for the first years in other ways. Thirdly, one would have to refuse absolutely, as we did for many years, to publish anything unless we thought it worth publishing or the author worth publishing. I think that "thirdly" is the most important of the three conditions of success. Most small publishers perish by trying to become too big too quickly. One reason why the Press survived was because for many years our object was, not to expand, but to keep it small. In business the road to bankruptcy is paved with what the accountant calls "overheads" and too many publishers allow their "overheads" to dictate to them the size of their business and the kind of books they publish. My theory was that the main object of a publisher, as business man, should be to keep his overheads as near to zero as possible, and, if he did that, he could forget about them and publish only what he wanted to publish. I still think that this had a great deal to do with the survival of The Hogarth Press.

Cobra: helicopter gunship

S. O. P.

To build a "gook stretcher," all you need is:
Two helicopters
Two long, strong ropes,
And one elastic gook.

—*Larry Rottmann*

A poem and drawing by Larry Rottmann from the 1st Casualty Press edition of *Winning Hearts and Minds: War Poems by Vietnam Veterans*. Copyright © 1972 by 1st Casualty Press.

1ST CASUALTY PRESS

by Larry Rottmann

LARRY ROTTMANN *founded* 1st Casualty Press *with other members of the* Vietnam Veterans Against the War *to create a forum for writings about the Indochina experience. With Jan Barry and Basil T. Paquet, Rottmann edited a first book of poems,* Winning Hearts and Minds. *A second book,* Free Fire Zone: Short Stories by Vietnam Veterans, *has just been published.* 1st Casualty Press *is located in Coventry, Connecticut.*

I wrote my very first poem while serving with the 25th
Infantry Division in Vietnam. Titled "Fuzzy Commitment," it was a product of my growing awareness about
a war for which I had volunteered, but for reasons
that I soon discovered were either invalid or nonexistent. I sent the poem to a friend back in the States,
and he (unbeknownst to me) forwarded it to a GI antiwar newspaper. The first I knew about being a "published poet" was as the subject of an investigation by the
Criminal Investigation Division of the Department of
the Army. Two CID agents had flown all the way from
Washington, D.C., to Cu Chi, Vietnam, to question me
about my loyalty and "possible charges of subversion,"
a real demonstration of the potential power of poetry.
      After my release from active duty, I began writ-
ing. Slowly at first, but soon the words were pouring
out almost faster then I could put them down. I was
working with Vietnam Veterans for Gene McCarthy at the
time, and I began using my poems in my speeches. There
were two distinct reactions--disbelief at what I said
("That's not what we've read in the papers.") and a-
mazement that a vet could possibly articulate in an art
form the horror and racism of the Indochina War. Both
Carl Rogers (another VV for McG) and I began to realize
that poetry by ex-GI's could be an effective tool for
political struggle. However, tentative, and later on,
concentrated attempts to have the poetry published were
fruitless. The material was good. The source unim-
peachable. But no newspapers or magazines (other than
a few underground types) were interested.
      Over the next three years, while working with the
Vietnam Veterans Against the War, I began collecting
poems and stories by vets for use in the VVAW newspaper. Gradually, it grew from a handful of material

into a huge collection of over ten thousand unedited pages. Stuff was sent in directly by veterans, some was submitted by teachers and family, and sympathetic editors began to refer vets' manuscripts to us.

In the spring of 1971, another veteran, Jan Barry Crumb, and I began approaching publishers with the idea of having one of them do some kind of vets' writing anthology. We personally visited over forty-two publishers, from the biggies like Doubleday and McGraw-Hill to the alternative types like New England Free Press and Ramparts Press. Editors admitted that the writing moved them to tears, but none of them wanted to see the project through. The few who were interested backed out at the last minute. There were the usual excuses: "We don't publish unpublished writers " "The war is winding down " "Sorry, but we're only looking for the Vietnam 'Norman Mailer'."

In September, Jan and I were joined by Basil T. Paquet, a vet and poet, who felt that the sheer bulk and uneven quality of our thirty-pound manuscript was the primary reason for the rejections. We spent the next five months on just the poetry, editing and shaping it into a tight, emotional and chronological narrative. We called the 106-page volume *Winning Hearts and Minds: War Poems by Vietnam Veterans*.

Two months later, after taking the new manuscript around to all the publishers again and getting all the same old excuses, we felt we were up against a brick wall. The war was still raging, the power and truth of the veterans' literary testimony was more important than ever, but all possible channels of mass communication with the American people seemed to be cut off.

We were by now wholly confident in the literary quality of *W.H.A.M.* and realized that the publishing world's repeated rejection of our manuscript (while it continued to churn out thousands of bad books on the war) was due to the effectiveness of the volume's message. The poetry was reaching them, and they just couldn't handle it personally. The fact they were editors and publishers didn't mean they could necessarily separate themselves from their complicity, and their reluctance is part of our entire nation's conspiracy of conscience about the war. Such desperate denials of guilt and awareness is what the poetry was aimed at exposing.

It should be noted that during this period we sought the encouragement and support of "movement" poets and literati and were surprised and disappointed by their lack of support. Their general attitude was not that much different from the publishing companies' in that both wished us success, but expressed doubt that what we were trying to do was important or would be "saleable." Even those New-Left writers who understood our project weren't eager or even willing to help out a whole new batch of good poets. Politics (or morality) aside, they seemed to feel that the whole idea smacked of too much competition in an already too-tight poetry market.

So we decided to publish *Winning Hearts and Minds* ourselves. With the help of several donors, plus a personal loan, we raised enough money to print ten thousand copies in paperback. We formed a nonprofit corporation and called it 1st Casualty Press (from Aeschylus' "In war, truth is the first casualty."). With the help of friends, we set the type, did the design and layout, pasted up the camera-ready copy, and ran off the books at a small Quaker press.

On April 1, 1972, *W.H.A.M.* was released, the very first copy being sold to a plainclothes cop at the Berrigans' Harrisburg rally. On May 14th, a long review of the book by John Seelye appeared in *The New York Times Book Review*. Fifteen poems were quoted, many in their entirety, and Seelye said, "...if one, or more, or the impact of all these poems does not make you weep, then by Jesus Christ you are not human, and ought to destroy your Social Security card."

For the next few months, Jan and Basil traveled up and down the East Coast doing readings and badgering bookstores ("We don't stock little-press books.") into carrying *W.H.A.M.* Meanwhile, I took off in my truck, The Great White Whale, on a coast-to-coast pilgrimage, doing talk shows, sweet-talking cynical bookreview editors ("We don't review little-press books."), staging impromptu readings, and peddling books out of the back of the Chevy. By June, *W.H.A.M.* had twenty-three reviews (including ones in *Newsweek*, *New Republic*, and the *Louisville Courier-Journal*), and *Winning Hearts and Minds*/1st Casualty were the subject of forty-three articles (in the *Chicago Sun-Times*, *New York Daily News*, *WIN* magazine, etc.). And our entire first printing had sold out.

In July, we ran a second printing and began contract negotiations with McGraw-Hill. On September 18, they released a new paperback edition and the first hardcover printing. By contractual arrangement, 1st Casualty continues to handle individual mail orders and movement organizations, while McGraw-Hill does world-wide distribution to bookstores, schools, and libraries.

On Valentine's Day, 1973, with the help of our new vet editor, Wayne Karlin, we released the second book in our projected series of five, *Free Fire Zone: Short Stories by Vietnam Veterans*. McGraw-Hill will print and distribute a second paperback edition and the hardcover. Similar arrangements are anticipated for subsequent volumes. This mutual publishing agreement allows 1st Casualty to remain financially viable and in editorial control. No matter how hard we might try, we couldn't possibly put our books in all the bookstores, supermarkets, and drugstores in America--which is where they have to go if they are to reach the people. Our experience with the "underground" distributors taught us that they demand the same--or an even larger--percentage as major publishers, and that they express near contempt for professionalism and mass distribution methods.

We are now working on our third volume, *Postmortem: Poems and Stories by Vietnam Veterans*, and are considering publishing a novel and book of photos and drawings as our fourth and fifth efforts. So far we have managed to break even financially, and have donated all profits above contributors' fees and office expenses to medical aid for Indochina. It has not been easy. And it has not been fun. But we feel we are doing what we set out to do, in a manner that is personally, politically, and morally acceptable. In these days and times, and in publishing, that's no small accomplishment.

> *"And, of course, the nice thing about the story is that now you have heard it, what happened is part of you, too."*
>
> Jim Aitken, "Lederer's Legacy"
> *Free Fire Zone*

KITCHEN-COUNTER

PUBLISHING

by Oliver Lange

OLIVER LANGE used the pen name "Carl Schrader" to self-publish Buckman Summers. "Oliver Lange" is still another pen name this writer used for Vandenberg, a Stein and Day best seller in 1971. This year the same company will publish his Incident at La Junta, another potential best seller. As Carl Schrader he limited his edition to twenty-five copies, and was happy about it. Buckman Summers is "an autobiographical excerpt in the form of essays, stories, fragments, and print-outs," and deals with the author and his friends, who live in Santa Fe.

In reply to the question of why self-publish, some literary sleuthing is in order. Here goes:

Writers of any conceivable age or gender too often are convinced that Gotham City's "publishing community" exists to provide midwifery--assistance at the accouchement of any given literary child. They forget, broadly speaking, that publishers love writers the way owls love mice, and either forget or ignore the insuperable dichotomy between writing and publishing--at their best, the first is art while the latter is a mercantile adventure.

Advice, then, to writers (good, bad, or ghastly): to publish conventionally is to join a team dedicated to honing, paring, clipping, *producing* a merchantable product. The proverbial package is much with us today: hardcover, paper rights, television and radio guest-shot promos, getting up and blathering in front of women's clubs in West Pork Chop, Oklahoma, book fairs, cocktail lunches at the Algonquin and the Plaza, and the like.

I'm not exactly knocking all this. Most writers don't mind such frolics and may in fact relish the attention and fuss. Probably an understandable compensation device to counter those years of pecking away in the back of a converted garage under the glare of a two-buck fluorescent desk lamp purchased down at Good Will.

For me, however, it's all a waste of time and pretty much of a pain in the ass too. My "pleasure" in writing terminates at the moment I hand a manuscript over the counter at the post office. I'm uneasy with editing or layout or PR-promos or having some astigmatic mongoloid sidle up to me at an autograph party to stutter a request for the old John Henry.

So, then, myself. I'd dropped out quite a few years back. Born and raised in New York (consider it

my operational turf, which may provide a small insight
into what is still, really, a criminal mentality).
Worked in publishing there for a few years. Ended up
in New Mexico. Got divorced. Married again; more kids.
Always broke. Was for years a candidate for Richard
Milhaus' poverty-level losers.
     The usual Gordian knot. How to support oneself
and family? Needs relatively simple. Like Faulkner,
you know, who claimed that all he needed was a little
tobacco, liquor, and a place to type.
     Academia always anathema in my book, although many
(maybe most) writers end up in that slot. So there was
instead the usual boring inventory of surrogate occupa-
tions: construction worker, night watchman, psychiatric
aide. Always marginal salaries. Debilitating, those
marginal salaries, because I knew well that Ph.D. pals
and baccalaureate buddies who'd taken out citizenship
in Academialand were knocking down from twelve to twenty-five a year, and were wearing J. Press suits and
gargling with Tanqueray gin (or at least Beefeaters),
while I was maintaining vital life-signs with blue
jeans, Paisano wine, and all the other good chemicals
that are grown nowadays in sunny California.
     Another point. I had the flaming reds about get-
ting locked into a conventional life-style. Like the
neat little house with the neat little thirty-year-long
mortgage; and the snazzy car with thirty-four remaining
installment payments. All that. A form of slavery.
My mythic folk-deities still include gadflies and drop-
outs like Ferdinand Lundberg, Thoreau, Malcolm Lowry,
Illich, Agee.
     So, what to do? Joined the full-time labor force
on a temporary basis. Bought a hill and meadow (this
is being typed from the hilltop). Built a house. Wife
and I. Ten rooms. That is, we built it--single-handed.
No great shakes, but a place to live. Low taxes, etc.
No liens...free and clear. Gasoline, car repairs, bu-
tane, food, clothes, and Faulkner's "some tobacco and
liquor." Not the best of all possible worlds, but not
the worst. Nearest damned neighbor miles off. No electricity: kerosene and Coleman lanterns for almost eight
years now. A family of coyotes have a den on the next
ridge, and they sing to us at night. A friendly, easy-
going kind of house. Pals visit: we have some good parties.

As I said, not the worst of all possible worlds.
Was astonished to learn that certain staider acquaintances hewed to the notion that I was some kind of aging
hippie. Furthest thought from my mind. I wasn't trying to prove anything. Piss on holy poverty. The thing
is, I knew I couldn't last long in *any* job, and so had
better address myself to the problem of lining up an
economical life. My theory about surviving in this in-
sane country is that there's no point in trying to earn
ten or twenty thou a year: Grubsville. There are only
two comfortable ways to hack it in this era. Either
you are super-rich, or else you figure out a way to live
on virtually nothing. (By that I mean getting by in a
decent and civilized fashion, with food on the table
and booze and books to read and enough time for thinking. Yes, time, that's the nut, always time.) No option being open to riches, I chose the latter, and for
years we made it on net incomes of, well, like fifteen
hundred to two thousand annually. Didn't live badly
either.
       One digression to this scheme: a wife. I was lucky
enough to liaison with a girl who would put up with my
weird thinking. The drinking, the paranoia, the writing, the isolation: all of it. A rather fantastic woman really. So that's very fine, having a wife like
that.
       Well, we were up on this hilltop, and I was writ-
ing, and we were living this life that frequently was
lovely but also was often grim.
       Another theory of mine is that anyone interested
in writing has to spend ten or fifteen years at it and
get his rudimentary two or three million words of original copy out of the way, and I was out to do this.
(There are something like eighteen or nineteen books in
my files, mostly junk, but that's okay.)
       I'd published a novel in the fifties using my
"real" name. Young man, intriguing talent, great promise, that sort of thing. Good reviews (translated,
this means lousy sales). Nothing during the interven-
ing years except a few short pieces. I was still courting the publishing community with well-made novels.
And growing more debilitated over those below-poverty-
level incomes.
       You know, that's one way almost no American can
beat the racket. Because this is a materialistically-

oriented society. Over the long mile I missed not being able to indulge in at least a few things my wife and kids and I might have enjoyed.

Anyway, I reached a fine, rare, vintage distillation of testiness a few years ago, and the interior dialogue went something like this: "Shit, I've been writing these conventional books for years, and just for once in my life I'm going to write something that *I* pick up on, not a manuscript that I think (and secretly hope!) will trigger hosannahs from the editorial cadre-system that is the basis of the trade."
So I did, all one autumn and winter. The result was *Buckman Summers*. Bought a second-hand mimeo, an antique hand-cranker. And a hundred dollars worth of paper, ink, stencils. For the modest sum of six bucks, *Buckman* was copyrighted at the U.S. Library of Congress under a vague imprint I invented: The Mestizo Press.
I knew nothing about bookbinding--didn't even know what a signature was. (A signature is made up of several sheets on each of which is printed four pages, so that when one is folded in half you have something like pages 23, 24, 66, and 67; and the following sheet-insert would have pages 25, 26, 64, and 65.) I practically lost my mind figuring out how everything was supposed to fit together, but finally got some useful insights as to what a book is all about by carefully disassembling a hardcover of *The Greening of America*. Anyway, *Buckman* was hand-collated and hand-sewn (heavy upholsterer's thread and a sailmaker's needle will do). The jacket art--a line drawing of our ranch house-- was individually drawn on each copy. Linoleum-block technique produced the large, boldface jacket printing. The book has more than its share of typos and misspellings, and graphically it would probably make most slick-mag layout dudes wince. Even so, it still provided an astonishing experience...to have total option, you see, just for once: content! editing! layout! promotion! (so what's to promote with twenty-five copies?) distribution!
This is what I have come to call Kitchen-Counter Publishing. Twenty-five copies of a 161-page book for under two hundred, a sum surely within the reach of any serious writer. At twenty-five cents a copy, the first printing was an instant sellout. The mentality of

charging two bits a throw is significant. I mean, it
doesn't make *sense*, and that's precisely what I was after, because by then *Buckman* had become a labor of love,
and its value (or worthlessness) had nothing to do with
the cost of ink, stencils, or the thousand or so man-
hours that went into it.

For me the quality of writing in *B.S.* ranges from
the sublime to the atrocious. But what a breath of
fresh air it provided. Copies went out to writer pals,
teachers, and various underground contacts, with an invitation to have each copy circulated chain-letter fashion. I imagine that by now several hundred have gotten
into those twenty-five copies, and reports still drift
in from readers. One writer called it "a prose home-
movie of Schrader in action," and a friend, Marc Jaffe,
who heads up Bantam Books, wrote to say that it was
"certainly in the tradition of the greatest personal
and private confession-journals, but I can understand
why you'd want it published under another name." I'm
not sure I understand what he means by that. Probably
the best reaction came from John Humphreys, another
friend, who operates some advanced creative-writing encounters at Columbia. He liked his copy well enough
to include it as required reading for his students, and
it promptly disappeared, to resurface a year later, ap-
parently having been handed around campus on a person-
to-person basis, the copy itself by then so tattered
that it was held together with rubber bands.

Offhand I can think of no better validations for
Kitchen-Counter Publishing than the above anecdotes.

Interestingly, even hiding out on this crazy New
Mexican hilltop, I feel much in contact with the contemporary writing scene. With some reservations I am interested in experimental (sic: "unpublishable") writing,
and have been turned on lately by such items as *Panache*
and *Assembling*, put out by Richard Kostelanetz. I take
umbrage with a lot of it, but then I've done that for
years with conventional publishing, and will continue,
if possible, to maintain a brigand mentality toward the
whole "industry."

As a human, I ally myself with no groups, movements, or cliques. Belong to no clubs or associations.
Don't believe in God or the American voting system, and
am fond of thinking of myself as a bona fide, practicing

existential outlaw. The closest I'll come to admitting
kinship in our intellectual community is to say that I
am for "good" writing (if you want to know what I mean
by "good," I'll probably reply, "None of your business!") If I didn't feel that much, I wouldn't be con-
tributing this article. I still value E. B. White's
much-quoted remark about being a shareholder with one
vote in the management of the human race, and, like him,
I don't think much of the board of directors' policies,
to the point where I speak my mind.

Personal credo: I try to live in dignity and style,
in grace and in remission. Try not to damage others
(not always successful here), and operate with a minimum of hypocrisy and phoniness (ditto not always successful).

Writing credo: I write what I like, using the crippled cerebral equipment I have at my disposal. Am too
easily wooed by those two old one-eyed stand-up literary whores: the well-turned phrase, and rhetorical so-
nority.

Some thoughts. Why write under various pen names?
I'll say this much: Identity is really meaningless as
well as temporary. Something is written. Who cares if
Carl Schrader or Oliver Lange gets the credits? The
writing is what counts. (The royalty checks are made
out to my "real" name, but all they really provide is
a livelihood wherein I continue to produce items under
other names.)

Pen names also self-protective. America feeds on
personalities, gobbles them up at the rate of fifty a
week. Witness Hemingway. Many others.

Exposure doubly perilous for the quasi-personality.
Television, for example, which is really a blenderized
analgesic for non-thinking non-readers. What do you
end up with? Capote, a second-rater, singularly defi-
cient in formidable talents, who is dedicated to illustrating that anyone in this Horatio-Algerland, including chubby   no-talents , can make it big, oh wow! Or
Mailer. Certainly one of the more consistently interesting writers around, except on television. Some writ-
er-friends and I are working up a slush fund wherein we
chip in all our loose change left over from an evening's
barhopping, the purpose of which is to buy Mailer a lar-
yngectomy. We figure we'll be doing him a real service.

150

With the *Vandenberg* book, you know, I did the
Frost Show and others. A dehumanizing experience.
Nothing to do with writing, or any form of communica-
tion really.

That trick was done to soothe my publisher. Commercial publishers have a thing where they get hot
flashes around pub date. They've done what they can,
but feel more must yet be accomplished. Hence, the PR-
promos and all that *dreck*. Well, I'd have to say this.
My publisher is a sensitive and intelligent man. And
no bullshitter--that is, he turned out to be a man of
his word. Surprised hell out of me. As far as that
goes, a lot of editors are decent types. A friend once
said that considering the exigencies of the profession
"editors are far more intelligent than we [writers]
have a right to expect." I guess I'd buy that. Still,
they're working with a product, and the score is kept
in ledgers divided into black and red.

On Kitchen-Counter Publishing, then, I'd recommend
it. It's not that expensive, even for a full-length
novel (discounting, of course, one's own time and labor). And, for me, the experience provided cogent ther-
apy. Tangentially, with the attempt I produced the one
piece of writing I really feel okay about. Using the
Oliver Lange persona, I've gotten all kinds of ego-
strokes, but such *kudoi* tend to make me uneasy. Another way of saying that the values I once cherished as a
younger writer have now palled.

Religious inclinations: To hold forth the candle.
To maintain the vision. Of what? A cherished image of
myself and my fellow men as three-dimensional human be-
ings. Bantu bushman and outback aboriginal; Chavez's
grape-pickers, bless! Fingersnappingly hostile Harlem
spades and pomaded Puerto Ricans, bless! Blackjackpack-
ing killer-cops, geriatric closet-queens, yes, even unto the German mentality which to this day blithely side-
steps the memory of Schwarz-Bart's six million. Even
unto Richard Milhaus, surely a treacherous man; and our
own Baltimore Torquemada, Agnew (though here the elasticity of my love is sorely tested). Bless! Yes, the
inequalities of our human condition are such that I cannot idly stand by but must fistshakingly contribute my
two cents' worth. My thoughts hinge on B. Traven,
Isaac Babel, and *One Day in the Life of*...

The ultimate goal of the writer is silence. As
Trilling said: "Nothing in literature is quite so mar-
velously effective as a period placed in precisely the
right spot." I look forward to this. Bless!
    I place enormous value on *individualism*. On this
basis alone I value myself. But also many others. A
surprisingly large number. I sometimes get to sit
around and booze and rap with these types. A hearten-
ing experience.

    So. Identity meaningless. All an existential
joke. Also fame, wealth, and concomitant fringe benefits. I can report to you that at this date I fragment
my days with reading, writing, loving, trying to be a
decent husband/father, and so on. Time left over is
devoted to thinking. As I said, not the worst of all
possible worlds.

    A crippled postscript to this. Three or four weeks
after carapace-shucking myself of *Buckman Summers*, the
other book, *Vandenberg*, sold. According to the *London
Times* it made a lot of money (journalists bandy figures
about as casually as they do facts: the best of them
are shitstick hacks). Even so, there's enough for a
few years' quiet living. I'm trying vodka instead of
rotgut-red, but my liver is hostile to Smirnoff's and
shows signs of rejecting what I consider a significant
upgrading.
    It strikes me that Volume II of *Buckman Summers* is
somewhere in the offing. A book for writers and, again,
a Kitchen-Counter attempt. I like to think that this
article might serve as a preface to such an endeavor.
    Meanwhile spring approaches. Damned rotten winter.
Not all that cold, but a lot of snow and mud (Santa Fe
is at seven thousand feet and gets no-nonsense Alpine
conditions). So we do the firewood thing, and four-
wheel drive, and there are the coyotes and no neighbors
for miles. Love from the hilltop.

PUBLISHING FROM

PRISON

by Frank Earl Andrews &

Albert Dickens

FRANK EARL ANDREWS and ALBERT DICKENS are doing time (more than a century of it together) in Rahway State Prison, New Jersey. Publishing their fiction anthology, Voices From The Big House, in 1972 was a triumph over all the usual odds against self-publishers plus the handicaps of prison life. Andrews and Dickens both contributed to their collection along with nine other inmates, including "Hurricane" Carter, the boxing champ.

Pyramid Publications has recently bought the reprint rights to Voices From The Big House and will publish Andrews' and Dickens' next book.

Several years ago, while in the State prison at Trenton, New Jersey, our mutual interest in writing led us to the idea of compiling and editing an anthology of fiction written solely by convicts. However, before we could really get our project underway, Al was transferred to Rahway and the idea of "prison inmates doing it themselves" fell into limbo. Fortunately, a few months later we found ourselves reunited and working in the Rahway State Prison Shoe Shop with a lot of free time on our hands. It wasn't long before we were talking again of *Voices*, and the more we talked, the more ambitious we became. Finally, we decided that we would also try to publish the book from our cells.

Collecting material proved to be an easy matter, since writing is one of the few positive things a convict can do. Also, because we wanted to make certain that our book would be doubly appealing to the public, we concentrated on eliciting material from only those prisoners who were considered the most incorrigible by the prison administrations. We set down to work, making grapevine contact with Trenton through the weekly shipments between the two prisons, and after several months we were ready with sixteen original stories that included the work of ten convict-writers. The authors differed in color, thought, religion, and just about everything else, except the enormous amount of time each one was serving.

Here are the Voices:

Rubin (Hurricane) Carter	Triple Life
Jimmy Coates (Cover Artist)	Life
William (Shoe Willie) Edwards	Life
Paul M. Fitzsimmons	Life

Eugene (Samad) Watson	Life
Frank Earl Andrews	67 Years
John J. Jones	65 Years
William (Willie) Selph	65 Years
Albert Dickens	51 Years
Herman Louis McMillan	30 Years
James (55X) Washington	30 Years

Our next step was to find a printer, so we went
to the prison library and leafed through some old
*Writer's Digest*s, jotting down the addresses of four
who specialized in book printing. We then wrote four
duplicate letters, outlining our situation in life,
mentioning the many extras we would need aside from
the printing and binding service. Prison regulations
forbade an inmate from receiving more than ten books
during any one month, so we would need a warehouser
and distributor. Prison regulations imposed a monthly
limitation on the number of letters a convict could
mail out or receive, and we would need someone to fill
orders and invoice sales also. In other words, we
needed more than just a printer, we needed someone who
would get involved.

A month passed before we had all four replies,
and we settled on Harlo, a Detroit printing firm, who
responded quite warmly. Among their services were:
mailing out review copies, making advertising circulars
to our specifications, filling orders, invoicing, and
also stamping their imprint on the spine, thus adding
a bit more prestige to the book. They would also have
the book copyrighted, see that we were listed in all
of the appropriate library and book-dealer magazines,
and help us to prepare an attractive press release.

We sent our manuscript to Detroit and two weeks
later Harlo replied with a quote of $2,244 as the cost
of printing and binding in cloth one thousand copies.
This price did not include the cost of producing one
thousand dust jackets, as we had recently swooped up
convict-artist Jimmy Coates, who went to work designing our cover art. The jacket production later came
to $248.

Now came the big problem, that age-old paradox
of man--*MONEY*. Both of us had been selling articles
to little magazines, yet we hadn't saved nearly $2,500.
We started borrowing, begging, and soliciting money

from everyone we knew, even asking people we didn't
know. Two months later we had $2,000 and the promise
of $1,000 more. We sent the check to Harlo and told
them to get the show on the road.

Producing a 5.5 by 8.5 hardcover book using the
linotype method takes from twelve to sixteen weeks.
This is good, since it allows the self-publisher time
to start promoting his efforts. We knew that we would
have to place advertisements, since people can't buy a
product unless they know of its existence, so we wrote
the Chicago Advertising Agency and asked them for a
list of advertising rates--and almost died! A small
three-inch ad in a major newspaper or large-circula-
tion magazine would cost more than what we had paid
for the entire production of the first printing of
Voices From The Big House. It was an ironic turn of
events, because there wasn't a man of the eleven who
hadn't commanded national attention when society's laws
were broken. Now we had no choice but to hit the begging trail again, though we doubted if any of the top
publications would help us.

Fortunately, all mail restrictions had been lifted
due to negotiations between an inmate committee and the
governor, following a riot. Our first letters were
directed at those publications whose content centered
around prisons, prisoners, and their problems. We
asked for advertising space and to be trusted for payment. The responses were practically nonexistent, so
we turned our attention to the larger magazines. We
didn't hold out much hope at this juncture, especially
since our own people had chosen to ignore us, but we
were determined to leave no stone unturned. The closer
we came to publication day, the more apprehensive we
became. Without exposure, all we would have was a
stack of hardbound dreams, gathering dust in some
printer's warehouse.

Then came Leonora Burton of *Coronet*: "Send us a
half-page mechanical, and there'll be no charge."
Louis B. Dotti of *Sports Illustrated* wrote: "We'll run
three-inch ads for you at no cost." Hoyt W. Fuller
could not run free advertising in *Black World*, but he
could make mention of us as a news item. K. Richard
Greene of the Woodbridge State Library alerted *Library
Journal* and endorsed *Voices* in the New Jersey librarians' *Newsletter*. Two weeks later he wrote and asked

us the name of our book, having risked an endorsement of it without seeing it. *Sepia* would give us ads and bill us, but if we couldn't pay, no bill collectors would be breathing down our necks. Len Oswald of the *National Informer* requested bound page proof and wrote a favorable review; so did Tom Ricke of the *Detroit Free Press*. Louis Botto asked for bound pages, then came into the prison and interviewed us for *True* magazine. *The Elk's Magazine* offered us free space; so did *The Eagle*, *The American Legion*, *Commonweal*, and others. Charles Green and Jeff Dixon previewed *Voices* on WNJR, New Jersey's largest radio station, then sent us a half-hour tape and told us to say what we wanted to. A little dynamite attorney named Ted Gast offered to be our legal adviser. When we told him we were flat broke, he grinned and told us not to worry about it. It has been over six months and we still haven't seen a bill. Finally, to add topping to the cake, a lady by the name of Mrs. Olaf H. Hage came into our lives, wanting to handle the promotion of *Voices*. She was backed by a husband made out of pure gold. Refusing to take a dime even for expenses, this fabulous woman started running all over the United States, trying to make "our dream" into a reality. She is still very active in our behalf, and it is due mostly to her efforts that we have been approached by several paperback publishers and book clubs. As of this writing, it appears that the deep chasm separating those things listed as "winner" and "loser" has been bridged.

SOME HINTS AND SUGGESTIONS. Above all else, avoid the subsidy or vanity publishers. There has been a great deal of bad publicity concerning these people and, unfortunately, we must add our voices to the negative vibrations. Our first instinct was to contract a subsidy publisher, since their services seemed ideally suited to our needs. After we read the conditions of their contract, we changed our minds in a hurry. Vanity publishers print in editions of about three thousand copies, and charge around $3,800 for a 200-page hardbound book. The author receives 40 per cent of whatever the book sells for. In case a second printing is needed, the subsidy company will produce the books at its cost, but the royalties paid to the author drop to 20 per cent. In other words, once the book displays signs of becoming successful, the vanity man moves in to take off the cream. Furthermore, only twenty copies of the book the author paid to have published are his. If he wants more books, he will have to buy them. Stay away from these people. You will get a better deal from a printer and probably as much promotion. You also own all books.

It is wise to start with a small initial printing, in order to test the sales potential of your book. If needed, subsequent printings can be produced quickly and at a reduced cost, using the offset lithography process.

The most coveted way of gaining exposure for a book is to get it reviewed. Admittedly, big-time reviewers usually devote their time to reviewing books from big-time publishers, but the more books that are sent out, the better the chances of getting reviewed. It may hurt, but the self-publisher cannot afford to pass up any opportunities, however slim.

Advertising too is important, but quite expensive. Major publishers think nothing of investing $30,000, $40,000, or more in advertising best sellers. Consistency too is important, as one advertisement in the largest-circulation newspaper or magazine in the world won't sell many books unless it is followed up. Ads should be placed with care, because a book about baking cakes or raising babies just isn't going to appeal to the readers of *Playboy*.

The most effective way we found of advertising was directly to bookstores and libraries. Addresses can be obtained already printed on #10 envelopes. We simply had Harlo make up a batch of attractive circulars, slipped them into the envelopes, and put them in the mailbox. Remember though that book dealers and libraries are in business and are entitled to a discount. The standards are 40 per cent off to bookstores and 25 per cent off to libraries. Another good thought is to stock bookstores (fifteen or twenty copies) "on consignment." This puts the bookseller in a receptive frame of mind, because if he cannot sell your books, he can simply ship them back to you at no risk to himself.

Another good idea, provided the self-publisher doesn't have space to warehouse his books, is to contact a fulfillment service. If the mailing and invoicing are left to the printer, he will probably charge around 30 per cent of each book sold. Fulfillment services will pack, apply the correct postage, and mail the book. Rates are about thirty cents per book shipped and $1.60 per square foot used for warehousing. Besides the lower cost, using a warehouser/ fulfillment service gives added assurance that what the printer has been paid for is in fact delivered.

Self-publishing is a precarious business, abundant with potholes and pitfalls. From a monetary point of view, it is a horrible investment. For those who think a fortune lies in self-publishing, don't believe it! The stories of authors who financed their own material and took the literary world by storm wouldn't fill a thimble.

Yet there are other reasons why people publish their own books: Some find it impossible to obtain a foothold in today's hard-core "realm of the written word." Others simply want to see themselves in print. *Voices From The Big House* was published for these reasons and a few others: We had grown weary of reading about only the gory and bloody shortcomings of prisons and prisoners, and we wanted to show the other side of the coin, that we were not all standing around in corners crying about the food, that we were not all insensitive vampires, just waiting for an opportunity to bayonet society's babies. Furthermore, we wanted to provide a medium of expression for ourselves, while eliminating the strict editorial requirements of major publishers.

If writing is your bag but you are having trouble breaking into print, keep in mind that you are competing with an army of already established professionals. The number of new books published each year by new authors wouldn't overload the trunk of your Volkswagon.

If you have been thinking about self-publication and you are financially able--*DO IT!* Self-publishing is a short cut and the sale of only one book places you in the ranks of the professionals. You will probably lose money, but if you aren't willing to invest in yourself, don't affect an attitude because others won't either.

Like the prophet who couldn't go to the mountain, bring the mountain to yourself. During the course of your self-publishing adventure you will meet new

people, mostly nice folks, so many that you will sit
back and ask yourself where you've been hiding all
these years. If that's not enough, wait until you
hold your first book in your hands, and if you ever
manage to formulate the words that truly explain the
inner satisfaction, the sense of well-being, the feeling of finally arriving, write and tell us about it,
because we're still in a daze...

An illustration from page 11 of the Grassy Knoll Press
edition of *MacBird*. MacBird and Lady MacBird are dis-
cussing the forthcoming visit to the MacBird ranch by
Ken O'Dunc, the king. Says MacBird: "I dare do all that
may become a man. Who dares do more is none." Lady
MacBird responds: "I'm not a man. I am a lady and a
Southern hostess." Copyright © 1966 by Barbara Garson.
Drawing by Lisa Lyons.

MACBIRD, A PLAY

an interview with

Barbara Garson

In the mid 1960's, Barbara Garson and her husband Marvin self-published *MacBird*, a satirical Shakespearean parody about the Kennedy's and the Johnson's. Recently she was interviewed in her apartment over a self-cooked meal of *hoi-sin* chicken.

How did you write MacBird?

MacBird got written because I had the time and the money and because of spite. Back in 1964 Marvin and I were living in Berkeley, California, and I was collecting unemployment insurance. I had been a picket for the Amalgamated Clothing Workers at two dollars an hour. Now I was collecting twenty-five dollars a week from the Unemployment Office! And I had a lot of time on my hands. Marvin and I had knocked ourselves out twenty-four hours a day for four months with the Free Speech Movement. The F.S.M. subsided. I was tired and for once we had actually *won* something. Marvin wanted to do some further agitation that I didn't agree with. So I hung a sign on my door, "No Contacts. Just Friends Admitted." And you know what? No one rang the bell for three months. So I sat home and wrote a play.

At first I thought *MacBird* would be a short skit in prose and maybe we'd use it at an antiwar teach-in. Then I tried out iambic pentameter for a soliloquy and found it was fun. It's really easy to write in verse. All day I was alone there with *MacBird* and Marvin was running around with the F.S.M. epigone. So *MacBird* was kind of a spiteful act of independence. I would show Marvin that I could stay home and not need all that tumult. *MacBird* was done in three months.

How did you self-publish MacBird?

Among the Left in Berkeley back then, everybody who wrote anything automatically went to a printer or a mimeograph machine and got it around to friends. Here in New York writers automatically send their stuff off to publishers. Maybe because there just aren't those groups of friends. Getting *MacBird* published was nothing. We already had a press set up in a friend's basement to print leaflets for the Independent Socialist Club, the *Newsletter* of the F.S.M., and other things. Putting *MacBird* on the press was a reflex action. Getting it around campus was easy. The Independent Socialist Club was the actual publisher, and in April 1965 we walked around campus hawking copies of the play for fifty cents apiece. We didn't have any reviews to go on then. We used basic enthusiasm. "Hey, here's a far-out play! Want to buy it?" I'd sell a few copies on campus and then I'd have lunch money for that day.

I don't know how many we sold. We didn't keep very good books back then. As fast as an edition was sold out, we printed another one. I guess we did maybe five editions of a thousand each in Berkeley, but I'm not at all sure. The first one we set on an IBM typewriter. The response was so good that we did a better edition with hot type and offset and just tried to keep up with the demand. Somewhere along the line we came up with the name Grassy Knoll Press.

How did MacBird *arrive in New York?*

People in New York "discovered" *MacBird* like discovering America. A big commercial publisher brought me to New York like some kind of Indian! But they wanted me to do another book and wouldn't publish *MacBird*. So we continued on our own. The first big New York break came with Dwight MacDonald's generous and witty review in the *New York Review of Books*. We placed a mail-order ad in that issue. Then the orders flooded into Grassy Knoll. We took ads in magazines whenever we knew there was going to be a review or when we had arranged for excerpts to be printed. Ads by themselves did us little good when there wasn't a review or excerpt in that issue of the paper.

We had a New York printing of 10,000 and kept going back to press as the editions ran out. Total self-publishing sales were about 105,000 at ninety-five cents each before Grove Press took over. We took direct mail orders, wrote letters to bookstores, and relied on word-of-mouth advertising. A friend would see a friend's copy and order from that. It snowballed. We kept the supply just slightly below the demand. Bookstores had signs in their windows, "We have *MacBird*!"

My mother showed Marvin and me how to do double-entry bookkeeping. We started out in a backroom of our Flatbush Avenue apartment. Then we took a small office in order to stock copies and to have a couple of desks for the paper work and to be near a post office. From then on we filled orders. "Fulfillment," as it is called in the trade, is one of the dreariest jobs in the world, yet I did it myself for almost a year with great pleasure. At our office, we called back and forth to each other as we opened envelopes. "Hey look, there really is a Kalamazoo and they want ten copies there." Or, "A Marine Sergeant in Vietnam. Far out!" Or, "Look at this fancy stationery. Be sure to charge her the extra five cents for postage."

I recently interviewed many women at *Reader's Digest* who do basically the same work but with intense supervision and with intense boredom and often fear. That isn't how I experienced the work. When I got tired of wrapping packages, I went on to stamp envelopes. Toward the end of the day we counted the money--with great glee. Sometimes it was a long, tedious count, thousands of one-dollar bills, but it never got boring to me. Then we entered the totals into the books and hauled the sacks and boxes down to the post office.

At Grassy Knoll Press I didn't just choose my own methods of work, I also selected the goal. I could do a repetitive task with enthusiasm because it was my own play--it was my own message. It was also my own money, which made it a lot of fun to count. I worked fast and furious because I wanted the play to reach Kalamazoo. And if I felt like slowing down, that was my choice too. I enjoyed the work because I understood and approved of the whole process. It was an awful lot of fun to run a small business.

It's so nice to be your own publisher. For instance, we had complete control of layout. When Grove Press took over publication, I told them no ads in *MacBird*. I put it into the contract. Even so they ran an ad right in the middle of the book, for *Evergreen Review*! Yich! I raised hell, and they took it out of the next edition. But a self-publisher controls all such matters, including how the book is to be promoted-- no obnoxious publicity. We picked the reviews to use in advertising too, like those on the back of the book, which include Lyndon Johnson's remark, "To the artists of the stage, who give us all mankind in all its disguises and so give us ourselves as truly we are, I pay tribute..." To get a commercial publisher to use that line would have meant all sorts of hassles.

MacBird never had an official publication date, which is the practice. It just grew like topsy. We started on a small scale and systematically made sure we got reviews and followed up the reviews.

Why did you sell rights of MacBird *to Grove?*

We got tired. We had other things we wanted to do (like have a baby). We'd reached the end of the easily accessible market. So it seemed like the step to take. Grove sold the next 300,000 copies at less profit to us than the first 100,000 copies we sold ourselves. But we got tired and we literally sold out.

STORY OF A

PUBLISHER

by Alan Swallow

ALAN SWALLOW, *founder of Swallow Press, was one of the
veterans of the small-press movement. He died in 1966.
The following article is reprinted by permission from*
New Mexico Quarterly, *volume XXXVL:4 (Winter 1966-1967),
pp. 301-324, copyright 1966 by The University of New
Mexico Press. In a tribute to Swallow at the end of
that article Gus Blaisdell said, "Alan could have been
many things: anything he put his hand to he did exceptionally well. He was a maverick, one of the great
ones."*

Why does one do it? Why does one attempt publishing
without training in the publishing centers? How does
one get the arrogance, if it may be called that, to
feel that a mantle of destiny has fallen onto his
shoulders? The reasons are difficult to analyze. Probably the best I can do is to sketch a bit of intellectual autobiography.

I grew up on an irrigated farm in northwestern
Wyoming near the town of Powell. Quite early I became
an omniverous reader of all the materials at hand.
These consisted of popular magazines, popular fiction
and nonfiction; in addition, I early acquired a tremendous interest in science and technology, particularly
mechanics. And, like many another adolescent of the
time, I fooled around a great deal with old cars and
motorcycles.

My adolescent intent was to become an engineer,
probably in the aeronautical field. I do not recall
just when I first picked up an interest in serious literature, which early meant poetry and philosophy.
There must have been some interest in the spring of the
year I turned sixteen, because I recall that I rode
into town to sell a motorcycle I had for a year or two.
Then my parents took me to Gardner, Montana, which is
the north entrance to Yellowstone National Park, and
that summer of 1931 I ran a filling station in Gardner
for a family which maintained a summer tourist business
there. This business consisted of a grocery store and
soda fountain in a large building and a filling station
next door ; it was my job to run the filling station.
My hours were long in that I worked from six in the
morning until eight or eight-thirty at night. But typical tourist business of that time was spotty, and there
would be rushes of thirty minutes of hard work and

then periods of fifteen or thirty minutes in which there wouldn't be much to do.

I did not have much money for books, but I discovered then the Haldeman-Julius publications. One could buy the Little Blue Books twenty for a dollar and the larger books ten for a dollar, and during the summer I bought probably two hundred fifty. I also acquired a few other books and magazines, including, I recall, Will Durant on philosophy and such magazines as *The Thinker*. I did a great deal of reading, then, during this summer, primarily in the fields of poetry, plays, philosophy, socialism, free thought. It was during that summer also that I first started to write poetry.

I was tremendously attracted by several things that I learned then: first, by the effort of Haldeman-Julius to provide good literature at inexpensive prices --and I suppose that there was planted a small seed of the idea of publishing at some time; second, through Haldeman-Julius publications of magazines and through reading other materials, I became aware of the group we call the "little magazines." I was certainly impressed with the idealism and the efforts of these magazines to put out a quality work without consideration for commercial results.

During the next two years, my senior year in high school and first year at the University of Wyoming, I became more and more interested in the "little magazines." I was sending out my own verse, and I had my first acceptances in two or three of these magazines during that period. In my sophomore year at the University of Wyoming, I decided to start a little magazine of my own. The idea was to start with local talent, in the hope that gradually the magazine could extend beyond the campus to reach for additional talent and more mature talent and also for reading response. The magazine was called *Sage* and was mimeographed. Several issues were issued during the year, and I had the help of a number of students. I particularly remember the help of Madeline Shorey, who, as a competent typist, did the stencils for the publication.

This idea was not a new one, and this pattern for the "little magazine" has been tried by many others since. I believe that in most cases it is not a sound idea for launching a magazine. At any rate, during what would have been my junior year at college I went to

Laramie and registered, but shortly returned home and worked during that year in a bank at Powell. The reasons were confusion and uncertainty about where I was going with a college education and my personal future. During that year, of course, I had nothing to do with the magazine *Sage*, although some other students at the University did get out one or two issues, and that was the last of that particular magazine.

On returning to the University to finish two more years of undergraduate work, I had the opportunity to do some editorial work with magazines. Ann Winslow, who was the executive secretary of the College Society of America, had moved to the University of Wyoming, and with her had moved the magazine published by the Society, called *College Verse*. My poems were appearing in the magazine, and under an NYA grant I was able to assist her with the work. In addition, there were two students' magazines--one called *Wyoming Quill*, sponsored by a local society; and a magazine of the student body which I edited at the time.

From these experiences I resolved that at some time I would return to publishing a magazine, but I also resolved that the next time would be under other circumstances. I wished it to be printed, and I wished to start less with a local situation and to be able to publish more mature writers whom I admired.

The three years from June 1937, to June 1940, were spent in Baton Rouge in graduate study at the Louisiana State University, and during half of that period my wife, Mae, was secretary for *The Southern Review*. A good many of us had arrived there because of the work of Robert Penn Warren and Cleanth Brooks.

The last of those years, the school year 1939-40, I thought that possibly the opportunity had come for which I had been looking. On the campus were a number of promising young writers who had been publishing in the little magazines as I had been. Two of these students, Sheila Corley and Frederick Brantley, proposed that there ought to be an anthology of the writings by some of the students who had gathered to work with Warren and Brooks.

In the fall of 1939, then, I borrowed one hundred dollars from my father and secured a secondhand 5-by-8 Kelsey handpress. I bought the necessary furniture and type cases, and also several fonts of type and some paper. This outfit was set up in the garage of the apartment where we lived. The library at the Louisiana State University, to my good fortune, had good holdings in the areas of the history of type, of printing and typography. I read all of these books I could to learn as much as possible in a short time about these materials, and I set out to print. The book being printed was an anthology, called *Signets: An Anthology of Beginnings*, and the procedure was to set one page at a time, print the copies on the handpress, then distribute the type back in the cases. Several of the students came day after day to aid in distributing the type in the cases.

I recall one of the exciting moments of the year. Corley and Brantley told me of a new student on the campus by the name of Thomas McGrath, who was writing verse and had published a few things in the magazines. They brought me some of his manuscripts and I sat down by the wall of the garage and read them through. Reading them gave me great elation and a great shock to think that we had such a fine and exciting talent. Subsequently, after knowing McGrath, I resolved that my first venture, other than the anthology, would be a small collection of his poems.

In March 1940, the anthology appeared and the following month, McGrath's *First Manifesto*, as number one of the Swallow Pamphlets. The reason for the pamphlet idea was that I still had the notion, gained from reading the Haldeman-Julius materials, that good literature ought to be put out at a very inexpensive price, and these pamphlets were projected at twenty-five cents each.

At this time, twenty-six years later, I am not sure that I can recall fully what was going on in my mind. Clearly, I was fired by the idealism of the little magazine movement. Yet the first two publications had been a book and a pamphlet, not a magazine. Somehow, I knew that the purpose of what I had done was to be able to have a little magazine, and I resolved that I would not have any period in my life in which I did not have active editorial, and probably publishing, control of such an outlet. And that resolve has been fulfilled.

Clearly, also, I had provided myself with some training. At this perspective of time, it seems that

the training might have been haphazard, yet it consisted of active selection of manuscripts, and it consisted
of sufficient technical training that I knew I could
put on paper in a workmanlike fashion some of the things
I would be wanting to publish.
Another factor was at work. Perhaps my readers
will feel this is a kind of mysticism, but I am sure
that it is not. From my account so far, the reader will
have perceived that I grew up in an environment of work.
My original home was, indeed, very close to the fron-
tier: the first water had been turned on the land, which
I called my home, just a few years before I was born; my
grandfather had homesteaded this land but had died before he could live on it; my father started farming it
when he was seventeen; I was born two years later. I
believe that I have one tendency which is significant
in these facts; it is a tendency that I inherited, although I would not say that all persons who grow up in
the environment will necessarily respond to the tendency. That tendency is to act upon one's beliefs and
ideas. I value this inheritance probably more than any
other. Translated to the situation in 1940 when I had
finished two jobs with my handpress, it meant that I
would be compelled by my own character to *act*, that is,
that I would do what I felt should be done, and those
things that I felt should be done were informed by the
idealism I have mentioned.
These factors--the somewhat haphazard training, the
knowledge and skills sufficient to *do*, the flair for
idealism, and the innate character trait toward action--
fell into place at one time in a way which I suppose is
rare in one's life. (Another set of circumstances fell
into place for me some fourteen years later, as I shall
indicate.) These led to one other idea which I cannot
spot exactly in time, but my concepts of publishing developed beyond that of the little magazine. This development, I suppose, has identified my publishing work
since that time. As a poet, I was concerned with the
problems of the poet. I realized that those problems,
in the publishing sense, extended beyond the outlets
of the little magazines. The ripened concept was that
there was even a greater need in the realm of book publishing than there was in the realm of the little magazine world for the effort which was analogous to the
dedication found often in the little magazines. The

concept was what I later came to call the "little publisher." The term "little" refers, of course, to an attitude, not to size. The analogy is that book publishing should be informed by the same noncommercial dedication as characterized at least the best of the little magazines.

Thus was added to the factors already mentioned a particular idea of what I could do in book publishing. The excitement of discovering McGrath and printing some other impressive work drove this intention deeper into me. And for the next fourteen years I worked from these abilities and concepts. I had two years in Army service, but even during those two years, I worked actively as poetry editor of *New Mexico Quarterly Review* (as the magazine was then called) so that I was never out of active decision-making in an editorial sense. Basically, the method was that I made a living as a teacher, first at the University of New Mexico for two years, 1940-42, and Western State College in Colorado for one year, 1942-43, and then after the war at the University of Denver for eight and a half years, from January 1946, to August 1954. The publishing was done part time as an avocation, technically. This means that during that period no money was taken out of publishing. Small amounts, such as could be taken from a teacher's salary, were put in. But at least ninety per cent of the values that were put in were in the form of labor. This included, of course, continuous and incessant labor of my own; but at various times I had the help of my family, friends, and students who volunteered; and at two different periods, the help, in separate organizations, of Horace Critchlow.

To try to tell the story chronologically during those years until 1954 would involve so many strands that the story would probably be confusing. So permit me to project ahead the story of the magazine effort alone and then return to book publishing.

Essential to the story are certain attitudes that I have had or that I have developed about the little magazines. The reader should recall that, in the first two decades of the little-magazine movement in this country, the chief effort was to publish creative work that was not acceptable in the commercial magazines: poems, short fiction, sometimes long fiction published

over several issues, plays, various experimental works
hard to classify. During the 1930's and the early 40's,
especially under the impact of the *Hound and Horn* and
The Southern Review, a different pattern developed,
which I have called the "quarterly review" type of magazine. The pattern for the "quarterly review" was to
publish more nonfiction prose than creative work, although each issue normally contained one or more stories
and a selection of poems. This type of magazine, together with the books which quickly followed, became
the publishing arm of the revolutionary critical movement which so completely changed much of our thinking
about literature, both in criticism and in the profession of teaching.

The "quarterly review" pattern became dominant and
until very recently has remained dominant in the little-
magazine field. The difficulty with the pattern is that
in the hands of its second generation (of whom I must
consider myself one), the critical materials became
repetitious and dull; that is, after the tremendous il-
lumination gained by the works of such men as Winters,
Tate, Ransom, Blackmur, Burke, and other men of their
generation, the magazines quickly seemed to be filled
with minor developments on the old insights and often
became dull. In the later 1940's, I published an essay
about the postwar little magazines, and I felt that the
need for the little-magazine movement was to return pre-
dominantly to creative work. Gradually, this has come
about until today, with the so-called "mimeograph revolution," the creative work seems to pop out from almost
every garret in America.

By the end of 1940, with my handpress equipment,
I was ready to launch a serious effort. In 1941 I published four issues of the magazine *Modern Verse*, printed from handset type always--at first on the handpress
and later on the larger press I shall mention. The
title indicates the purpose: to publish poems. The
only prose was a small effort at reviewing. In this
period, Dudley Wynn had become editor of *New Mexico
Quarterly* and had changed the name to *New Mexico Quarterly Review*, projecting the former magazine more particularly into the "quarterly review" pattern. He asked me to become poetry editor of *NMQR*, and I turned o-
ver the small subscription list for *Modern Verse* in
accepting this position. From 1942 to 1948, when

Dudley Wynn relinquished the magazine in order to go to the University of Colorado, I continued as poetry editor. As I look back on this experience, I believe that we had an important magazine of the "quarterly review" type. The prose fiction selected by Dudley Wynn was challenging and often very distinguished, including the work of many persons now widely known. The nonfiction had, appropriately, many important materials about the Southwest, but also included literary criticism. In poetry, I was able to have space which permitted me to publish even more poems per quarter than I had been able to use in *Modern Verse* and also to conduct a review section covering my commentary on some eighty volumes of verse per year. Although a part of a larger magazine, this effort was clearly one of the larger efforts concerned with verse in the literary field of the time, and it would be a pleasure to have the space to spell out the names of the poets who contributed.

As I was editing poetry for *NMQR*, I thought I detected a number of poets working in experimental ways that were not merely offshoots of the old experimentalism. I published some of this work, but it was clear that with the eclectic policy I had for my poetry selections, I did not have space for the job I felt they needed. On my initiative, Meade Harwell and I sent a letter to the poets I thought were involved, proposing the formation of a cooperative group and the publication of a new magazine to concentrate upon this experimental work. A group was formed and the magazine *Experiment* was begun. During its first or second year, I was its editor; it was continued by other hands until it now seems to have gone out of the picture.

After 1948, no longer having the poetry editorship of *NMQR*, I worked in various ways in the little-magazine movement. One of my objectives had been to try to find a means of being helpful to the best magazines. An early experiment was the publication of *The Advance Guard* for the four issues in the period of 1947-48. This magazine did not publish creative material but attempted to give precise commentary upon serious literary publications in book and magazine form (my readers will detect an idea here which reached some fruition in the "current bibliography" sections of *Twentieth Century Literature* several years later); it also provided brief histories of significant little magazines. As my ideas developed, *The Advance Guard* became the *Index to Little Magazines*. Indeed, the first volume of the *Index* in 1948 was published simultaneously as the last issue of *The Advance Guard*. I had finally developed a project which I felt would be the most helpful one I could do for the best little magazines. This project has continued, and it is also being projected backwards to cover the historic past of the little magazines.

Active editorship in creative materials for little magazines was confined for a short time to minor positions as associate editor and advisory editor for various magazines. But, under my feeling that the chief effort in little magazines had to be the publication of creative work, once more, in 1953, I started my magazine *PS* (poems and stories). As the name indicates, this magazine contains no critical work, not even reviews. It is purely an occasional magazine and has seemed to average about one issue every eighteen months. I consider it primarily an adjunct to the book publishing, an opportunity to publish briefer things by some writers whose work interests me.

In 1955, with the help of some of my former students, as a cooperative endeavor, *Twentieth Century Literature: A Critical and Scholarly Journal*, was begun. It has been published continuously and just as it crosses its twelfth volume, the journal will be given to Immaculate Heart College of Los Angeles so that it may be institutionalized and so that, also, it will be assured a place without dependency upon my personal health and time. I have been proud that it has been the only privately sponsored critical and scholarly magazine in the literary field in this country. It has prospered and has become too large a burden for me, taking too much time away from my publishing. *PS*, however, will be continued.

Now I can return to the much larger effort involved with book publishing under my concept of the "little publisher." In the spring of 1940, after completion of the first two works with the handpress, and thinking about a first full book of poetry to offer on the market, I had asked Robert Penn Warren if he knew any good poets who had remained unpublished in book form. He suggested two, of whom one was Lincoln Fitzell. I contacted Fitzell, whose work I had seen in magazines and

admired, and entered into the first contract for a
book of this nature.

The printing equipment and the new type and the
plans for Fitzell's book, *In Plato's Garden*, were pack-
ed into the car and taken to Powell for the summer,
inasmuch as I was going to the University of New Mexico
that fall to begin full-time teaching. During the summer I kept working away at the printing of the Fitzell
book--a page at a time--and I have always felt that
this was one of the best printing jobs I ever did. All
this was taken to Albuquerque in September, and the
printing was finished in the fall. I was lucky to discover Hazel Dreis, surely acknowledged to be the best
bookbinder in the United States at the time, in Santa
Fe, where she had a binding shop. She became interested in the work and prepared a very nice case binding
for the Fitzell book at as low a price as she could,
and I issued the book that fall. This was followed
immediately by some additions to the Swallow Pamphlet
series.

The work to this time was poetry, as was the work
with *Modern Verse*, and this is a good place to indicate
some general attitudes about publishing poetry. A
basic position I have had is this: it is not possible,
volume after volume, to sell enough copies of a book
of poems to pay commercial prices for production and
to pay royalties. Of course, there will be individual
variations, and an individual volume may do very well.
Against this, if one is persistent and publishes book
after book, many will sell very poorly indeed. Therefore, the publishing of poetry in our culture involves
finding a means of making up this deficit. The means
are several: so-called "vanity" publishing makes up
the difference at the author's expense; supporting the
monetary loss by monetary gains elsewhere; seeking the
help of an "angel," which in our culture sometimes can
involve not so much an individual as a foundation or
an educational institution.

To my mind, all of these are to be rejected. The
dependency upon the author is not in the best interests
of poetry or poets, and certainly there is no correla-
tion between the ability of a poet and his ability to
finance publication of his work. The second is presumably the method used by our large publishing houses,
some of whom pride themselves upon sufficient literary

taste to take a loss which will be made up by best
selling books. It is to be noted that many of these
publishers hedge on this matter in various ways, but
it is also to be noted that after a period in which the
number of publishers who thus prized their literary
qualifications had declined considerably, their number
has somewhat increased in recent years. The third
method I have chosen to reject wholly. The reason is
that I regard as significant the value of individual
editorial judgment and I have therefore been wary of
ever getting into a situation whereby a gift might impose a kind of control or obligation. And the sorts
of other outside support usually involve the viciousness of "committeeitis," that is, the filtering of the
judgment through a kind of averaging-out of several individual judgments. In our time, a vigorous publishing
program for poetry has been carried on by Wesleyan
University Press. To my mind, although I feel it is
an admirable effort, the editorial judgments involved
have been to some extent blunted by the advisory-com-
mittee approach.

Rejecting these, yet determined to publish poetry
on my own judgments, the training I had given myself
in printing was the answer, just as it was the answer
to the problem of publishing the little magazine. My
position was simple: by throwing in my own work without cost against the book, I could reduce the out-of-
pocket expenses of producing a volume of poems to the
extent that sales would earn back all the expense plus
a royalty for the author. As my list has built, the
average sales have increased, so that the dependency
upon my own manual work is less. For example, whereas
I set the first books by hand and thus saved composition expense, I now buy composition commercially. But
for most of the books of poetry I still do my own work
at the "stone" and my own presswork. It should be noted that in a pinch I could get out a book with almost
no out-of-pocket expense. I have not taught myself to
make paper, but I could do so; but I have, with the
help of friends in the bindery, done every other process of getting materials and of preparing a book.

The idea has worked as well as the extent of the
labor I could put into the books. This has been sufficient to publish for nearly twenty years more volumes
of poetry under a royalty contract, as I have publicly

claimed, than any other publisher in the nation. At
least for me and my basic position of action upon my
judgments, I cannot think of another device as a solution to the problem of publishing poetry in our society.
Now, what of the taste and philosophy behind the
judgments ? If the judgment was generally faulty, all
this work would have been a false, nearly useless, accomplishment. I have one interesting test for my enthusiasms; for it is the momentary enthusiasms which
are likely to endanger the independent judgment, so
long, at least, as one may assume that the independent
judgment is reasonably grounded on a useful critical
position. That test is this: I normally will have
handled the poems a good many times before a book is
ready. I try to read each book, before acceptance, a
minimum of twice carefully, and usually three times.
This delays the final judgment sometimes, but it does
protect the author and me from possible decisions on
quick impressions and momentary enthusiasms. Then in
reading proofs and in the actual pressrun--during which
time I will be reading also--the work can become "old
hat." By the time the process is finished, I know a
great deal about the poems. If my enthusiasm remains
after those trials, I issue the work with all the critical assurance I can command. I test my critical
judgment against the laborious process of printing, and
I cannot think of a better test. It reminds me of my
early way of determining how much I would want to purchase something from the Montgomery Ward catalog; I
would translate the dollar amounts into the number of
hours of labor that I would have to put out in work to
acquire the wanted possession. And I can think of only
one title which, when I was through, had failed this
test and I felt I had largely wasted my time. There
have been a few other books, but very few, that I have
not been proud of at the end of the process; these were
books in which I would shorten my own process because
of the strong recommendation or enthusiasm of someone
else whose judgment I respected. These have not been
bad, by any means, but in a few cases I confess that my
own critical judgment did not sufficiently accord with
the other judgments. To put it another way, on an occasional individual volume, out of respect for others,
I have succumbed to what I call the vice of "committeeitis" and in many of those cases I have been regretful.

An interesting sidelight to me: the method I have outlined makes me so familiar with the work that I am a little affected by the review comment that my books of poetry receive. I feel it in my bones, as it were, that I am so much more inside these poems than the reviewer is likely to be. I respect many reviewers, but I know their handicaps. And until I find that rare one who has come as close to the poems as I have, I know that my judgment should not be effected by the review comments. I am betting my judgment for the long haul against the judgment of any reviewer or critic. This may sound like a lot of arrogance, but I do not know how a person could possibly act on his judgments so continuously without finally taking that position.

With the proud position occupied on my list by the poetry of J. V. Cunningham, Yvor Winters, Edgar Bowers, Alan Stephens, Allen Tate, and others who might be identified as working within the older traditions of English poetry, obviously my taste for the resources of that tradition showed plainly in my editorial judgments. However, I have many times been annoyed by some public comment that would classify my publishing within this range. I have been eclectic; I have published the work of experimental writers, including at times special efforts that linked poetry with drawing (although I think this is very clearly a fruitless endeavor); I have published a good many people working within what seems to be considered the "modern temper," as some of the characteristic definitions of poetry are thought of today. I have been proud to publish Thomas McGrath who is, in a sense, none of these. Indeed, I find that most of the critics who wish to categorize are themselves working with a narrow definition and might approve one or another book that I have done; but because I have done so many others not within that definition, they feel that I have not worked hard enough for those particular notions. Shift the notions from critic to critic, and you cover the spectrum.

A man by the name of Horace Critchlow was a graduate student at the University of New Mexico that school year of 1940-41 and we became acquainted. He was somewhat older than the usual graduate student and had a bit of money. He was keenly interested in the publishing and thought he would like to work with me on it; so he bought out a small plant of printing equipment which a man had used as a part-time activity in the basement of his house. It consisted of a Chandler and Price 10-by-15 press, type cases and furniture and several fonts of type, mostly adapted to job printing. We installed this equipment, together with what I had, in a garage we rented near the University and formed a partnership called Swallow and Critchlow. For something like a year we published together under that name. We had an idea that we could pay for some of the cost of publishing by doing odd jobs of printing for hire. In much of the time available at the press, I printed letterheads for a church, stationery and invitations for sororities, one leaflet for a boys' ranch, and similar work. We called this facility Big Mountain Press. We bought linotype composition from a Baptist publication in Albuquerque, where a preacher ran a linotype.

While Critchlow and I were working together, we had the notion of expanding beyond the realm of poetry. Particularly interested in the problems of the literature of the West, we thought this expansion might move in that direction. We published two books, one of them paperbound, and the other, both hardbound and paperbound (and thus perhaps one of the many, many precursors of the "paperback revolution" which is usually attributed at its start to Anchor books) on which first appeared the reincarnation of the word "Sage." We called these two titles, "Sage Books." One consisted of translations, *Three Spanish American Poets*; the other, the anthology *Rocky Mountain Stories* edited by Ray B. West, Jr.

In 1942 Critchlow was called into the army, and we had to break up the partnership. We decided to dissolve it on approximately the way we had gone into it--that is, I kept my handpress and the type I had had, and the titles, since I knew I would be going on with publishing, and Critchlow took the larger press and the other equipment he had purchased. That equipment was moved near Santa Fe and then, I discovered later, landed in Denver during the war.

That fall I went to teach at Western State College in Gunnison, Colorado, and during the following school year I issued a few titles, all poetry, using the handpress.

In the fall of 1943 I went into the Army for a

184

little more than two years. When I was in the Army,
I was not able to issue any books, although I did continue the editorial work for the *New Mexico Quarterly
Review*. I came out of the Army late in 1945 and arrived in Denver in January 1946, to teach at the University of Denver.

I had been thinking about a new idea for my publishing. I thought that it was possible for a small
personal publisher to cooperate with a commercial firm,
and drew up some plans which were submitted to a number
of New York publishers during the winter of 1946. My
idea was that I would do some of the smaller things as
before with the small press and with the Alan Swallow
imprint in Denver, but that certain types of books
might well make a go of it on the commercial market
through a joint arrangement with a New York publisher.
William Morrow and Company was the first to take an interest in my plan, and in May 1946, we concluded an arrangement for joint publication under the imprint The
Swallow Press and William Morrow & Co.

The first joint imprint title appeared in 1947 and
during the next four years some twenty-one titles appeared thus. A number of these were poetry, but others
provided an extensive experience with literary criticism, literary bibliography, and fiction. I may as
well use this reference as an opportunity to talk about
these types of books, just as I have previously talked
about my philosophy in publishing poetry.

One of the first two titles in the joint imprint
was *In Defense of Reason*, by Yvor Winters. This was
followed by critical books by Alan Tate and Wallace
Fowlie. They demonstrate that I have been interested,
if I publish literary criticism, almost exclusively in
books which had what I would call a "seminal" position.
I have had very little interest in many of the books
which are often published as literary criticism. One
of these is the ordinary collection of disparate essays
of a person who happens to have published a number of
articles in the quarterly reviews. Another is the usual study of an individual writer. I have felt that
the publishing situation for such books is fairly well
provided for; particularly did this become more true
when Ford Foundation funds became available to university presses. I have considered this a happy circum-

stance. The problem of the "little publisher" in this
whole realm, it seems to me, is to keep from frittering
away his time and energy over the useful but derivative.
At least I have wanted, and I am proud to have achieved,
in the three critics mentioned and also later in publishing the criticism of J. V. Cunningham, the publishing of books with these characteristics: a definite and
"seminal" point of view, that is, a type of criticism
informed by new critical thinking as well as containing
useful scholarship and useful commentary on the individual works. I am interested in what I have called
the "whole critic," that type of critical work which
demonstrates a union of aesthetic and critical ideas
with the ability to see the particular literary work.
The publication of the Winters criticism began here and
continues on into the present; I have indicated elsewhere that I feel that he is the outstanding example of
the "whole critic." Tate's work, although it is a collection of disparate essays and although Tate has not
provided a fully stated critical position, certainly
suggests these qualities. Fowlie was breaking new
ground in attempting a rationale for surrealism and
other modern movements. Then Cunningham came along
with the most succinct arguments of position and detail
that I have ever seen.
       I have violated this editorial stand by doing an
occasional book about a particular author. I recall
particularly the book on Sherwood Anderson by James
Schevill (published at the University of Denver Press)
and the recent book by R. K. Meiners on the work of
Allen Tate. The reason for doing these, which seem outside my editorial position, is that I believe that each
made a particularly needed contribution which might not
have been published elsewhere and thus fell within the
special functions of the "little publisher."
       As an offshoot from my position about literary
criticism, I have had a considerable interest in literary biography, particularly that type which can provide
some biographical information while at the same time
providing some useful, although brief, critical awareness of the writer's work. This accounts for the publication at various times of such a series as the English Novelists, so far as I know, the first series of
such compact books in our time, and the volume on Frost
written by Elizabeth Isaacs. Considered either as

biography or as criticism, such volumes are of secondary values. But as a working teacher, I have been interested in the very considerable values of such books
when they are well done. I may say that I have been
glad that this type of book, now proliferated in several series such as the Twayne series and the Minnesota
pamphlets can now seem to be done successfully without
the need of a special dedication of the "little publisher." My only other passing comment on such books is
that I wish they were not so rigidly conceived in pattern, but I suppose if one must face the task of being
certain that dozens and dozens of writers must be covered, one somehow has to shepherd the effort. It is
not, frankly, the kind of editorial work and editorial
judgment in which I would have any interest.

Still another offshoot from my critical interest
has been, if I may say so, a demonstration of the use-
fulness of the "little publisher." This involves what
I call "literary bibliography." A prototype testing of
this kind of work was the volume *Poetry Explication*,
first done by George Arms and Joseph Kuntz and published in the joint imprint in 1950. This compilation of
critical references was a new concept and it was very
hard to sell at first. I will say that at the time the
joint imprint of Swallow Press and Morrow was given up
and the titles moved to Denver, we had some unbound
sheets of this title which were remaindered because the
sale had been so poor. But I could not leave this concept alone and persisted by publishing additional volumes of this type. Gradually, over a decade, the concept caught hold. When *Poetry Explication*, for example, went out of print in its first edition, it was
more in demand than ever before, and since we had the
idea that these books should be revised approximately
each decade, a simple reprinting would not have suf-
ficed. Instead, the time had to be taken to do the revised edition. Since then *Poetry Explication* has been
through several printings as have its companion volumes, *American Novel*, *English Novel*, and *Short Fiction
Criticism*. The series will be rounded out by the addition of two volumes of drama criticism this winter, and
the intention is to keep each of the volumes revised
each decade.

Twentieth Century Literature linked up with this
group of editorial ideas in that it, in its attitudes,

eschewed the work primarily of explication but demanded that its articles have something of critical awareness or scholarly contribution. Then it immediately projected itself into literary bibliography by its "current bibliography" section and by its publication of individual bibliographies. The latter feature made it feasible for me to issue some of the bibliographies also as books, since costs could be shared in the two appearances. Three or four years ago, *College English* had a survey of useful materials for the teacher and student, and of the thirty-five titles mentioned, I was proud that seven were Swallow publications.

I have approached the publishing of fiction also with some particular attitudes. One of those was in effect programmed by one of the first two books published under the joint Swallow Press-Morrow effort, a book I edited entitled *Anchor in the Sea: An Anthology of Psychological Fiction*. This attempted to point out a particular type of fiction that had been the concern of many of our finest writers of recent times. I would say that my editorial interest in publishing fiction has remained somewhat close to that original conception except that, as I have gotten more deliberately into it in the last decade, other ideas have become a part of the editorial concern. Perhaps the best way that I can summarize the position is this: a small publisher really should, if he can, stay away from the publication of fiction. The entire apparatus of the publication, reception, and sale of new fiction is something outside his method of operation. And the procedure I have outlined whereby one could manage a continuous effort in the publication of poetry will not work for fiction. The reason for this is merely mechanical: most books of fiction are long and the small press will have to devote so much time to a single volume that the printer could be doing several shorter books with the same effort. I have done a few books of fiction in which part of the manufacture was provided by my own labor, but most of this work I have had to hire others to do because of the factor of time. That is, the time that I had available for production was centered on the poetry and I was unwilling to give up several volumes of poetry for one volume of fiction.

Despite these attitudes about publishing fiction, I have persisted in doing so. The primary reason is

that I have from time to time found works which I admire greatly and which for some reason were not being
taken up by the large publishers. Thus I felt compelled , again by my judgment of value, to do everything I
could to see that some particular works were published.
Besides individual volumes that I could mention, chief
effort has gone into such as these: the making available of the historical novels of Janet Lewis; completion of Vardis Fisher's gigantic Testament of Man and
then pulling together a good many of his works; the
assertion of the value which had been neglected in the
work of Frank Waters; the publication of the works of
Anaïs Nin; the publication of two titles by Edward
Loomis and various works by N. V. M. Gonzales, Thomas
Bledsoe, Richard McBride, and quite a few others; doing several books by Frederick Manfred at a critical
time for him. How have I managed it? Situations for
individual volumes vary a good deal, but at this moment
I can say that I have not been hurt by doing this. I
have had to feel that with serious work the "little
publisher" may not be at quite such a disadvantage as
it would first appear. Being devoted to the works, he
is prepared to neglect the immediate reaction, which
counts so much in the larger marketplace for fiction.
In other words, again he is asserting his judgment on
a long-range basis; he is willing to expect that the
better fiction is not completely subject to that marketplace and that it will continue to sell instead of die.
Some of the works have attained a steady sale, a few in
quite good volume. An example of which I am particularly proud is the Frank Waters' novel, *The Man Who Killed
the Deer*. When I issued this at the University of Denver Press about 1951, then taken over by my imprint in
1953, there was practically no sale available. But I
managed to continue a sale at an accelerated pace ever
since until now in its two editions it has a very substantial sale; every year it is more and more accepted.
        Incidentally, I believe that the University of
Denver Press was the first university press in the nation to publish original fiction, not reprints.

        In the joint-imprint plan I had thought that some
of my titles would be able to assume the tremendous
overhead costs involved in New York commercial publishing and, further, that a by-product of my work with

some of the authors for my specialized literary imprint would be an occasional book of even more popular demand, which would be a money-maker for such a firm as Morrow.

Experience indicated that I did turn out two or three manuscripts of interest to them. But on the whole, the idea was not very satisfactory. I found that the authors with whom I was working were not very frequently commercially feasible in terms of New York publishing. I found, further, that despite the advantage of salesmen and the normal operations of a New York publisher, the titles in which I was specifically interested did not sell so well that they could stand the extra costs involved. So, by friendly and mutual agreement, in 1951 the joint imprint was dissolved with Morrow, and all the titles remaining that had been published thus were moved out to Denver.

Several other things had been going on: I continued to publish under the Alan Swallow imprint with verse and some fiction. I discovered that Mr. Critchlow was in Denver also, and that the press we had used in Albuquerque was in Denver in the basement of the home of Rudolph Gilbert, the Unitarian minister . I was able to make arrangements to use that press. Mr. Gilbert, in fact, was using it, as well as a treadle Pearl Press that he had, for the printing of church bulletins and programs. With both presses available, much more work could be turned out than with my small handpress. For several years I did my printing under those conditions, and a number of my students took an interest in the publishing and would lend aid, particularly John Williams, who learned to print and operated the press quite often for a couple of years while he was studying at the University of Denver. A number of other students also aided in one way or another, either by printing or by folding printed sheets for binding at the open-house gatherings I held periodically for students.

Critchlow also indicated continued interest and faith in publishing. With the Swallow Press arrangement with Morrow and with continuation of the smaller editions of the literary material under the Alan Swallow imprint, the spot that seemed to me wide open for similar activity and development of a market was that of regional books--books about the Rocky Mountain West. Critchlow and I picked up this idea from our brief beginnings some five years earlier when we formed the

small corporation called Sage Books, Inc., to work in this field.
Then the University of Denver decided to make an effort in publishing, and founded the University of Denver Press. I was asked to become director of that effort, although it was to be part-time, since I continued to teach.
For a period of a few years, I was responsible for the books coming out under four different imprints: Alan Swallow, Sage Books, Swallow Press and William Morrow & Co., and the University of Denver Press. This was reduced, of course, when the Swallow Press and Morrow & Co. imprint was dissolved. Because those titles came to Denver, the number of titles did not reduce, and the effort involved in the joint imprint was actually transferred to Denver and continued with the Alan Swallow imprint.
In 1951, with the death of Margaret Bartlett, *Author and Journalist* came on the market and Critchlow, Raymond Johnson--who had founded a firm interested especially in publication printing--and David Raffelock of the National Writers' Club decided to buy the magazine. I was asked to come into the group to edit it. A part of the arrangement was to provide some space for the press, which I moved out of Gilbert's basement, and for storage and shipping, which had become a real problem and had been informally handled through the aid of friends who would put books up and sometimes do some of the packaging. For a period of two years, then, that side of the work was handled in a building *Author and Journalist* had rented. In 1953 the *Author and Journalist* was sold to Nelson Antrim Crawford in Topeka, and it became necessary to make other arrangements for space. One of my students, Bruce Woodford, provided basic storage in the basement of a home he and his wife owned, and then later I rented a garage to store the books. That year we added to our home and provided a small room in which I could place the press itself and do the actual shipping, replenishing a small supply of the titles by going to the storage facility. This served temporarily until in 1954 I secured on a competitive bid the publication of the *United States Quarterly Book Review* from the Library of Congress, and with the income from this contract (the suspension of *USQBR* came in 1956), we added a building on the back of our pro-

perty, which has been used since for printing and shipping and storage facilities. In 1953 Mr. Critchlow decided to leave Denver and ultimately moved to California, so again we had to dissolve our association.

The experience with Sage Books, Inc., and the University of Denver Press had interested me in the problems of a regional list; and I was determined to pursue it. So the arrangement was that I took over the stock of Sage Books titles and made the imprint itself--without the "Inc." since the corporation was dissolved--a sub-imprint of mine; and I have carried it on since, with approximately one half of the publishing effort going into the books under that imprint.

In September 1953, The University of Denver, under stress of change and financial difficulty, had decided to drop the University of Denver Press operation. During that school year I worked at disposing of University of Denver Press titles. I was thoroughly convinced of the value of a number of these, for which we could not get what seemed to be equitable offers from other publishers; so I secured some credit, and entered into long-range contract with the University of Denver on some of them, and acquired a number of them to add to my list. Most of these tied into the regional effort of Sage Books, a field we had devoted much effort to at the University of Denver Press also.

I mentioned earlier that there had been a second time in which factors of my own character and determination as well as events around me seemed to "jell" into a pattern. This second period came in the spring of 1954. I had taken over solely the Sage Books imprint, I had brought together titles of the Alan Swallow and Swallow Press-Morrow imprints, and I had acquired some titles from the University of Denver Press. When these were put together, I had a fairly substantial list in one place resulting from those previous areas of effort. Furthermore, under the stresses of time at the University of Denver, the Department of English had been reduced so much for the moment that I felt that I could not encourage graduate students to come into the writing program as strongly as I had before.

In that year, I resigned from the University of Denver and decided to cast my lot full time with the

publishing. This was the first year that we had taken
money out of publishing. I told my family that I did
not truly believe that a person could make a living in
this country publishing the books that I wished to publish, but I was mistaken. The living, of course, must
be reasonably modest; but over the years the values
have increased and the amount of effort in terms of
number of titles and variety of titles had increased.

Since 1954 the effort has been channeled principally in the two imprints--Alan Swallow and Sage Books.
These are, of course, the imprints for the literary
works (poetry, literary criticism, bibliography, and
fiction) and for what I call "books about the American
West." The latter terminology is intended to be quite
broad. I see a need for small editions in the narrow
category, "Western Americana." But this work interests
me very little. I have concentrated upon trade editions
over a broad span, and even the references to the American West have sometimes been stretched a tiny bit.
But the books have included a wide range from science
through biography and memoirs to guide books, history,
and even cookbooks.
In 1959 I decided to enter the fashionable and
rising field of the quality paperback. At first, the
work of this type was concentrated in Swallow Paperbacks, that is, in the paperback offshoot from the Alan
Swallow imprint. A little later, I added Western Sage
Paperbacks, a paperback development from Sage Books.
The effort in paperbacks warrants a comment because of my particular approach to it. I had done occasional titles in paper where the form of binding
seemed suitable for presentation of a particular work,
and the Swallow Pamphlet series had been continued with
occasional editions. But I had resisted going into the
"paperback revolution" because I felt that it had an
editorial position contrary to my own. That is, although it was extremely valuable to publish package
works neatly and was relatively inexpensive, it was
ninety per cent or more what I call "leech" publishing.
I mean by this that editorial judgment is not extended
to new work and the reputation of the publishing is not
standing or falling on the judgment of untried work.
Instead, the scramble soon was on in the "paperback revolution" to find titles that had been published and

made their reputations. That they brought many of
these back into print is, aside from the price, the big
claim that paperback publishing can make.

I began to feel, however, that because paperback
publishing created, in part, a new market--the expansion of the college bookstores into trade-book departments, which primarily became paperback departments,
and the creation of a new group of bookstores which
handled paperbacks only--I should do all that I could
to offer this market to my own authors. This was my
reason for entry into the paperback field. With one or
two exceptions, I have not sought the out-of-print book,
and with one exception, I have not gone to other publishers to get paperback rights. Instead, the paperback titles have been developed from my own list, according to that philosophy.

Furthermore, with my bent toward asserting an active editorial judgment, I quickly became interested in
exploring the possibilities of the "paperback revolution" for the original work, the untried work. This
effort takes two forms: (1) to publish something originally and solely in paperback, as I have in the series called Poets in Swallow Paperbooks and Fiction in
Swallow Paperbooks; (2) the simultaneous publication
of many titles in both clothbound and paperbound form.
The first of these two methods is quite difficult because the developed market is so closely keyed to the
reprint, and the review media also so closely tuned to
the conception that in handling paperbacks they are
noticing reprints, that the "original" in paperbook
form has little place in the entire development. This
is particularly true of original fiction, and after trying a number of original titles in paper alone, and
finding that the stores could not make a place for them
and that the review media took no notice of them as
original contributions, I modified that particular plan
and now publish a clothbound edition alongside the Fiction in Swallow Paperbooks edition. The original in
paperback works a little better in poetry, and the method adds flexibility to the presentation of poetry.
Within a limited range, I now prize the technique. I
can now, according to the way I see a manuscript of
poems and the problems of presentation, publish in any
form among the following choices: hardback, simultaneous hardback and paperback, paperback original alone,

and the Swallow Pamphlet. I find this flexibility significant, and I wish that a similar flexibility will be available to other works. But in this sense, the "paperback revolution" has not demonstrated that it is a mature kind of publishing.

My work with fiction in original paperbacks had been with the long standing feeling that the "little publisher" was needed in the area of short fiction, that is, the short story, novelette, and short novel, all of which find a difficult time in the patterns of large-scale publishing. From my original entry into publishing fiction, I have been interested in this particular problem. I had hoped that the paperback development would be a help in solving the problems of presenting short fiction, and it is a disappointment that so far it has not been a help. However, I am not so sure that this picture will not be changed by patient and continuous work, since I cannot help feeling that at some time we will all become impatient with the lacks in paperback publishing and expect it to do more. To my mind, the form is there and sometime it can be more successfully used.

A word should be said about a third imprint, Big Mountain Press. As I have indicated, this name dates back to the days in Albuquerque in which Critchlow and I called our printing facility Big Mountain Press. During the years that we had the *Author and Journalist* magazine, we decided to do something about the vicious practice of vanity publishers. That something was to revive Big Mountain Press as a printing-for-hire facility so that those authors who felt compelled to self-publish would be able to secure a fair deal. The term for such editions is "private editions," in which the author seeks book production and owns *all* books produced and *all* rights in the work.

We are aware that the "private edition" or the sometimes cooperatively sponsored book (I mean by this term that a group might sponsor rather than the private individual) is essential to American publishing because certain works of specialized thought, of ideas not acceptable to our publishing market, sometimes of poetry, and of similar limited needs, would not make a place in the normal commercial market. Yet if they have inherent values, even of a local nature, they must not be denied a chance. Such books might be sponsored by institutional and governmental processes, but they usually are not. Advantage of this need had been taken by the group of publishers we call "vanity," and quite a large industry had developed, which, to my mind, flourished at the authors' expense.

Big Mountain Press developed in perhaps unusual ways because it was in a geographical area with rather little know-how in professional book manufacture. Therefore, it has become a service as much for institutional work as it has for the private edition. Universities, colleges, museums, historical societies, churches, other publishers, and other organizations have sought it out as a means of getting professional production. A service of Big Mountain Press has also extended, when desired, to aid in distribution and selling of the books manufactured, this done purely on a commission basis. Once into such commission work, and having the only recognized trade publishing firm in a particular area, I have also handled distribution of other works on a commission basis, most noticeably the Bancroft Booklets.

The entire endeavor of my publishing has increased with such vigor that at times it has stretched beyond my abilities to keep as close to each detail as I would like. As of the present time, something between fifty and sixty titles are coming forth each year, of which approximately forty-five are in the two imprints Alan Swallow and Sage Books, normally about equally divided between the two, and in the remaining eight or ten, the service work is performed by Big Mountain Press. The size disturbs me, but so long as I have the time and ability to assert the center of the effort, that is, the editorial judgment of value in new work, I feel that the development can be only helpful. And certainly it does provide an assured, strong and flexible base: that the judgment need never fail merely because of lack of facility to back it up.

THE GREAT

AMERICAN NOVEL

by Luke Walton

LUKE WALTON's comic novel, The Galapagos Kid, *considers the all-American fantasies of a fourteen-year-old
boy. Like the hero of his book, Walton reached puber-
ty on Philadelphia's Main Line. He spent six years
writing* Kid, *self-published it in North Plainfield,
N.J., and has since become a recluse.*

Sexual fantasy sustained me through a decade of attempts at The Great American Novel. I dreamed of the New York Pub Day Cocktail Party Girls. I'd read of Ernest Hemingway's, Dylan Thomas', and Norman Mailer's intoxications and fornications, and I imagined the Pub Day Party was an institution. When my turn came all those literary groupies would tumble for me with my first Bill Faulkner straight bourbon on the rocks. Like thousands of Great American Novelists, I sought truth, beauty, fame, fortune, and immortality. But what I really wanted was literary stallionship.

I had first planned a Great American Novel at age seventeen. Then a decent, virginal kid, I exposed corruption. Naturra, an idealistic African chief conceived through Thoreau and Emerson, paddled to America where he discovered rampant materialism and sex. After twenty-six pages he paddled back to his jungle disgusted, and the novel ended.

At college, I decided it was again time to fulfill my destiny. I jotted down the seven crucial facts of the age. Without further planning--since genius relies on intuition--I started to draft my second Great American Novel. The facts were: (1) There is no sense of permanence in America. (2) Americans are rich. (3) Americans are lonely. (4) Americans are greedy. (5) The Bomb may drop. (6) The old American values are dead. (7) There is no sense of community in America. This final no-community fact was imitation Paul Goodman. I had just read Goodman's *Growing Up Absurd* and was overwhelmed by him. I was overwhelmed by most good writers.

I spent the year worrying through drafts of the novel, disturbed about my writing for community be-

hind a constantly shut door. I decided to maintain my
solitude for a higher calling. Real community could
wait. Besides, I didn't like anybody in the dorm.
That novel was about a Vassar girl names Sudye
who had jilted me. Sudye was lonely, living in a non-
community, and preyed upon by characters like Porfirio
Vaseline, Clarence Buffalo, and Mayor Trueblood, com-
posites of relatives I didn't like. Lippincott rejected it fast and I dropped my year's work into a drawer.
I figured my mistake was lack of planning. Next
time I would be prepared.
Harvard gave me a graduate fellowship. I loiter-
ed for two weeks at Harvard, then got Bill-Faulkner —
drunk on the train home. My parents were upset. I
smashed a glass on the kitchen floor and yelled, "I
want to be a writer!"
The military threatened. I resolved to dodge the
killing in order to write. I'd escape to Canada, finish my Great American Novel (a patriotic duty), attend
the Pub Day Cocktail Party, then prove my bravery by
suicide. But schoolteachering was a less traumatic
way to avoid the Kennedy draft. I planned a year of
writing short stories. After classes, I napped from
three to four; then dinner, coffee, and five hours of
work. I did an outline the first week, rough draft
the second, and clean copy by the end of the month. I
finished six short stories. The subjects were: a black
Princeton student; a minister who is beaten up by his
church janitor; a skinny IBM employee; a lovelorn lady
teacher; a cub scout who loves his sister; a druggist
who saves a sick whore in Juarez. I'd never been to
either a whore or Juarez, and I knew not much more
about the other subjects.
I tried the usual *Atlantic-Esquire-Harpers* circuit and received all the usual form rejections. When
a friend suggested the little literary magazines, I
snapped it was the big time or no time.
In Paris, I rented a closet-sized room on the
seventh floor of a walk-up hotel. The floor buckled
in the middle, mice chewed my manuscripts, and I was
bothered by the typewriter racket of other resident
Great American Novelists.
My best Paris piece was about an optimistic, innocent American teenager named Kip, based on me. *The
Paris Review* said: "Dear Mr. Sonabend, Some parts of

'Kip' are very fine. We would like to see more of
your things." Sonabend was not my name and I didn't
like my stories described as "things." I ripped up
the note.
        But I had been touched. This was the first time
I had written about what I knew--me. I planned a week
of note-taking about my life. The week stretched on.
Thirteen months, seven notebooks, and 1,734 pages.
        Was my kindergarten teacher big and fat, or did I
just think she was because I was so small? Did I vomit
before my fifth-grade Christmas trumpet solo or after?
Did I drop that infield pop in my right eye or my left
eye, and was my sixth-grade girl friend laughing nearby or across the field?
        In the mornings I attended the Sorbonne for the
draft board; then I reserved two hours for coffee recall of my past and the remainder of the day for total
wine recall. Wine recall was the most productive. I
refused to read books, since I didn't want to be influenced. I worried about influence as I trimmed my
Bill Faulkner mustache in a sliver of mirror. Sex-
starved because the French women didn't like my dipso,
soulful-writer act, calorie-starved with only one meal
a day on a bedside camping burner, I kept at it.
        When my father died, I returned to the United
States and wrote about him and me in the notebooks.
For the draft board I registered at the University of
Pennsylvania and continued to recall with Schlitz in
the back of a bar where old men slept on tables. The
University discovered I wasn't much of a student. English professors had scant sympathy for this new novelist who threatened their career heroes. They informed
the draft board.
        I had finished the notebooks, but where was the
plot in all those 1,734 pages? Draft board and plot-
lessness drove me on benders. A distant cousin died
and left me $1,500. I visited a psychiatrist.
        After a few months, the shrink came up with a
plot outline. Better still, he explained my alcohol-
ism to the draft board. After that the draft board
didn't want me and since I had my outline, I didn't
need the shrink.
        I began the first draft with a private ceremony:
I wrote and received a special-delivery letter from
Kip on Mt. Olympus. "Smack the gods in the face,"

Kip advised.

During the writing years, booze was reserved for Saturday nights. Sundays were for the hangovers. Other days were for a clear head and coffee. I locked up my private-school P.-R. office after work, napped on the office floor with a chair cushion for a pillow, and rose with the alarm clock. After a light dinner, I opened the windows or turned on the air conditioner until the room was well below sixty degrees and started five hours of typing. At that temperature I had to keep busy or shiver.

On the wall next to the typewriter I hung some rules:

"As you attempt a heavy Great American Novel, pretend that you intend only fun. Entertain the reader. If the reader suspects you are up to something serious he will fall asleep or turn on the television.

"Imagine that your reader will be intelligent. Don't explain anything twice. You may find that your reader is definitely *not* intelligent. But you must imagine. Otherwise the reader will sense that you took him for a dummy.

"Keep moving. Readers like happenings. (E.g., the novel will open with Kip in jail, immediately flash back, and then flash forward to the arrest of this last great all-American teenage boy. English professors will remember the structure of Nabokov's *Invitation to a Beheading*.)

"If you want to write an immortal classic, write it at four or five simultaneous levels. English professors decide what is or is not an immortal classic. You must give them levels of meaning to explain endlessly to other professors. (E.g., Kip's girl friend, Mirabella, should become a fish in grade school. Embarrassed by her scaly affection, Kip will try and fail to faith-heal her. Levels: (1) Mirabella's chasing Kip will announce plot theme of chaser being chased--professors will recall Melville's *Mardi* and might declare that you are in Melville's tradition; (2) they will notice Kip's coming of age sexually and expect more sex; (3) wide-awake critics will see that Kip's failed faith-healing announces religious doubts; (4) Mirabella's fishiness introduces evolution theme--professors might recall the tradition of H. P. Lovecraft; (5) Mirabella's mutation announces fantasy and

will set up multilayered fantasy finale for the professors to discuss--do-gooder Kip will enter the school's
science contest and mutate his autistic sister into a
loving firefly."
The manuscript grew to 360 pages. Twice I endur-
ed a week in bed, immobilized by back-spasms from
bouts at the typewriter.
I tape-recorded several of the ten drafts. I
played the tapes, stopping here and there to listen to
a word, jumping forward and backward through the novel.
Each of the sixty to eighty thousand words had to look
and sound exactly right or be dropped.
I devised a fire and flood insurance that was act-
of-God proof. I xeroxed each draft and distributed
the copies between my mother's house, my apartment, and
my office. A copy of early drafts was kept in my car's
glove compartment. When the car burned up one evening,
I was still many-copies safe. I didn't care about the
car.
Temporarily thinking I had done all I could, I
invested $8 for first class registered postage both
ways, and entered the novel in the Harper Prize Novel
Contest. I waited four months for Harper's reply. I
let my hair grow long. At least I'd look like a writer.
One day, very hairy, I called fiction editor David
Segal. He said the manuscript was on his desk. He
would read it over the weekend. I'd made it through
almost a thousand entries to the big fellow. I went
out and got a hair cut.
I was sure I had approached David Segal and Harpers correctly. Write the best you can; mail the novel with a short letter saying only that you are enclosing return postage, nothing about past publication
in college literary magazines or your mother's opinion
of the book. That was the Quality-Faith approach.
You write quality and have faith that publishers are
interested in quality.
David Segal's rejection encouraged me: "We all
feel that it is better than the average unsolicited
manuscript." That sounded like scads of editors had
read the novel. I wrote to Segal and asked him what
I should do now. He said: "The question you raise in
your letter is that ancient and sad question of who
publishes serious fiction these days. I would suggest
that you try Farrar, Straus & Giroux; Viking; Little,

Brown; Houghton Mifflin; and Knopf, more or less in
that order; and good luck with the book."
     Segal knew I'd written "serious fiction"! Top
publishers should see it! Quality-Faith was right.
     But I soon stumbled onto the Friend-of-a-Friend
approach. A friend of mine knew an editor at Knopf.
The editor responded to my letter, "I'd be delighted
to read your novel." Delighted!
     I met the editor at the friend's wedding, made
sure she noticed me leading a song to the bridegroom,
bought her a 2 A.M. Sunday *Times*. She seemed shy.
Was she awed by my book and me? She wrote: "I think
you will have to find someone who responds to your
very special kind of humor."
     She suggested Christopher Cerf at Random House
and offered to take it to him. Christopher Cerf!
Bennett Cerf's son! I could hear the chatter of The
Party groupies.   Cerf's unsigned, printed reply
plunged me into my first rejection-slip bender. When
I recovered, I decided to take David Segal's publishers
in order.
     Farrar, Straus & Giroux neglected to confirm manu-
script receipt. When I called them they mistook my
query and mailed the manuscript back the next day via
special delivery. I sent it to Viking and then to
Little, Brown. I rearranged my name, using the ini-
tials W. C., like W. C. Fields or W. C. Handy. Would
"W. C." rescue the manuscript from the slush pile?
While waiting for Little, Brown I got married. My wife
had been warned about my Great American Novel obsession. I didn't tell her about Pub Party groupies.
     I telephoned a college acquaintance, John Nichols.
His novel, *The Sterile Cuckoo*, had just been published.
There would be a movie with Liza Minelli. His publisher put his picture in a full-page *Times* ad. My voice
cracked when I talked to him. I couldn't just ask him
straight out to read my novel. Finally he asked *me* if
he could read it.
     Revising between rejection slips, I was then in
the middle of my sixth draft. I paid a highschool
student $75 to type most of the 325 pages for Nichols.
She caught the flu. An aunt did the rest for another
$25.
     I met Nichols in New York's McSorley's Pub and he
axed the novel like a pro. He bought the beer, pro-

posed that *we* writers were the best of buddies, that
he understood how I made so many mistakes, he'd made
them all himself years ago. My novel was impossible.
He couldn't stand fantasies. Besides it was two times
too long.

I got drunk, difficult to get rid of, smoked pot
with his wife, made a halfhearted pass at her, and
staggered out of his apartment with my one-hundred-
dollar typing job under my arm.

Little, Brown's rejection slip waited for me at
home in Philadelphia. I phoned demanding why. The
managing editor fished a card out of his files. My
characters were too fantastic.

"What did they mean fantasy was unpublishable!
Don't they realize that we live in a world of fantasy!"
I raged at my wife.

Gambit was new and small. Maybe they *needed* me.
They didn't. "There is no doubt that you can write,
but..." the editor-in-chief said. When I called Boston to ask why she rejected it, she suggested I tight-
en the plot. I wouldn't cut the fantasy, but I did
cut the manuscript until the original outline-skeleton
was sticking through. Had I regressed to the outline
after all these years? I collapsed for a week, my
back in spasm.

At McGraw-Hill I tried the Loyal-Alumnus approach
on the director, a graduate of my college. For this
I received the universal form rejection: "Doesn't meet
our present needs," and headed for the bar. At Doubleday I tried the Advertising-Sleuth approach. Writers'
magazines advised authors to study house requirements
by reading house ads. Doubleday was advertising *Yellow
Back Radio Broke Down* by Ishmael Reed, a fantasy twice
as far out as mine. Obviously Doubleday wanted fantasies.

My wife had become a graduate student at Princeton. Instead of our street address I used a Princeton
University address on Doubleday. Doubleday was unimpressed by the address and didn't want my fantasy
either.

In a state of depression, I considered the promises of vanity houses. "Hundreds of thousands of
copies sold! Nationwide television appearances for
our author!" boasted the vanities, omitting hundreds
of thousands of authors who hocked their tvs and homes

to pay for unsaleable, unreviewable books. I wasn't quite ready for vanity.

I was bewildered. I had worked hard. I was a good writer, plenty of editors had told me that. Then why wasn't I published? What was the secret?

Finally an agent, recommended by a friend of a friend, wrote that he "really did like" the novel and wanted me as a client. When my wife and I visited his Forest Hills home, the agent served us champagne! In the afternoon! I had been accepted by the establishment. My wife and I skipped down the sidewalks in boozy joy.

We rented a farm house by the Seine in Normandy, and my wife began writing a book of her own. Confidently I began another novel, employing the same ideas but in hack form. Hacks like Hailey and Susann sold big. Maybe hack work was what New York really wanted.

Mail in Normandy is delivered by motorbike. I trained my ear so that I could hear the mailman coming a half mile away. A delivery and I dashed for the gate. Every two months, the agent's letter of regret about my Great American Novel, now titled *The Galápagos Kid*, was badly ripped in my haste to get it open.

Broke and searching for jobs, my wife and I headed for England. I dropped off a copy of *The Galápagos Kid* at Calder and Boyars in London, expecting nothing. In Oxford, we answered ads for bartender and barmaid. Unemployed and unemployable we cashed our last travelers checks for a plane ride home to my mother's house in Philadelphia.

Even my hack novel was rejected.

I had failed to solve the publishing mystery.

When my wife's book was accepted on first submission, I was sure that I was a dunce, that my wife would soon leave me, that if I couldn't solve the mystery from the outside, I'd go to New York and get inside.

I went to New York. Publishers looked at my bookless résumé and returned me to Philadelphia. I scattered résumés around the country. Rejections of all types, plus some cheap wine, threatened my sanity. An uncle in North Plainfield, N.J., rescued me. The uncle issued a magazine for a camping association. He told me I could work for him.

Then Calder and Boyars, in an airmail rejection,

called my Great American Novel not only a good novel
but a "very good" novel (their underline). This from
the publishers of Nobel Prize winner Samuel Beckett.
I never did like Beckett's stuff, but now I walked
around repeating, "Samuel Beckett! Nobel Prize!" *
        Lurking in the back of my mind was the idea of
printing a few copies myself. At least this would end
the nightmare of a yellowing manuscript in the attic.
Somebody, if only a person I might meet in a bar, would
read the book. But if somehow I could invent a house
to back the novel...
        My uncle had some funds. A big-hearted, adven-
turesome man, he agreed to produce a few other books
if I paid for all the expenses of my novel, donated
the income to the company, and ran the entire operation.
        The Carolina Quarterly accepted my short story,
"The Kid That Could"--the story that became the novel.
"We needed a crazy and you came through with a champ,"
they said, and offered me $70 for it. They wanted a
reply by return mail, plus biography and information
about works in progress.
        After a leaping dance around the living room with
my wife, I realized I faced a crisis. Our sales teams
of commissioned representatives were already wary
about this untried house. Bookstores don't readily buy
self-published books. If the reps knew our star novel
was written by the chief editor, or if bookstores found
out, we were done. I needed a pseudonym.
        I had hours to change my name and inform the *Quar-
terly*. Confusion. My name was my tradition, my tie
to my past. Wasn't that important? I decided I would
gladly forget both tradition and past.
        But what had I been struggling for these years if
not to let people know that *I* had written something
fine? I figured the only people I wanted to impress
were my friends. Why I needed to impress them I didn't
know. The rest of the world didn't give a damn about
me and never would, at least not an affectionate damn.
I'd confess to my half-dozen friends and use the pseudonym.
        I considered many names, particularly that of a
Horatio Alger character, Luke Walton. I liked the
name Luke--unusual, masculine, biblical. Walton was a

*Editor's Note: The importance of advance reviews and
opinions before doing anything should be stressed.
Often the worst judge of a manuscript is the author.*

newsboy who knocked himself out buying a sewing machine for his poor mother and rescuing his dead father's
stolen gold fortune--a perfect all-American author
for a Great American Novel.

I called the *Quarterly* and told them to by-line
me as Luke Walton. When I hung up the phone I felt
like I hadn't since fundamentalist tent meetings of my
childhood. I was a new person with a clean slate!
Anything was possible for Luke Walton! Twenty-nine
years had vanished. If I used my name wisely, Luke
Walton could be somebody to reckon with. Born again!

There was another extra: the Lone Ranger syndrome.
Who was that masked man? I imagined myself stepping
to the podium and watching the questions in the eyes
of the audience: who is Luke Walton? A Texas Ranger?
A Prince? A Great Lover? I was mysterious.

Deciding not to fight the large publishers for
Christmas review space, I picked an early-fall pub
date nine months away--September 15.

I searched for a printer in the pages of *Literary
Market Place* and soon learned that only short-run book
printers were interested in talking to me. I located
a nonunion printing company that operates in Brooklyn
with antique machinery and stays small so the union
won't notice. The president, who works in a tee shirt
and types his own letters, supplied me with a batch of
extra galleys so that I could get advance-of-pub-date
reviews. With advance reviews I hoped to attract
media reviews.

To find my advance-review people I paged through
the public library's *Contemporary Authors* and listed
every author I'd heard of--forty-eight. Six months
before pub date I wrote to these authors quoting "Samuel Beckett's London publisher" and stating my judgment as editor that the galleys of Luke Walton's book
were certainly worth a look. And wouldn't they like
their quotes in our national ads for this fine first
novel?

Kurt Vonnegut's wife replied that Kurt didn't
have time to read galleys. I sent them via special
delivery anyway, with no results. Lawrence Ferlinghetti said he couldn't read the galleys ("We are too
busy with our own unknown authors.") as did Isaac
Asimov ("My gorge rises at the thought of galleys.
I've read too many of my own.") and Herbert Gold,

Peter DeVries, Jonathan Yardley, Richard Eberhardt, and Lionel Trilling. Some said they wanted to see the finished book.

Ralph Ellison, George Plimpton, James Farrell, Robert Penn Warren, Harry Petrakis, John Updike, Calder Willingham, Isaac Singer, Vladimir Nabokov, Hannah Arendt, Bruce Jay Friedman, Paul Gallico, Allen Ginsburg, Paul Goodman, Walker Percy, Eudora Welty, John Ciardi, Philip Wylie, Philip Roth, J. D. Salinger, Noam Chomsky, Robert Cromie, James Dickey, Thomas Berger, Richard Lattimore, Hortense Calisher, Bernard Malamud, and Mark Van Doren never answered the letters. Letters to Shirley Ann Grau, Shirley Hazzard, and David Slavitt were returned as undeliverable. Nat Hentoff, Dore Schary, and Christopher Isherwood said okay, send the galleys, but did not reply later.

Six people who received galleys did reply. Frank Jennings, then editor-at-large for *Saturday Review*, said: "If *The Galápagos Kid* is indeed a 'first novel' then Luke Walton has announced his competence and displayed his controlled gifts brilliantly. Those gifts are difficult and demanding: an antic sense of fantasy, a capacity to distort reality into meaningfulness, an accurate ear for spoken language, and almost total recall of the adolescent's hunger for ineluctable truth."

I upped the print order from five hundred to a thousand.

Oliver Lange, whose *Vandenberg* had just made *The New York Times* best seller list, said: "*The Kid* is a delightful book. I particularly relished Walton's loose-jointed, free-style use of fantasy and whimsy in telling what is really a very scary story."

Max Wylie said: "An irresistibly ridiculous gluesniffing trip that will make every Presbyterian jump off the Ganges and swim the Eiffel Tower! Original sin never had such a Nantucket sleigh ride nor Lucifer such a body slam. Celestially irreverent, joyously cockeyed! Luke Walton, after tipping over every icon in the seminary, powders them, sprinkles the dust with homemade holy water, and brings off a new resurrection of the human spirit. There are moments in this wonderful nonsense when Jonathan Swift might wish he'd said it all."

Novelists Charles Calitri and Roy Friedman approved as did the editor of *The Carolina Quarterly*.

Calitri compared Kip to Holden Caulfield and Peter Pan.
The *Quarterly* editor mentioned *Catch 22*. I upped the
print order to two thousand and planned a $10,000 ad-
vertising campaign.
     But my wife and I were broke again. Her book's
advance had been donated for printing, binding, and
jacketing *The Kid*. I asked my mother and brother to be
advertising angels. They said $4,000 was their limit.
They'd been stung by my schemes before.
     I trumpeted *The Kid* to New York advertising agen-
cies, certain they knew the magic of creating best
sellers. The agencies sniffed. Four thousand dollars
was nothing, barely covering a full page in the *Times
Book Review*. I picked a small agency, not realizing
some agencies are small because they deserve to be.
After their dull full-page ad in *Publishers Weekly*, I
realized the agency knew no magic.
     Three months before pub date the bound books ar-
rived, sheathed in the most expensive three-color (red,
white, and blue), laminated jacket that New York printers could provide. The advance reviews were plastered
across the back of the jacket so that reviewers couldn't
fail to notice. On the flaps I said that the advance
reviews suggested a "comic masterpiece"--fine revenge
for all those publishers' rejections, and the exclusive privilege of the self-published author.
     I immediately mailed a hundred review copies with
a letter of editorial sound-and-fury to major reviewers listed in *Literary Market Place*. Arriving a month
and a half too soon, the books were tucked away on
shelves to wait for pub day, and some were forgotten.
     Five weeks before pub day, I mailed a reminder
letter from the editor about Luke Walton. I also peti-
tioned an additional 120 newspapers of under 100,000
circulation with a jacket and invitation to request
review copies.
     Shortly before pub date, the first review, a
three-column feature, appeared in *The Atlanta Journal*:
"In *The Galápagos Kid* American myths come home to
roost....Walton is an expert in the art of Brinkman-
ship--pushing reality to its outer edges....Nor must
one overlook the comedy in *The Galápagos Kid*. It's
painful comedy, but made much easier to bear by Walton's fertile imagination....Walton plays hell with
our minds. Conclusions? Walton could be headed for

a successful career if this first novel is any indication of his ability. Take four cuts above the 50's
Holden Caulfield, more above the 60's Giles Goat Boy,
add a seasoning of Yossarian--and you've got *The Galápagos Kid*...a continuing fascination at every reading."
Pub day arrived. Instead of the New York Pub Day
Cocktail Party, I savored my wife's Veal Suisse, salade
á la Greque with Portugese rosé. We toasted my book
with champagne. My wife's sister sent me a "Luke Walton" tee shirt. With galloping confidence I told the
agency to place a full-column ad in the *Times Book Review* running three consecutive Sundays at $800 per Sun-
day.

On the Monday after the first *Times* ad I sat back
and waited for the office phone to ring. I thought of
all the money the big publishers spent in the *Times*, of
how many books they had to sell to pay for those ads,
of the hot reviews featured in the ad. I walked among
the 1,400 books in the office basement, wondering if
the stock would last the week.

On Monday the phone didn't ring. On Tuesday the
phone didn't ring. On Wednesday I received a mimeographed appeal for free books from a Maine charity plus
two letters from buyers of publishers' overstocks.

I ignored these omens. After all, our salesmen--
with considerable phone and leg work by myself--had
managed to stock 450 advance copies in bookstores before pub date. Obviously the readers of the *Times* ad
were jamming into Brentano's, Doubleday, and many smaller stores. They'd be sold out in a week or so, I
thought. Then the phone would ring.

But orders arrived in ones and twos. The phone
remained quiet. When the *New York Review of Books* ad
appeared twice in October ($250 per ad), a few profes-
sors requested copies, free.

Reviews trickled in, among them: *The Philadelphia
Bulletin* said that I was "witty" and featured my photo
with Ernest Hemingway's--mine was larger. The *Nash-
ville Banner* said: "It's rather possible you've never
read anything like this...chock full of interesting
ideas." *The Miami Herald* called *The Kid* "explosive...
like walking on a field of firecrackers." The Palm
Springs, Calif., *Herald-Call-Enterprise* reviewer didn't
bother to read the novel. She merely reprinted the
jacket copy. *The San Antonio Express* said: "At its

best *The Galápagos Kid* is reminiscent of Evelyn Waugh's satires." *The Sunday Home News*, New Brunswick, N.J., did a half page feature on Luke Walton and mentioned that he and his wife had been living on fish cakes and cheap wine, and that his best pants had recently split out at the seat. *The New York Times Book Review* said: "an existential fantasy that does not have a frame of reference."

I spoke about fiction on a fundamentalist radio station and about publishing to an adult writing class consisting of housewives and a retired Navy Captain. I autographed copies and addressed the Plainfield Book and Author Luncheon, trying to make the scowling ladies laugh. One of the ladies decided *Kid* was dirty and returned it before dawn to our front porch, taped in a plain brown wrapper.

The New Jersey Association of English Teachers handed two authors' awards to my wife and me. The local bookstore held autograph parties for both of our books and I sold five copies of *Kid* to friends.

When my wife's book was reviewed in the *Times*, I made it big--I was pictured hugging my wife.

I collected my reviews into a mailing piece to 3,500 large libraries. I admitted I self-published the novel in the tradition of Walt Whitman, Ezra Pound, Anaïs Nin, and Edwin Arlington Robinson. The libraries didn't panic getting orders in, perhaps mistrusting the self-published author, or Luke Walton's name dropping.

Bookstores began returning unsold copies. Sales peaked at about five hundred copies, respectable enough for the serious, underground sort that Luke Walton now imagined he was.

But where was my immortality, fame, fortune, and all the rest? Where was my classic--would professors *ever* begin their arguments about my meanings? And where were the literary groupies? And what did I, a married man, want with groupies now? The fewer groupies the better.

But I had made a few friends. I'd been reviewed in the *Times*. I'd tasted the bitch goddess and wasn't very impressed. And I had discovered the secret of publishing. Publishers exist to make money and make money to exist. My novel, and many like it, was rejected not because it was of poor quality or unloved, but because it would not contribute to profits. I knew that now from my own profit and loss sheet:

Profit:
 None. All income from the first thousand copies
reserved for the company. Five hundred sold at 40 per
cent discount to stores, less to libraries. Sales representatives received commission of 12.5 per cent.

Loss: *
  $1,500.00 -- shrink's fee to produce the plot
                 outline
   2,500.00 -- bill for printing and binding 2,000
                 copies
     800.00 -- bill for two editions of jacket
     280.00 -- postage for library mailing
     107.00 -- list rental for mailing
   4,000.00 -- advertising, repayable to angels by
                 author
      98.00 -- xeroxing for fire and theft protec-
                 tion
      20.00 -- total doctor's bill for spasmed-back
                 incidents
       5.00 -- hot water bottle for spasmed back
      30.00 -- five reams of erasable typing paper
     150.00 -- review clipping service fee
       5.00 -- typewriter ribbons
     100.00 -- typing charge, Nichol's copy
      64.00 -- postage, mailing manuscript to pub-
                 lishers with return stamps
      12.00 -- postage to one English professor,
                 one agent and Nichols
      50.00 -- tape recorder and tapes for listen-
                 ing to novel
       7.50 -- copyright charges, with notary public
                 bill
      20.00 -- gasoline and travel expenses to pick
                 up books from bindery
      80.00 -- artist's fee for rendering jacket
      45.00 -- *Carolina Quarterly* and Charles Cali-
                 tri reading fee total
     100.00 -- other postage costs
 $10,873.50 -- total loss to Luke Walton for *The
                 Galápagos Kid.*

*Editor's Note -- Luke Walton's novel has just been
published as a Pushcart Paperback.*

213

An illustration from page 24 of Irena Kirshman's forty-eight-page cookbook titled *Spaghetti Lovers*. Copyright for the drawing © 1971 by Bob Penny.

COOKBOOKS:

POTPOURRI PRESS

by Irena Kirshman

IRENA KIRSHMAN's cookbooks are almost as unusual as her self-publishing history--the books are wonderfully designed (some are about the dimensions of a necktie), thin, decorative, to the point, and able to be disassembled into file cards. Her Potpourri adventure *began in Greensboro, North Carolina, but she currently writes from her home in Port Washington, New York, turning out titles such as* Chicken, Meat, Soup, Desserts, Spaghetti, Eggs, *and* Chops.

Fads erupt in a tumbling profusion. Suddenly hair is long, clothes are short, blue jeans are frayed, and natural food is healthy. *Love* is a new word created by the valiant crew of the Yellow Submarine, and all the little buttons say *SMILE*. Maybe many conditions have to be right for a new grin to be accepted from the fickle Cheshire cat, or maybe it is all just chance, like the fondue thing...

Overnight, fondue pots appeared everywhere, in gift shops, department stores, hardware stores--everywhere. There were hundreds of pots evoking visions of snow-clad Swiss mountains, lithe fur-fringed skiers, and hot bubbling creamy cheese. More shops bought more fondue pots, and in no time at all the wholesalers had sold so many fondue pots that it looked like a movement. We too were convinced and bought six pots for our own tiny gourmet shop and French cooking school. Six beautiful, gleaming, expensive pots, and the next day they were still there, and the next day, and the next. It is difficult to know what to do when you are in the midst of a movement and nothing is moving.

We decided to launch a local fondue-education program. An advertisement was placed in the newspaper, and the entire circulation was invited to come and taste our glorious creation. They came and tasted, and said they liked it, and tasted some more, and then they all went home. We still have our six fondue pots, one slightly used.

A little puzzled, we tried another approach. We thought it would be a good idea to show people how to make fondue themselves and then perhaps they would buy our pots. We hunted for fondue recipes. There weren't any. Well yes, there were a few, one in one book, one in another. After all, who needs a recipe for fondue?

It is simply melted cheese. Nevertheless, we decided
to have a flyer printed.

We called on our local printer, who was dubious
about the whole scheme. With the earnest wisdom of a
corporate lawyer, he advised us against the whole idea.
Not only did he explain the entire mysterious workings
of a printing plant, but showed us rows and rows of
figures to prove his points. He assured us that it
would cost almost as much to print a four-color flyer
as to produce a small book in black and white.

We learned that the costs of printing in color are
so much greater than in black and white that we had to
stop and decide exactly where we were going, what we
wanted to say and to whom. Our hope was to sell fondue
pots and at the same time give some really helpful information on how to use the pot and what to cook in it.
After a little more thought we decided against the idea
of a flashy flier because, realistically, we suspected
that it would not only fail to influence the buyer but
even if the huge piece of paper was taken home there
wouldn't be enough room in the kitchen to unfold it and
make practical use of the recipes. Everything seemed
to point to the book idea.

The book had to be as inexpensive as possible so
that the total purchase price of both the book and the
pot would not deter the potential double sale.

We discovered that our printer had several type
faces from which to choose and we selected one which we
thought was cheerful and would not look too much like
textbook print. Assuming that our customer was willing
and enthusiastic to learn something new, we thought it
would be wise to make the book look as clear and easy
as possible.

We didn't want to frighten the buyer away with a
slick professional-looking photograph of a fondue and
purposely designed a simple, almost naive-looking cover
for the book. The copy was kept to a minimum, so the
book wouldn't look too complicated. We used an economical trim size to make maximum use of the paper without wastage. Once the original art fees were paid, and
the plates were made, it made relatively little difference in cost whether we printed six copies or three
thousand.

So now we had three thousand black and white fondue books in addition to our five and a half fondue

pots. We had a solution to the problem of how to sell
the pots which defied all reason. It would have been
less expensive to just give the pots away!
The next question was what to do with the books.
We could buy three thousand pots and give the books
away or try to sell the books on the assumption that
other stores might also be faced with the same difficulty in trying to sell their pots.
We had heard of Marshall Fields but didn't know
exactly where it was, so we sent a letter to the store
addressed simply, "Marshall Fields, Downtown, Chicago,"
and enclosed a fondue book. An order came back immediately. Encouraged, we tried several more stores and
reprinted the book, 5,000 copies this time. By the end
of the year, we were reprinting 50,000 copies at a
time, and within twelve months we had sold well over a
million books and four fondue pots.
At the same time other people were writing and
publishing fondue books, and it appeared fondue was the
"in" thing. People were sitting or standing in groups
of four or six or more eating fondue with cocktails,
serving it at teenage parties, or having it for lunch
or dinner. It was a new inexpensive dish at a time
when food prices were rising rapidly. It was quickly
and easily prepared, and it tasted good. Of course
this was why the stores bought the pots in the beginning!
Our fondue book was first published in 1967. Even
at that time hundreds of cookbooks were flooding the
market, and we realized that the saturation point had
probably been reached. I had been teaching French cooking and lecturing around the country, and I gradually
became convinced that there was a market for a different kind of cookbook. We decided to try to apply our
experience with the fondue book to a series of books
that were designed as "teaching" books and hopefully
answered some of the questions which had been raised
in the cooking school. We defined our potential market
to include those people who wanted to know how to cook
one single dish or a single group of dishes. The aim
was to produce very simple books which gave explicit
details of how to make a crêpe, a soufflé, or an omelette. We sacrificed the mystique of cooking in an effort to show the principles and techniques of preparing
good food. The books were light and conversational in

tone but had an underlying seriousness and respect for the ingredients themselves.

This series of books was received with enthusiasm by the stores because a small book could be sold with a crêpe pan, a soufflé dish, or an omelette pan. The customers bought the books for gifts, or for themselves. They were inexpensive enough that if somebody bought the book and then changed his mind about making a soufflé, he could throw the book away with the Sunday newspaper and not feel guilty about having bought a big, glossy volume which was not used. We were immediately and immoderately proud that a few people even collected them!

Though this article appears to be all about cookbooks, the same principle can be applied to publishing in many other fields. If you have looked for a book on a specific subject and cannot find one, the chances are good that others would also welcome that book. You then have the choice of either publishing and selling the book yourself, or asking a special interest group to commission a book and let it distribute the book through its trade organization, magazine, or club membership.

I am convinced that our success was due partly to our knowing that a particular market existed and partly to our complete ignorance of the established mores of publishing. If we had taken our fondue-book idea to a prestigious book publisher it undoubtedly would have been turned down several weeks or months later. Publishers are very polite and prefer not to hurt anybody's feelings. Rather than come right out and say they do not like your creation they simply remain silent or constantly leave their offices for extended vacations. By printing the book ourselves we did not have to humbly admit that we had never written a book before. (Publishers generally seem to prefer authors who have already been authors.) We, unfortunately, did not have any credentials whatever. Consequently, there were no charming lunches with editors, no somber projections of sales by funereal accountants, and no advertising budgets to concern us. We simply wrote the manuscripts on pieces of yellow, lined paper and gave them directly to the printer. In this way we were able to print very quickly and in small quantities. We tested the water before plunging in with a large printing and so were able to minimize our risk. We tried to listen carefully to those whom we considered to be our potential customers and tried to write books that filled a specific need.

We made several mistakes along the way and wasted a considerable amount of money on advertising. We also decided to become more sophisticated and designed the books so they would look beautiful. Oddly, by doing this, it seems we became part of the cookbook establishment and the new books were not accepted as readily as the simpler, earlier efforts. So we changed the style back again.

Now, sixty odd books later, we have embarked on a new field and have a group of craftsmen writing books about their own particular corner of life, and "teaching" the reader everything from how to cut a pair of jeans into a skirt to the best way of stitching a piece of leather.

Though we have acquired a team of typists, who never write on yellow, lined paper; a computer which never forgets Marshall Field's address, and an office building to call our own, we are still essentially a group of three: a publisher whose primary interest was in his group of specialty gift shops, an artist who was temporarily out of work as a salesman, and a housewife (me) who was teaching French cooking as a hobby.

If you have an idea that you believe in and know with whom you would like to share it, publishing a book is like an opening night at the theater with all the butterflies and all the wishing it could have been better, but it gives a unique sense of satisfaction and allows you to retain a measure of independence. There is a wonderful sense of freedom in writing a book. You can lie in the sun with your eyes closed and, if challenged, say you are thinking. The next best thing to publishing your own book is to imply that you are just about to.

A concrete poem from *Notpoems* by Adele Aldridge. Copyright © 1971 by Adele Aldridge.

NOTPOEMS & CHANGES

by Adele Aldridge

ADELE ALDRIDGE publishes from her home in Riverside, Connecticut. She combines the various talents of painter, printmaker, graphic designer, and publisher. Recent works include Notpoems, *a book of visual poetry, and* Changes, *a visual interpretation of the* I Ching *in two volumes: one color, the other black and white.*

I came to publishing, not from the verbal world of a
writer, but from the visual world of a painter. My
background was in painting, printmaking, and other visual mediums. I had had several one-woman shows, one
in New York City, one in Connecticut, and had partici-
pated in many group shows. During all this I had always been aware that the creative act of painting had
nothing whatever to do with the problem of getting the
work into a gallery and to the public. The alternative of keeping one's work in the attic was not very
satisfactory because, more than money, an artist needs
feedback.

The process of going from painter to publisher
was a slow one and still continues. There were basically three stages out of which evolved my visual and
physical awareness of books. I was painting and printmaking concurrently when I began to incorporate printing techniques into my paintings. Then I began printing in series, which propelled me into making these
series into hand-bound books. The last stage was
thinking in terms of the actual publishing of these
books.

A writer who presents a manuscript to a publisher
and then waits to see it in book form usually has very
little awareness of the steps involved in putting a
book together. The choosing of type, paper, layout,
and cover all contribute to the look of the book. A
book is more than words on a page.

Everything that I have learned about putting a
book together has been through a slow, self-taught
process. In the beginning, I had no thought of publishing. Everything that developed did so primarily
out of inner needs, not out of conscious decisions.

Of the varied printmaking techniques, I focused

in on woodcuts because, unlike etching, I could easily
manage this in my home studio. I became so involved
in the marvelous effect of transparency of color one
gets with overprinting that I began to paint with wood
instead of with a brush. By this I mean I would design blocks and print them onto large sheets of rice
paper and then laminate the whole sheet onto a canvas.
The effect is like painting, yet it was made by printing. The act of printing was so fascinating to me that
it took over, even though I still called myself a
painter.

The results of this print-painting were a series
of about thirty paintings. The next series, also
print-painted, were of semi-abstract figures. Words
began to creep into the paintings. I had worked with
a calligraphic look in the previous series but in this
I started using letters as integral parts of the statement in the paintings.

Often at night, when I was too tired to paint and
before going to bed, I worked out word designs. I collected these doodles over a period of a year and put
them aside as ideas for future use. These words were
visual images of a statement that had to be read to be
understood, but could not be read out loud to get the
full meaning. In other words, the physical layout of
the words was an integral part of the total statement.
This was a way of working out my feeling that letters
are beautiful shapes in and of themselves. I wanted
to coordinate these shapes with a literal statement,
yet make the statement one. Later I learned that this
kind of expression is called concrete poetry. My collection of visual poetry was put aside, having mounted
into a pile of scribbles.

Next came my love affair with the *I Ching*. Because the *I Ching* is a book, my visualization of it
became a series that I wanted to be in book form too.
My print-paintings had been experiments with the var-
iables of color and placement of shape on a page, making different statements while using the same elements.
In effect, this is exactly what any alphabet does, but
I did it in a pictorial way. In my effort to understand the *I Ching* I found that its basic structure was
a similiar idea: taking eight units and interrelating
them with each other, forming sixty-four separate units.
My understanding was of the book's mathematical clarity

of structure, its computer-like essence. This is what
I wanted to show, change through shape.
The *I Ching* interpretation was the first project
in which I went through all the basic steps of con-
structing a book. It was a work of art and in no way
commercial. Again, making the book was done out of a
need to have my work presented in a way I thought suitable. I did not yet think consciously of publishing.
I was still making rarified art in my studio with no
thought of a wide audience.
In making this book, I hand-printed each page.
The book was printed in black on white in an edition
of two. It took me an entire summer to do the actual
printing. When I was finished and needed to put the
book together, I found a woman in New York City, Catherine Stanescu, a professional hand bookbinder, who
gave classes in her studio. I studied with her one
day a week for almost a year.
I learned the tedious and time-consuming but rewarding technique of how to put my work into finished
book form. The results were two very elegant, 16- by
20-inch books, covered in raw burlap with the title
hand-embroidered. The end papers were a beautiful,
thick Japanese rice paper.
Making hand-bound books is not only time consuming
but essentially unprofitable; however it is satisfying
on the aesthetic level. I enjoyed seeing my idea grow
from inception to completion in physical form, and I
learned a lot in the process.
My next step toward publishing happened as a direct result of the bookbinding course. I learned that
it is much more economical to be working on the binding
of several books at once. For example, while one book
is drying in a press, another can be sewn. Unlike the
other students, who were binding old family books and
antiques found in shops, I felt I had to come up with
another book of my own. The result was my series of
concrete poetry.
"What is concrete poetry?" so many people asked.
And so many times I found myself answering, "Well,
they're not poems." The title *Notpoems* resulted. I
put the book together and took it to a printer. I
wanted to bind ten books, but learned it would cost me
just as much to have ten as to have two hundred printed, so I took the two hundred.

After hand-binding the ten books I found it impossible to put a price on them. Anything under $35 was a give away, and people did not appreciate a price of $35 and over for such a tiny book. Because I had many requests for the book, I took 150 copies and made a paperback version, putting it together with rings. I signed and numbered each book, like a limited edition, and sold them at $5 each.

This side venture, as it seemed then, became a turning point in my career. These turning points in artistic expression, in hindsight, have always been interwoven with personal events in my life. What seemed unrelated later is shown to be an integral part of the whole pattern.

There were varied results from publishing *Notpoems* in my limited edition. I was surprised how pleased I was to have many people possess the book, even though the volume and its price were small. Selling paintings at much higher prices is gratifying in that someone thinks enough of my work to want to own them, but this happens infrequently. Many more people are willing to pay five dollars for an art object, and I began to think about that more and more.

I enjoyed people ordering one and two books and then coming back for more. In the world of commercial publishing, a 150-copy edition is hardly considered publishing, but compared to selling a single painting, that represented a great deal of activity to me. The knowledge that many more people were in touch with my work had a big influence on my turning toward publishing.

Because I had bound my poems into a book, they were easy to show to people for other uses. Some of the Notpoems were printed on the covers and inside pages of *Aphra*, *Black Maria*, and *Omen*, and while these are small literary magazines and paid very little for the use of my work, I was pleased to have an even *wider* audience. Then Scholastic Books bought a poem and had it printed in color for a poster they used in the school systems all over the country.

While I designed *Notpoems* with press type and had a printer photo offset it, I became more and more interested in type itself. I bought an old treadle press and had it hauled to my third floor attic. Then I heard of a man who was selling a smaller antique

treadle press along with some trays of type. That
press was also hauled up to the attic, and then, along
with my table etching press, which I used as a proof
press, my studio had grown into a print shop.

At this point, the hardest thing was learning how
to set type. I had a few hours of instruction from a
friend, but mostly had to teach myself. This was a
trial-and-error process with the type falling out of
the chase, poor impressions made, and a variety of
technical problems, including the bigger press' crack-
ing in the middle of the run on a project.

The next thing that propelled me toward publishing
was an all-consuming desire to translate my *I Ching*
book into full color and print it so that I could sell
many copies. The size of the book, 8 by 10 inches,
was limited by the size of the press. I had to hand-
turn the press, printing each page three times, once
for each color. I limited the book to 55 copies because 72 pages in color, plus a few more in black and
white, meant approximately 3,240 turns of the wheel.
I began to yearn for an offset press, although I am
sure the effect would not be of the handmade quality.

The difference between what I printed and what is
printed in a regular book with illustrations is that
my pages are all original prints. A single print of
this size usually sells for anywhere from $10 to $100
each and I priced my book at $75--less than a dollar
per page.

The decision to print my *I Ching* in color was not
taken because I am a glutton for physical exertion,
but because I could not afford to pay a printer to do
that kind of work in color. My urgency, as usual, was
to see the finished product. When an idea is strong
in my mind it wants to force itself out into a physical reality.

I highly recommend that all poets learn to set
type by hand. It not only gives one a respect for the
look of the word on the page, but forces a new conden-
sation of style. One sees how the organization of
thoughts affects the work as a total expression. When
something is written down on a piece of paper and presented to someone else, the look of it has its own impact alongside the impact of what the words actually
say. Some books look like they want to be picked up,
others do not. Typesetting is a slow and tedious

process and not something I recommend doing for life, but it is an act that affects the writing itself and cannot be fully appreciated until tried.

Putting a series of prints into book form, making them portable and not dependent upon a complicated gallery arrangement, brings the work into the world. The original need for books in the world was to send the message out to more than one person at a time. I find this need a basic element in me, and, in comparison to doing single paintings, there is more feedback per project. I find putting my work into books is a step beyond working things out in the studio, with far less ego damage than I always experienced when taking paintings around to galleries. In asking approval for my paintings I found myself much too close to the work, as if the painting were me. Somehow the process of making a book, even though it has been all my work, leaves me feeling one step removed and less vulnerable to opinion. If things do get published I am pleased, but in the meantime I do not have to wait. Although this means putting forth great effort, the rewards have been worth it.

The third phase in my publishing sprang from my past actions and proceeds onward. My studio-made books bore the imprint of The Mandala Press. *Mandala* means "magic circle." The rest of my story is about how Magic Circle Press was formed by my partner, Valerie Sheehan, a writer and photographer, and me.

A strong influence in my life has been Anaïs Nin's diary. I was helped by her at the time I was thinking of printing my first *I Ching* book. I had doubts about the justification for the work itself. I was reading the third volume of Nin's diary at the time and was moved by her efforts to publish her own work when no one else would. I saw that without a strong belief in one's own work, one was lost. I was deeply touched by how Anaïs Nin did what she had to do in spite of great odds. Reading about her struggles years after they happened gave them more validity because I could see the outcome. Had she not pursued her goal perhaps we would not be reading her books now. In other words, one has to take risks. Nothing happens by itself.

With a great amount of energy, daring, and love for Nin, Valerie Sheehan and I started Magic Circles in April 1972 and created a weekend called *Celebration*,

A Weekend with Anaïs Nin. During the weekend artists discussed the making of creative books. Some of the original books printed by Anaïs Nin were on display. She talked about her press, as did Daisy Aldan, I myself, and others who were making books by hand.

Valerie and I don't know yet where Magic Circle Press will go, but it is exciting to discover. Our aim is to be in control of the work we do. The first book we have published is a revised and enlarged edition of *Notpoems*. We are compiling a book documenting the Anaïs Nin Celebration. One goal is to sponsor more Magic Circle weekends, creating a book from each. These will be intimate dialogues, always celebrating a living artist. Our books will make the intimacy available to a wider audience.

Another major goal of our press is to make books that are works of fine art in themselves. These are books in signed, limited editions, often in color, always done by the hand of the artist. We intend to have people enjoy our books by returning to the way they were made originally, as objects to be loved, pleasing to the eye and hand, using graphic design in presentation of material to heighten nuances of meaning and tone. We intend to maximize the potential in words and images, strongly emphasizing visual and literary wholeness. We also hope to keep prices low by sticking to paperback covers.

My path toward publishing was a long one more or less particular to me. But however a person comes to publishing, he usually arrives there for the same reason I did: a strong desire to get one's work out into the world. And why not?

Illustrations of how to alter a jacket shoulder and how to make trousers lower waisted from *Garment Altering and Repairing and Tailor Shop Management*. Copyright © by Clarence Poulin.

TRADE & CRAFT

TEXTBOOKS

by Clarence Poulin

CLARENCE POULIN *is a journeyman tailor and poet. He works and publishes in bucolic Penacook, New Hampshire. Besides several self-published books of poetry, he has issued his own tailoring textbooks, which he discusses here. The lessons he learned from writing and publishing textbooks on his trade may be applied to almost any trade or craft how-to book.*

Over twenty years ago, the idea occurred to me that a how-to book about my trade, custom tailoring, might find a publisher. I had sold some of my writings in other fields, so putting words together was no great problem. Besides, having received a fairly good art education I could illustrate my instructions with step-by-step line drawings. I shipped this manuscript with the drawings to the Charles A. Bennett Co., Inc., of Peoria, Illinois, and they accepted the book for publication. Once released under the title, *Tailoring Suits the Professional Way*, it found its way quickly into trade schools and libraries. After twenty years in print, I revised it this year and look forward to its continued life for another couple of decades.

This first work, however, was mainly about suit making for men. Many tailoring students and teachers wrote me that I should prepare a book of lessons on garment altering and repairing, and also on the operation of a tailor shop.

So gradually I typed out and illustrated some forty-two lessons under the title, *Garment Altering and Repairing and Tailor Shop Management*, and had them printed by offset in a small first edition of two hundred copies. It was something that I had been told was far too "specialized" for a publisher to risk money on, and I had an idea it would sell slowly. But also, I knew that there was a need for such a book, and that if I priced it sufficiently high I need not lose money in the long run.

The printing cost by offset was quite reasonable, and I found that if I bound the copies in Gaylamount covers, or shelf-binders, and stamped titles on them, the schools would accept them. The page size was 8.5″ by 11″, and my illustrations were sufficiently detailed and clear to serve their purpose. The book contained over 160 illustrations, and I am sure that its sale depended almost wholly on them.

How was I to advertise this book? At first I placed classified ads in the needles-crafts magazines and received a number of responses every week; but soon it became evident that I must not cater only to "home sewers."

Then one day I read in a writers' magazine the sage advice: "Write for the schools!" I wasn't sure that *Garment Altering and Repairing* was printed in a nice enough format for schools, but I took a chance with them and began sending out descriptive circulars to universities, vocational schools, State departments of education, and also the larger libraries. Quite a few asked me to send them a copy on examination.

Here the market proved receptive, especially in the fall and at the beginning of the year. And with the schools, copies sold in quantities--five, ten, or even twenty copies in a single order.

Again I received letters from student tailors who wanted more instruction on ladies' suit tailoring and the use of model patterns in cutting suits for both men and women. I therefore wrote another profusely illustrated, 8.5-by-11 book on these subjects, which I titled *Women's and Men's Suit Tailoring*. This too was bound in Gaylamount board covers and proved acceptable to the schools and libraries.

Having written myself out on the subject with these three books, I had a circular printed listing their contents in detail, and this is sent out in response to requests for prices.

I should mention that the first two books have been listed each year in Bowker's *Books in Print*. Any title of a useful book can be listed very economically in this great book directory, which is kept in every major library and bookstore in the land, and this is an advertising source that every self-publishing author should utilize.

To obtain reviews for such books is difficult, as most reviewers will not trouble themselves with a book not professionally printed and not bound in cloth, no matter how good it is. So I sent out no copies to reviewers, though some brief descriptions appeared in certain periodicals all the same. It is the teacher and students who must be depended on to find out for themselves if such books are good, and then the advertising is done by them. Books, like people, make friends on their merits, and very loyal friends indeed! And it is they who gradually boost sales over the years. In general, they don't mind if a book is typed and is bound in boards. In fact, this rather recommends it.

In my advertising campaign, I did try mailing to commercial names-lists, i.e. lists of names and addresses that can be bought for mailings to firms or persons interested in your product, but found results rather poor. Lists of trade and vocational schools are available in directories kept in most public libraries, and these generally bring good responses.

The financial outlay is something that we must return to. If one intends to put out a professionally printed and bound job on any highly specialized book, it would be better to try to place it with a regular publisher. Letterpress printing, the services of an artist, the binding in cloth, and the jacketing--these expenses may kill all the chances of making a profit for the author-publisher. An inexpensive publishing job, therefore, is a sine qua non. Offset reproduction of your pages, as you have typed and illustrated them, is the best course; and even then one should find a "reasonable" offset printer. Many charge almost as high as letterpress printers, and a bit of shopping around may cut one's bill by almost half.

Printing by mimeograph, I have found, is best done on one side of the sheet, and the order should stipulate that the copies be collated and side-stitched, but without covers.

The Gaylamount cardboard covers can be purchased in the proper spine thickness and a bit larger than the book page, preferably cut with rounded corners. These covers, which are brown and may be easily and durably glued to the spine of the book, may be obtained from Gaylord Brothers, Inc., P.O. Box 61, Syracuse, N.Y. 13201.

The title on the front cover can be printed acceptably with a rubber stamp done in script lettering, using black ink. Printing on the spine is not necessary, and dust jackets are best omitted due to their high cost, especially on books with such large covers.

The price of my garment-altering book is current-

ly $15 per single copy and $12 per copy in quantities
of two or more. This may seem like a high price, but
for a specialized work which must be frequently revised, it is really not so. A number of the books are
sent to a bindery for binding in cloth, but as this
raises the price by about $4, most buyers prefer the
board-bound book.

There is much labor and many hidden costs in the
marketing of books--let there be no misconception a-
bout this. The large publisher has to employ many persons in various departments to do his work. The small,
independent publisher has to do all of it himself, or
have it done under his direct supervision. He must often be his own sales correspondent, publicity man,
binder, and shipper. He must keep his own accounts.
Printing costs and mailing costs are both high. Books
returned are usually damaged at the corners and must
be rebound. Refunds when demanded must be made cheer-
fully, and a policy of complete honesty must be followed in advertising and dealing with customers.

It is, of course, necessary to copyright such
books, and wise to add wording beneath the copyright
notice: "Reproduction of this work in whole or in part
is strictly prohibited." Since the advent of photo-
copying machines, many publishers have discovered that
their books are photo-copied by certain private schools.
One of the advantages of binding side-stitched is that
when a book is returned, one can tell by the strain
wrinkles on the covers when it has been photo-copied.
One could prosecute such schools under the copyright
law, of course. But in general, people are honest and
few are apt to go to the labor of copying an entire
book to save a few dollars.

The writing of tailoring books is something not
many writers can manage. First, one must be a master
tailor with years of experience behind him. Secondly,
one must be able to write clearly and in great detail
all the operations that are done in making coats, trousers, vests, skirts, and other apparel. Thirdly, one
must be a trained artist with the ability to make line
drawings in series. Fourthly, one must be able periodically to revise the book in keeping with the changes
occurring in the trade. And fifthly, if one is a self-
publisher, he also must be able to answer students'
letters of inquiry for further information on any pro-

blem of tailoring practice.

These qualifications possibly indicate some reasons why the big publishers find such books hard to keep on their list, at least in the United States. Perhaps the best tailoring authors are still the British, quite a few of whom have produced hefty volumes which, in England, are still subsidized by regular publishers and almost never published by the authors. Poole and Morris, for example, both have written monumental authoritative works on garment cutting and pattern drafting, which would never have found a publisher in America. Perhaps this is because in England as in some other European countries, all good craftsmen are accorded an esteem and respect which is not obtainable in our country by persons performing manual labor, however skilled.

The remarks that I make on tailoring books here may be taken to apply to books on the other trades. If one is going to write them, one must know the work thoroughly and be able to write clearly and to illustrate his work with sufficient line drawings. By writing clearly, I mean saying neither too little nor too much. It is possible to confuse a student by writing an exposition that is much too detailed. On the other hand, one must accept the fact that everything cannot be described in words or pictures--a limitation which explains certain lapses in every technical book.

Line drawings are done with drawing pens and India ink on heavy white typing paper. (Afterwards they are trimmed around and pasted with rubber cement on the typing sheet and the text typed around them.) A fine pen is used for detail and shading, and a coarser pen for outlining or emphasizing. Lines are best done boldly; better to have a few well-placed ones than too many. Such drawings are usually numbered and captioned. Placing them appropriately on the page requires some talent for artistic layout, but usually the writer determines the positions of the drawings by the referring text. Mistakes in such drawings may be painted out with white tempera paint or Chinese white water color.

The text in such books should, in my opinion, be a bit informal and chatty, and reasons should be given for doing things in the way advocated. In all trades, various writers give different preferences for ways of doing the same things. But too much detail may also turn out to be confusing, and ultimately the author's success must depend on his own talent for saying just enough without continuing too long in unessential directions.

I see no reason why an electrician, a carpenter, a plumber, a barber, if he can write and draw, cannot sit down and gradually produce a saleable book which will turn out to be a valuable, lasting contribution to the literature of his trade. I see no reason why he cannot print and market such a book at a profit.

Major publishers, of course, often pick up books that an author has successfully sold over a period of years. So if you, like myself, are "selling" your trade, be sure to keep all the orders you receive to show to interested publishers. Keep also the notices and letters that come to you relative to the book. Collectively, they will offer convincing proof that the book is good.

A question that might be asked is whether one can earn more income from a self-published work than from one placed with a royalty publisher. With my own books I have done rather better--or as well--than I would have under the usual royalty contract of 10 per cent. But aside from immediate financial gain is the advantage of retaining the control of your work so that you can revise it, change its price when and to the extent you wish, or sell publication rights for a good price when you wish. Once you have signed a royalty contract with a publisher, these rights and this control are forever lost to you, even though you are spared the efforts of marketing.

As to the gains to be derived from any how-to book, one should best expect them to be modest. A successful novel may sell so many copies in a couple of years that the author finds himself well off. But the selling life of craft books may well be from twenty to forty years, during which they accrue income. This is why they are good investments in time and effort, although they may not make their author wealthy.

A few remarks about the how-to of writing a craft book will perhaps be of service here, even if we repeat some points already raised.

First, you must know your field thoroughly. This means that you can do what you aim to teach others with uncommon skill, you can do it in the different

known ways, and you are fairly well acquainted with
the existing literature on it. It means that your
training and experience already qualify you as an expert; that your interest in your craft has led you to
do research of your own on it and to arrive at certain
definite conclusions as to how it ought to be taught.
     Secondly, about your writing skill. Craftsmen
are not literary men and no editor or reader expects
flawless grammar and punctuation from them. But there
can be no doubt that even such books are successful to
the degree that the writer puts down his thoughts interestingly, with spontaneity, color, and feeling.
Big words must not be used to impress. But the *right*
word is to be sought at all times.
     Thirdly, one must believe in oneself, in one's
authoritativeness. I bring up this point because so
many people who could write useful books dissuade themselves from the attempt with the query: "Why should I
write on a subject that has been handled before and
better than I could ever hope to?" To this one must
respond that while it is good to be humble and self-
effacing, most writers who have produced classics
would never have turned them out with that attitude.
Books, like other works, are the result of faith: faith
in your own unique potentialities as a creator. A
hundred men each could write a book on building a
house, and each book would be different from all the
others in style, scope of content, size, and mode of
exposition; yet each one might contain something that
all the others lacked. So if you know your subject
thoroughly, then believe that you can handle it *almost*
as well as the next fellow, and that once written it
will be unique among books as you are unique among
men!
     Now for some more specific remarks. Before you
start writing your book you need to make an outline
of its contents. The book will probably start with an
introduction telling why you wrote it and the reason
you included certain things and left out others. In
it you may also give credit to the authors whose work
you made use of in preparing your text. Chapter or
Lesson I may be devoted to listing the tools required
and their uses. Chapter II may discuss the materials
with which you are to work: cloths in tailoring, met-
als in forging, woods in cabinet making, or pipes

and fittings in plumbing. Chapter III may explain the basic techniques used repeatedly in the trade and which must be mastered before attempting any large project. Later chapters may discuss projects that require prolonged attention. The book will usually end with a glossary of trade terms, sometimes followed by a bibliography and an index.

While writing your text, you should remember to "slant" the material. The term merely means directing your book's appeal toward some particular group of readers: to men only or to women or to both sexes, to professional craftsmen only or to amateurs. Obviously the most successful books are slanted toward the widest field of readers. In writing my own books, therefore, I decided from the start that they should be addressed to all amateurs and students of both sexes interested in garment making. If I had written them just for professional men tailors, they would have sold comparatively few copies.

Your main task is, of course, to select from the vast amount of material that could be handled in the teaching of any craft, that which seems basic and essential to it. This job may not at first seem problematic to you, for most craftsmen labor under the delusion that what they know can be stated briefly. However, the moment one starts putting facts on paper, one finds one's subject getting more and more complex. This is often true even of simple crafts, because there are always several methods of doing the same things. Inevitably, one is forced to limit oneself to the discussion of one's own preferred ways of working and to fundamentals. One also discovers that, while some things which cannot be conveyed clearly in words can be shown in illustrations, other matters cannot be taught satisfactorily in either words or pictures. Your book like every other book will in the end suffer from some omissions, but you should be careful to have as few of these as possible.

In selecting material, you must always have at the back of your mind the questions, "What should I include and what should I delete to make my material clearer to the beginner?" Brevity will often be more conducive to clarity than much detailed analysis.

Pay attention to transitions in your work. A jerky change from subject to subject is characteristic of many how-to books. It may seem superfluous to write, "Having finished this particular operation, let us pass on to the next," but such a sentence does help the reader's mind to accept the change of subject as natural and in place.

With regard to the number of pages in your book, how-to books seem to vary more in length than any other kind of literature. Some are slender volumes, some bulky tomes. Perhaps most contain about two hundred pages, and most writers might do well to produce a first book of that size. Such a length can accommodate a pretty impressive text and set of illustrations while selling at a reasonable price.

Almost all beginners labor under the delusion that ideas can be copyrighted and therefore nothing stated in other books should be restated. The fact is that ideas are no one's property. It is only their expression in words or diagrams that can be copyrighted. Even if you have learned formulas, facts, techniques from other books, they are usually public property which you too may use if you wish. If you wish to quote material from someone else's book, write to its publisher for permission. This will be readily granted if the amount of material is not too large and you are willing to acknowledge its source in your own book.

New authors make lots of errors in word usage. They also overpunctuate, overitalicize, overcapitalize, and often use too many hyphens and dashes. Many write sentences that are too long, use clichés and bad similes. Modern writing favors economy in sentence length and punctuation.

Some parts of your book may have to be rewritten five or six times. But don't think badly of yourself if you must rewrite. Few persons dash things off correctly the first time. Be careful, however, not to destroy the spontaneity of your first draft by too much editing.

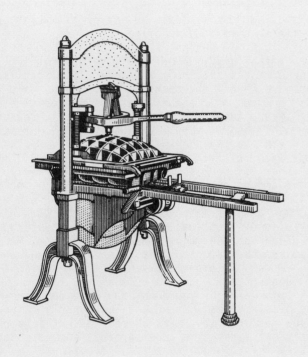

Drawing of a handpress from page 363 of *The Last Whole Earth Catalog*. Copyright © 1971 by Portola Institute, Inc.

WHOLE EARTH CATALOG

by Stewart Brand

The Whole Earth Catalog got started in a plane over
Nebraska in March 1968. I was returning to California
from my father's long dying and funeral that morning
in Illinois. The sun had set ahead of the plane while
I was reading *Spaceship Earth* by Barbara Ward. Between
chapters I gazed out the window into dark nothing and
slid into a reverie about my friends who were starting
their own civilization hither and yon in the sticks and
how I could help. The L. L. Bean Catalog of outdoor
stuff came to mind and I pondered upon Mr. Bean's service to humanity over the years. So many of the problems I could identify came down to a matter of access.
Where to buy a windmill. Where to get good information
on beekeeping. Where to lay hands on a computer without forfeiting freedom...

Shortly I was fantasizing access service. A truck-
store maybe, traveling around with information and
samples of what was worth getting and information where
to get it. A catalog too, continuously updated, in
part by the users. A catalog of goods that owed nothing to the suppliers and everything to the users. It
would be something I could put some years into.

Amid the fever I was in by this time, I remembered
Fuller's admonition that you have about ten minutes to
act on an idea before it recedes back into dreamland.
I started writing on the end papers of Barbara Ward's
book (never did finish reading it).

The next morning I approached Dick Raymond at Portola Institute with the idea. I'd been desultorily
working for him for about a half year, had helped in-
stigate one costly failure (an "Education Fair" which
aborted), and was partly into another doomed project I
called E-I-E-I-O (Electronic Interconnect Educated Intellect Operation).

I told him this access catalog was what I wanted
to do now. Dick listened gravely and asked a few questions I had no answers for (Who do you consider to be
the audience for this "catalog"? What kind of expenses
to do think you'll have in the first year? How often
would you publish it? How many copies?). All I could
tell him was that I felt serious enough about the project to put my own money into it, but not for a while
yet. I wanted to move into the scheme gradually, using
Portola's office, phone, stationery, and finances (which
were Dick's personal savings, dwindling fast). He said
okay.

For over a year Portola Institute had been nothing
but Dick, a secretary he shared, his office, and a few
expensive projects with big ideas and little to show.
So he rented a nearby set of cubicles that some archi-
tects were moving out of, to give us more room to make
mistakes in. I was working in my cubicle several weeks
later when Dick leaned in the door and asked, "By the
way, what do you think you'll call it?" My head filled
with the last success I'd had, a 1966 photograph-of-the-
whole-Earth campaign, which I felt was still incomplete.
I told him, "I dunno, *Whole Earth Catalog*, or something."

My activities at this time were mostly visiting
bookstores and looking at books. One of Dick's friends
at the Checkered Frog bookstore in Pacifica told me I
could "wholesale-buy" single copies of books from publishers if I joined the American Booksellers Association, a commitment of $25. Shortly after that I made
the big step and (holding my breath) spent $60 on note-
o-gram stationery from Modern Business Forms. Dick
helped me open a commercial account at a bank.

I was operating without pay but keeping track of my
time, to pay myself back-wages of five dollars an hour
if we ever started to make money. In July '68 I printed
up a mimeographed six-page "partial preliminary booklist" of what I'd gathered so far (*Tantra Art*, *Cyberne-
tics*, *The Indian Tipi*, *Recreational Equipment*, about
120 items). With samples of each in the back of our
truck Lois and I set out to visit the market--familiar
communes in New Mexico and Colorado. In about a month
the Whole Earth Truck Store did a stunning $200 of busi-
ness. No profit, but it didn't cost too much and was
good education.

On return in August I hired an employee, Sandra Tcherepnin, who came around part time to type and buoy my conviction that something was going on. In September Lois and I moved into Ortega Park (formerly Rancho Diablo), seventy acres and house newly leased by Portola Institute as a teachers' laboratory. She was housekeeper and I was caretaker in an empty mansion. It was a plush time.

Dick Raymond had introduced me to Joe Bonner, a talented teenage artist looking for work. He preferred to do layout than janitor for Portola so I took him to Gordon Ashby's design studio in San Francisco for a ten-minute course in layout. In October '68 we started production on the first *Whole Earth Catalog* in the garage in Ortega. Sandy fell in love with the IBM composer while Joe nailed together light tables out of scrap plywood. We got some electric heaters and started work. Joe did layout, Sandy typed, and I researched, reviewed, edited, and photographed. Whenever the typewriter, heaters, camera lights, and fry-pan of wax were on simultaneously the electricity went out. We'd spend an hour on projects like making an exotic border with the composer. A leisurely production. A month or so for sixty-four white-spacey pages.

We had the contents printed at Nowels Publications, a newspaper press just down the street from Portola Institute, and the cover printed at East Wind in San Francisco (using the picture from a Whole Earth poster we'd already had them print), and the binding done at another place, with us doing the transporting between. It was a terrible arrangement. The thousand copies we printed were a huge chore to cart around.

Our real luck was in finding Nowels Publications and Bob Parks. I've never met a man I'd rather do business with, and to find a printer who is fast, thorough, cooperative, creative, honest, and inexpensive is just unheard of. We had one *Catalog* printed elsewhere and regretted it.

I only dimly recall what we did with the first *Catalog*. We sent them to the fifty or so subscribers we'd got with mailers and personal contact. We carted some around to stores, who didn't want them, not even on consignment ("Too big. Too expensive. What is it?"). We traded some with other publications like *This Magazine is About Schools*, *Explorers Trademart Log*, and *Green*

Revolution.

Meanwhile we were starting a store. Dick Raymond had had his eye on the building at 558 Santa Cruz, Menlo Park, just across the alley from the cubicles he'd rented. Formerly a USO, then a Salvation Army store, then a printer's, the place had apartments upstairs and 4,000 square feet of big rooms downstairs and a nice store front. The printer had failed and the building was going to be sold. Dick got with the likeliest buyer and worked out a five-year lease for the downstairs part at $450 a month. We felt like we were really into the soup now. Five years! That's 1973.

At Thanksgiving we'd met a girl from New York named Annie Helmuth who had some familiarity with the publishing world, mostly on the publicity end. She was hired to take on publicity and help with research and typing since Sandy had left for woolier pastures. We soon found out that handling our own distribution was going to be impossible (bookstores wouldn't pay what they owed and hassled us with endless bizarre problems). Annie started looking around for other alternatives.

In December '68 we moved into 558 Santa Cruz. There wasn't much to move--a chair and some books. Joe set to work with free scrap wood making the store a funky pleasant wooden place. We sublet an office in the front to Dave Shapira and a space in the back to lawyer Jim Wolpman. That cut our rent to $250 a month. Joe made desks and tables out of doors and 2 by 4's. We never got around to changing the walls from institutional green.

From the beginning the pretty little Indian girl Lois, my wife, who still has to show her ID to bartenders, was the hard core of the business. She applied her math background to our bookkeeping, and her sharp tongue to our lazinesses and forgotten promises. She had the administrative qualities you look for in a good First Sergeant. In my experience every working organization has one overworked, underpaid woman in the middle of things carrying most of the load. None of the rest of us ever cleaned the bathrooms. Lois cleaned the bathrooms.

Annie was at the City Lights Bookstore in San Francisco one day talking to Shig, the manager, about where to look for a distributor. Shig suggested a new long-haired outfit in Berkeley called Book People. Annie went to them and was immediately taken with Don Gerrard and Don Burns. Pretty soon Book People was our distributor, and that was a big relief. We made no contracts or vows, but the *Catalog* stayed with Book People as sole distributor until the March '71 *Supplement* (when the *Realist* took half the distribution).

In January we had a grand opening party at the store, though we'd been open for a couple weeks. ("There's a customer in the store!" we'd whisper in the back room.) Annie and I invited all the newspapers and were surprised and hurt when none of them showed up. It was a nice party anyway. The readership was a small sort of cult then, most of whom seemed to know each other, or wanted to.

Also in January we produced our first "Difficult But Possible Supplement to the Whole Earth Catalog." It was a thirty-two-page newsprint collection of friends' letters, old pamphlets like Abbie Hoffman's "Fuck the System," a solar heater, new *Catalog* suggestions. We made it at the store.

About this time Tom Duckworth joined the scene. He lived in a truck with Connie and their kids and soon had a place to park at Ortega. His dream was to really do a traveling truck-store. In March we gave him a shakedown cruise to New Mexico when the Whole Store caravanned to ALLOY, a lusty, dusty gathering in New Mexico of outlaw designers such as Steve Baer, Lloyd Kahn, Jay Baldwin, Dean Fleming, Steve Durkee--so or so hardworking hippies. If I had to point to one thing that contains what the *Catalog* is about, I'd have to say it was ALLOY. We put it in the March *Supplement*, along with how much the *Supplement* cost to make, which Steve Baer had suggested at ALLOY. A good practice. We never regretted it.

When we started the *Catalog* I imagined that it would be a month of work, then an easy month to travel around and get the news, then a month of work, then... but it wasn't working out that way. None of us knew how to run a store and we were learning the hard way. We couldn't seem to find a mailing house that would do an even half-decent job of serving the subscribers. We had to try three places, each at big expense.

Our hassle with the post office, which continues to this very day, was in its surreal beginnings. (We're a periodical, in every spiritual and legal sense.

Periodicals are mailed Second Class, a faster, surer, and cheaper service than Third Class, which is Junk Mail. The classifications man in San Francisco said, "It says *Catalog* right here on the cover. Catalogs go Third Class." Dick Raymond cleared his throat, "*The Rolling Stone*," he said, "is not a stone." Through endless appeals the thing was ambled, letters to our Congressman Pete McCloskey, rulings, and re-rulings, to this result: we had to send *The Last Catalog* Third Class. When a mail truck gets stuck in the mud, Third Class is what they throw under the wheels.)

About this time Lois and I started living in the store. Joe and Annie and I, with editorial help from Lloyd Kahn, did the Spring '69 *Catalog* production amid the busy din of the store, a bad mistake. The *Catalog* was twice as big and a dollar cheaper. To clear my head after production, I hitchhiked to New Mexico for what turned out to be the Great Bus Race. Joe and Annie also headed for the desert, pending rendezvous in Albuquerque for the July *Supplement* production.

You should know that all this time Portola Institute was going through continual interesting changes that someone else is going to have to write about. Dick Raymond did one especially nice thing for us: he protected us from the vicissitudes.

Store and mailorder business was gradually picking up, so we hired Hal Hershey, a friend of Duckworth, who had worked in bookstores. We also hired Diana Shugart, a close buddy of Lois' and mine. At the store we had a chart on the wall that showed our income and expenses for each month. The income was gradually catching up.

While we were having a good July production at Steve and Holly Baer's house in Albuquerque, Hal and Donna were starting to face a heavy current in Menlo Park ("Fifty-two subscriptions today!"). Philip Morrison had written kindly of us in the June '69 *Scientific American*. We were being mentioned in a lot of underground papers such as the *East Village Other*. And then Nicholas von Hoffman wrote a full piece on the *Catalog* that got syndicated all over the United States. We were caught. We were famous.

(One interesting note. Of all the press notices we eventually got, from *Time* to *Vogue* to *Hotcha!*--in Germany--to the big article in *Esquire*, nothing had the business impact of one tiny mention in "Uncle Ben Sez" in the *Detroit Free Press*, where some reader asked, "How do we start a farm?" and Uncle Ben printed our address. We got hundreds and hundreds of subscriptions from that.)

Hal and Diana hired more people. Deposits at the bank were more frequent: the bank officers got more polite.

In September Joe and I returned to Ortega garage to work on the September *Supplement*. Annie had stayed on at Lama, so we hired a Kelly Girl to do the typing. As I was driving up the hill to work one day it suddenly hit me that I didn't want to. Instead of golden opportunity the publication was becoming a grim chore. I considered the alternatives of taking my medicine like a good boy or setting about passing on my job to somebody else. I'm sure I sighed unhappily. And then this other notion glimmered. Keep the job, finish the original assignment, and then stop. Stop a success and see what happens. Experiment going as well as coming. We printed in the September '69 *Supplement* that we would cease publication with a big *Catalog* in spring '71.

Meanwhile business was still growing. The morning mail was a daily heavy Santa Claus bag. We hired Tracy McCallum, Peter Ratner, Mary McCabe (a bit of uptown glamour amid the Hair), and a guy named Fred Richardson who had amazing talent for handling the world's hardware. Bernie Sproch and Megan Raymond came in periodically to handle our increasing load of filing and flyer-mailing and other chores. We were having group lunch at the store by now, Lois and Diana dishing it up.

I actually thought I could fit Liferaft Earth—which involved going foodless for a week in a crowded public place to personalize the inevitable overpopulated future—in between the September *Supplement* and the fall *Catalog*. Setting up the event was even harder than production. Then starving for a week was no way to recuperate. Dumb.

I went from Liferaft straight into fall *Catalog* production. We were late, so we had to do it in two weeks. Fred was going to take over the camera. We had a hot new typist, Cappy McClure. We had a big new Stat-King that wasn't worth it. Joe brought in his brother Jay to double our layout speed. We worked eighty hours a week. We got to the printer on time.

Then Christmas was on us. Everybody was overloaded

at the store. In January we had another burst of hiring, practically whoever came in the door. Les Rosen
the bookkeeping ex-Marine, John Clark, Russell Bass,
Jerry Fihn, Alan Burton, Leslie Acoca, the booklover
Laura Besserman. Pam Smith was cooking lunch. When
Tracy left to Canada, Pam's husband JD came in as manager. JD instituted a fine addition to the store front--
a Free Box ("take or leave"). Everybody should have
one; they really get used.

About this time I went over some edge. Minor tasks
became insurmountable obstacles. The thought of another
production filled me with hopeless dread. I couldn't
walk right. It was a nervous breakdown, garden variety.
I'd never had one before so I thought I was dying,
which stirred up a snowflurry of phobias that took more
than a year to disperse. I'm not happy to mention this,
but it seems an important part of the bookkeeping we're
doing here.

In retrospect what I particularly appreciate was
Dick Raymond's help and comfort, which was none at all.
He's an unusually merciful soul. He said out loud to
Esquire, "You have to let people have their own nervous
breakdowns." Correct.

I jittered through the January '70 production and
then asked Gurney Norman to handle March. He did, and
with bells on. Guest editorship had come to Whole
Earth. Joe Bonner left on the mystical road, and I was
worried, but Hal Hershey more than filled his shoes on
layout.

In January Fred built a volleyball court in back
of the store. I was too fucked up to play on it for a
while, which grieved me, because volleyball instantly
became a valuable part of the store routine. We played
two games after lunch every day. It improved our
health, got us out in the weather, loosened our ten-
sions, and--honest to God--built character.

Since we were playing on paid-for time, we naturally tried to stretch out the two games, so each day
the players spontaneously arranged themselves into always different but equal teams. Lunch and volleyball
kept us well acquainted. That, and the morning mail-
opening scene. We had some newcomers--Mary Jo Morra,
Soni Stoye the good cook, Austin Jenkins of good cheer.
. On the spring *Catalog* we went up to 144 pages and
lowered the price further to $3. (Later a friend at

Stanford Research Institute said he made the calculations one afternoon and figured out we would make the most money with a $4 price tag. Or $3.95, as they say.) A new face on spring production was Steamboat, who seldom spoke but could draw volumes.

In July Lois and I left to see the world and Expo and the Bakers in Japan. My old (and favorite) employer Gordon Ashby took on the July *Supplement* and totally changed our layout ways. We converted from wax to rubber cement.

JD, Nebraska's Marlon Brando, kept a strong crew busy at the Store and started gathering material for the fall '70 *Catalog* he was going to edit.

In September '70 Gurney came back from a summer in Kentucky with Wendell Berry and put out what came to be known as the Cracker issue of the *Supplement*. The BD-4 airplane kit we'd ordered started to arrive, and Fred and later Troll and Doug and Bob sawed and filed and puzzled and riveted at it in the back room.

Don Gerrard had left Book People and among his other projects was trying to find a big distributor for the *Last Catalog*. We wanted a contract by Christmas. Nobody in New York seemed very interested.

There were strong family feelings in the Store by now and a desire to do something else together. A restiveness. When the teacher's lab at Ortega finally failed and quit, JD and I pressed to get it as a home for most of the Truck Store staff, a commune. Idealism filled the air. It was never a very successful commune; it was a plenty educational one.

As fall production went on up the hill in the garage there were new laborers in the Store. Herald Hoyt, Dudley DeZonia, Francine Slate, Terry Gunesch, Diane Erickson. People's children were in the Store more often now. Marilyn's kids, Francine's, Diane's, Pam's. I was buried in the back of the office starting the long haul toward the *Last Catalog*.

During another ALLOY-type conference called "Peradam" near Santa Barbara, Steve Baer spoke of an ancestor of his named Divine Right at the same time that I was wishing that the *Last Catalog* could be a work of fiction. Gurney Norman swerved his own novel fantasies accordingly, and "Divine Right's Trip" came to pass. It was written to a weekly deadline during the production of the *Last Catalog* and printed by mini-story installments.

At Christmas there were memorable parties.

In January '71 some of us safaried to a remote un-named desert hot springs for an adventurous *Supplement* production.

Don Gerrard had gotten good offers from Dutton and Random House for distribution of the *Last Catalog*. We decided to go with Random, who was more businesslike.

I asked Richard Brautigan, Ken Kesey, and Paul Krassner if any of them would like to edit the March *Supplement*. Brautigan said he was already involved in a quaint project, writing a novel. Kesey said he would edit if Krassner would, and new levels of offense and tooldom were leveled at our readers in *The Last Supplement*.

The *Last Catalog* you know about.

A lot of other stuff happened too, ask anybody who was there. Ask Bernie Sproch to show you his **Whole Earth** stamp collection.

THE LITERARY AGENT

AS SELF-PUBLISHER

by Alex Jackinson

*ALEX JACKINSON is an outstanding New York literary a-
gent with a variety of books to his agency's credit.
Frustrated by publishers' rejections of manuscripts
that were good but uncommercial, he founded Impact
Press in 1964. His business autobiography,* The Barnum-
Cinderella World of Publishing, *was issued by Impact
in 1971 to excellent reviews. He plans a sequel for
1974,* A Personal Involvement: Twenty Years With Authors
and Editors.

I became a publisher for the same reasons that I had become a literary agent back in 1953--the challenge was formidable, and I had always liked to meet challenges head on.

An editor had said to me then: "I admire your courage, starting a literary agency in the midst of a publishing slump." I survived almost twenty years of agenting (some say that I even prospered)! As a unique publishing firm, Impact Press is ready, willing, and able to tackle some tough peaks.

Hazel Lin, M.D., was in my office once in 1964. She is a very attractive Chinese obstetrician, gynecologist, and surgeon. She also writes novels--*The Physicians*, *The Moon Vow*, *The House of Orchids*. I happened to remark somewhat casually that, if I had the means, I would publish some books, books which the large publishers turned down as "good but not saleable." This happens often enough to be my most recurring single lament. Dr. Lin understood perfectly; her own novels had gone the route. She offered to become a partner.

Dr. Lin's investment in Impact Press was nominal, six thousand dollars. To survive, I knew that I would have to balance the books which I *wanted* to publish, mostly poetry and offbeat novels, against the books which I thought might sell. I planned to publish one of each, starting with nonfiction.

I had then a skimpy manuscript, *Is Divorce An Evil?* by Jack Greenhill, a retired Los Angeles lawyer who was also a poet. I considered the manuscript completely inadequate. It was not full enough to be offered to the trade, and also too dated. Editing could work wonders, but it occurred to me to add a second part, to be comprised of essays on divorce and marriage. Mr. Greenhill agreed.

Letters began to go out, invariably to people I had previously been in touch with. The response was generous.

Back in 1928 I was a member of the Communist Party. Before total disillusionment came, it seemed that I was being groomed for the Lenin Institute. I was a steady contributor of articles and fiction for the *Daily Worker Sunday Magazine Supplement*. I was active in the "revolutionary" Fur Worker's Union, then the foremost union under Party control. I worked approximately six months as a fur cutter. That was "the season." The rest of the year I could do what I liked. Without economic pressure, I wrote what I pleased, proletarian poetry, essays, and book reviews for Left-oriented magazines. I also did commercial writing, which included humor. To gather varied experiences, I was a first reader for book publishers. Also for a literary agency.

In February of 1928 the *Daily Worker* sent me to the anthracite coal regions, ostensibly to write feature stories about "the starving miners." Miners were, indeed, up against it. There existed then a help-the-miners organization called the Penn-Ohio Relief Committee. "Openly" they disbursed relief checks to local unions, but the *real* aim was to pull the locals away from Lewis' United Mine Workers Union and bring them into the then-existing dual union which was under Communist control. I disbursed these checks. Fannie Hurst was then covering the mine situation for the Hearst newspapers. We met in Pittsburgh at a miners' relief benefit given by the magician, Thurston. A few years later I reviewed Miss Hurst's *Anitra's Dance* and sent her a copy of my review. She had thanked me for its perceptiveness. We were not in touch again until I asked her for an essay on divorce. She agreed almost by return mail.

Hers was the first article to arrive in 1964. Within a short time I had the following essays: "Divorce or Martyrdom" by Frank S. Caprio, M.D.; "Hypnosis in Marriage and Divorce" by Leo Wollman, M.D.; "Marriage--Divorce--Disaster" by Herbert A. Glieberman, an attorney; "Divorce--Depression--Drugs" by Erwin Di Cyan, Ph.D.; "Love is a Four Letter Word" by Thomas Bledsoe; "Divorce in England" by Dr. Harold Cross; "90% Unused" by Alfred Dorn, M.D.; "A Personal Message to Parents" by Judge Roger Alton Pfaff; and "Divorce Has Many Faces" by Fannie Hurst.

I now had a book!

Richard Taplinger of Taplinger Publishing Company was to be the distributor; Tom Bledsoe, then a senior editor at Macmillan, would do the copy editing. Stanley Leeds, a highly experienced book promoter, would handle publicity. I secured a good artist for the cover, a good advertising agency for cooperative ads with the Doubleday and Brentano bookstores. Impact Press was set.

When the jacket and a mailing piece were ready, copies went to the contributors. To my complete astonishment, two days later a letter arrived from Fannie Hurst's lawyers:

Our client, Miss Fannie Hurst, has forwarded for our attention your memo to her of September 23, 1965, together with book jacket of the proposed Work of Impact Press entitled *Some Syndromes Of Love* which you advise will be published on Friday, November 26th.

Neither Miss Hurst nor this office is aware of any authority by which you may include the article by Miss Hurst on the subject of divorce in this proposed Work.

Please be advised that in the event you or Impact Press proceed with plans for publication as stated by you, we shall on behalf of Miss Hurst, take all steps necessary and appropriate to stop the publication and recover such damages as may be incurred by her.

We await word from you that you are not going forward with this project...

As a consequence, I had to engage a lawyer, who replied:

My client, Mr. Alex Jackinson, has asked me to reply to your letter to him dated September 28, 1965, in which you question his right to include in a forthcoming publication an article written by Miss Fannie Hurst.

Mr. Jackinson has also forwarded to me his file containing correspondence with Miss Hurst, and after examining it I have concluded that there is no

question but that Miss Hurst has given her con-
sent to this publication.

Our offices are only a few blocks apart, and I
shall be glad to show the file to you if you will
let me know when it will be convenient for us to
meet. I think that this is preferable to an extended exchange of letters and preferable, also, to telephone conversations in which we could not both be
looking at the same papers.

I shall look forward to hearing from you...

Fannie Hurst had utterly no case, save that she
had agreed to appear in *Is Divorce An Evil?* and not
Some Syndromes Of Love. What accounted for that lawyer's letter? It was no news to her that publishers
habitually changed titles. My feeling was that she had
seen the jacket and not taken the time to *think*. Lawyers always find a *reason*, and came up with the fact
that no contracts were signed. There had been a formal
agreement only with Jack Greenhill; to the contributors
I outlined terms of payment, that 50 per cent of royalties would be set aside for distribution to the many
authors. Those I approached either sent in an essay or
declined. Some, like Lucy Freeman and Dr. Pinckney,
declined. Fannie Hurst had edited her own pages. She
had acted before seeing what would be *in* the book, and
I offered essays by qualified people who had something
trenchant to say.

It all would have blown over, save that a copy of
the first letter went to Taplinger; with a direct
threat of litigation, he refused to distribute the book,
and I could not blame him. I could arrange for no other distribution; "Taplinger" was stamped on each copy.
Stymied, I nevertheless went ahead. Review copies went
out, and the book was reviewed. Not in the key places,
but it was reviewed. The book was put on Recommended
Reading list by *MD*, the most prestigious of the medical-
oriented magazines. A prominent author-psychologist
who taught at Franklin Pierce College wrote me: "I have
now not only read *Some Syndromes Of Love*, but have made
eleven 8- by 9-inch pages of notes for use in my classes. There is much good and little nonsense in it." A
reviewer wrote: "The book is a must for college students
and educators who deal in human relations, and it is a
must for the average layman's library."

Ultimately there was a settlement drawn up by the two sets of lawyers. Fannie Hurst "won" absolutely nothing, but Impact Press lost very heavily. By the time that this inexplicable detour was righted, and I wrote to Richard Taplinger that we now had the green light, the assembly-line method of book publishing and distribution caught up with me. Taplinger wrote:

I don't know what we can do with *Some Syndromes Of Love* at this point. We started to sell it and had some advance orders, but found that we could not distribute it with any degree of legal safety, and now since the book has been published it will be impossible to get any decent publicity coverage for it, and it is also impossible to reintroduce it to the bookstores. In view of the rather confused situation, I suggest you continue as you have been going.

Lacking distribution set off a chain reaction. Stan Leeds, who took a very active interest, questioned the use of publicizing a book which was not in the bookstores. And he disagreed with my reluctance to exploit Fannie Hurst's threatened suit. To do *something*, Stan ran a joint Impact Press-Doubleday Bookstores ad in *The New York Times*. *Syndromes* did not sell--the book was not *known*, and thus was not asked for, or picked up, in sufficient quantity. There hadn't been that coordinated punch of an ad plus publicity, so that *Syndromes* might get *talked about*. A few copies were sold by mail order, but a short time later the book was remaindered, at thirty-five cents a copy. It had cost Impact Press $1.35 per copy to produce the book.

Impact Press was left comatose, but still breathing. There were no funds to put other books into production; I did not want to operate on credit. After four years of inactivity, Dr. Lin withdrew as a partner. The firm became "all mine," but what could I do with less than $500 in the till? There can no longer be a paperback sale, for social events badly dated *Syndromes*. There could be updating and then republication. This was suggested by one of the contributors, Alfred Dorn, M.D., who, with another active psychiatrist, Alfred E. Eyres, M.D., turned out two books which I delighted in handling as an agent: *Stress And Distress* (A. S.

Barnes) and *Sex: Its Uses and Abuses* (Information, Inc.). Dr. Dorn's book publication had started with *Syndromes*. For that he was grateful. So much so that he took over Dr. Lin's original role. He wanted to see Impact Press revived, and I certainly had no objections.

A third active participant is editor Charles Di Witt (a pseudonym), who had been with McGraw-Hill when we established our tie. That was 1963. Impact Press is unique in many ways, and one is that none of the partners wants to "make money" out of the firm. That is, not for personal gain. Each has his own source of income. The concept remained as originally planned, to balance nonprofitable books with commercial ones. If a novel, it would have to be a book we would take pride in publishing, but we'd also want to see movie possibilities and a paperback tie-in. If nonfiction, the book had to have a fairly predictable market. We all believed in good distribution and putting money into making a book known. To start, we needed a trail blazer. It turned out to be my own book, *The Barnum-Cinderella World of Publishing*.

The manuscript had an interesting travel history. Harris-Wolfe took the book--almost. A contract was negotiated between myself and William Breedlove, then the executive editor. Contracts arrived, were ratified by me, and returned. The firm unexpectedly went into a tailspin and crashed. The full story of this bizarre upset is told in my *Barnum-Cinderella*.

I tried other publishers, assiduously avoiding houses with which I had close submission ties as an agent. That excluded quite a few! A large number remained. While I would have liked a prestige firm, and I tried some, realistically I felt that my best chance lay with some new publisher. Robert B. Luce almost contracted. Silvermine in Norwalk, Connecticut, showed interest. "Contracts will go out next week," wrote William Atkin, the president. As with Harris-Wolfe, I wanted to know that I had a publisher and could coordinate ideas, but I was in no rush for publication. Contracts were always pending, and I preferred to await the outcome. Mine is a business of continuity, a business without an end (save *the* end). New events were always happening which I wanted to include in my book.

The agreement from Silvermine failed to come

264

through because their hoped-for expansion failed to materialize. I continued gathering rejection notes:
    World Publishing: "I really enjoyed reading your book. The range of your experience in the business puts *me* to shame. Lord, what a crazy business we're in!...Alas, I am going to stand aside on this one. The usual grim, sordid commercial reasons. I know there will be an interest in the profession at large, but I just can't predict whether or not it will break out into the general market."
    G. P. Putnam: "You provided me with a lot of solid entertainment, and this material really deserves presentation in hardcovers. But, I simply can't get anyone here to share my enthusiasm, despite the fact that I believe strongly that there's a lot of useful information presented. I repeat, there's a lot of excellent material here but we simply cannot work up the courage. Market jitters..."
    Macmillan: "Let me say that we consider your work extremely well written. However, it is our feeling that it is a bit too personal a memoir to attract the necessary readership outside of New York to warrant our making a publishing offer to you."
    Bobbs-Merrill: "I want to thank you very much for letting me see your manuscript. As an insider I found much of it entertaining but I couldn't really convince myself that there are enough members of the general public interested in our crazy business."
    Houghton Mifflin: "I'm regretfully returning your partially completed *The Barnum-Cinderella World Of Publishing* without making an offer for it. We found it entertaining and informative reading, but I'm afraid we feel that books on the publishing industry have little interest for the general market."
    E. P. Dutton: "Thank you very much for giving us a chance to look at your manuscript. In my opinion, much of the 'behind the scenes' approach to the material would probably make a fine basis for a popular novel, but I had real trouble envisioning a market for the book."
    I was dealing with the Barnum-Cinderella world of publishing where the unexpected can always be counted on to happen. In that context, this letter from Charles Di Witt is highly fitting.

Thanks for the Xerox copy of *Barnum-Cinderella* and the batch of rejection letters. The publishers are quite right--this is not a book for "the general public," to which my answer is: "and who cares?" It is very much a book for lovers (and buyers) of books. It is *very much* a book for writers (writers on all levels); it is certainly a book for students and teachers of creative writing. It is also a book for librarians--all sorts of libraries should have this book. Everywhere there is interest about how books are chosen, and not chosen, marketed, and, all too often, prematurely remaindered. Your expertise elicits admiration. Almost every other family boasts a writer of one sort or another. Your book will appeal to the much-published writer as well as the novice. You point out the pitfalls, but you do it with compassion. All sorts of writers will learn from your book. And they will tell others. I foresee a lot of word-of-mouth recommendation. In my view, a large market exists without the general public.

Had I continued the search, I am reasonably certain that I would have found a publisher; with Impact Press revived, the search terminated. I knew the mortality rate for small new publishers, but there was the challenge part.
There would be ten thousand dollars to work with, a tiny sum these high-cost production days, but I had always thrived on battling odds. At Impact there would be no editor's or other wages to pay. Also no rent, since we operate out of my office. I ran a one-man business. Matilda (spouse) donated her time and skill as a typist. Once the decision was made, I wanted to get my book out in the fall of 1971. This meant getting it into production not later than May. In turn, a cutoff for completion of my manuscript had to be set.
Distribution had to be seen to. I approached David McKay, Crown, E. P. Dutton, three of many large houses which distribute for small firms. This is a growing trend in the industry. If I had had a *list*, the firms would have been receptive, but they did not want to start with a single, specialized book. The alternative was to rely heavily on mail orders, which are a more immediate source of income.

I believe in advertising and promotion, which are extremely expensive. The first ad was in *The National Observer*. Cost, $800. I took the inside cover of the November 1971 *Writer's Digest*. $850. I ran an ad in *The New York Times Book Review*. That was $1,500. There you have $3,150, and that was only the start. It cost $8,054 simply to produce 3,000 bound copies of a 353-page book meant to sell at $5.95. Six thousand sheets were printed, and 6,000 jackets. Binding books is costly, but once the presses roll, it costs only a fraction more to run 6,000 sheets or jackets as half that amount.

Vail-Ballou, the book manufacturers who had also printed *Syndromes*, received $6,589. In their own spelling, it was for: "Frontmatter text; Ms. & order processing chaps nos & titles; rules; samples; 1122 extra page proofs; incorporating new changes & corrs chap 05, 17; authors alterations."

Jackets were produced by Tribune Litho, and they received $544. Copy editing cost $375. Art work on the jacket, $100. Potomac Electrotype received $96.94 for some stamping dies. Then there were delivery charges to bring books from Binghamton, New York, to my office in Manhattan. I had to buy Jiffy bags, order stacks of labels and envelopes. There were circulars to print. Postage is a heavy drain.

Did my ads bring results? This needs a lot of explaining. Responses did not nearly cover the costs, not even by a third. Yet I regard advertising as extremely important. I repeated a *Times* ad, and I plan to advertise more. It makes a book known. Libraries respond. Authors. I receive numerous letters which run in this vein: "I have read your book, would you please read mine?" A few manuscripts proved good enough for me to handle as an agent. Selling copies of my book is not all that I must consider in placing ads, as I will show.

On December 15, 1972, a little more than a year after publication, Gilbert A. Ralston wrote me: "Dear Alex: From whom do we order multiple copies of your new book? I want some for my writing class. I can order them from Pickwick in Los Angeles, but it takes ten million years for them to send books." I replied that my book should be ordered directly from me, Impact Press. All orders shipped on the day of arrival. I tend to the shipping.

Gil Ralston has impressive credits as a screen-television writer. His best known recent success was *Willard*, which paved the way for a sequel, *Ben*. He has also turned to the novel, *Cockatrice* and *The Frightful Sin of Cisco Newman*. Ralston has a passion for teaching creative writing. He had headed the communications department at Tahoe Paradise College, and is now president of Sierra Nevada College.

Also in December 1972, a pleasant-faced young man walked into my office. He showed me a crumpled coupon from one of my *Times* ads. The visitor paid cash for a copy. For my records, I asked who he was, and he replied: "I'm...a producer. I've an office at 1545 Broadway."

"Are you looking for plays?"

"Oh, yes. Very much so," he replied.

"Prentice-Hall," I told him, "recently published a novel, *End And Beginning* by Ken Edgar. The novel originally came to me as a play. Because so few serious plays are produced annually on Broadway, I suggested that the play be converted to a novel. Now we have both."

The producer walked off with a copy of the play. And a few other "properties," since he also served as story scout for a movie star and a motion-picture director. This chance visit, which may turn out to be an extremely important contact, illustrates the efficacy of advertising. It also gives me an opportunity to stress an important point.

I gave the producer some unpublished novels, and I said: "If movie interest develops, for the purpose of prior exploitation, I can guarantee hardcover publication. I can stress *guarantee* because of Impact Press. I'm not bound by lists, schedules, or previous commitments. I could put a book into production overnight."

One of the glories of being your own publisher is that you have control of all the connected tangents. I like that; I like to hold the reins.

Although my book was meant to be mail-ordered, orders are constantly arriving from bookstores and libraries. People hear about *Barnum-Cinderella* and place orders. My book is not going to be dated for a long time to come, just as my first book with a publishing background, *Cocktail Party For The Author*, published by Challenge Press, is still pleasing readers. That is the ultimate test of a book's value: whether or not it is pleasing the audience at which it was aimed. Many have bought *Barnum-Cinderella* and then ordered a copy for a friend. My book has something of importance to say to writers, as the following comments--only a few of those I received--show.

Publishers Weekly: "Alex Jackinson, as a literary agent in New York, has been guide, mentor, comforter, and man-up-front for authors trying to make it in publishing. He is often as entertaining in describing his experiences in that battered world between author and publisher that is an agent's lot as he is helpful in spelling out the problems and pitfalls of the literary life."

Detroit Free Press: "Solid, behind-the-scenes stuff on why some writers get published and some don't, how and when to pick an agent, the uses and abuses of fee-hungry 'literary counselors,' vanity publishing, writing schools, the obligations of a publisher to the writer and vice versa, selling tips, all drawn from the author's wide personal experience. He names names, too."

George Abbe (novelist, poet, teacher): "Your book is great entertainment and richly informative; I found it hard to put down. You are a lighthouse in the publishing dark, a house of integrity and kindness and hope for the new writer."

Harald J. Taub, executive editor, Rodale Press: "I found *Barnum-Cinderella* utterly fascinating and want to thank you for it. It could only have come from an agent whose vast knowledge of the business is matched by his contempt for growing personally rich. Every agent has such a book in him, of course, but I don't know any other who would dare to make as many enemies simply because he loves writers and wants to see them fairly dealt with. I hope many, many writers will read your book if only for the understanding they will gain of how to pick an agent for themselves."

As this article is written (at the end of 1972) half of the three thousand copies have been sold; the others will be. All involved in Impact Press are glad that we revived the firm. We are ready for the next steps.

The worries of being your own publisher are manifold, and the most important are the obvious *limitations*. With an assured movie sale for a book, there wouldn't be much of a problem in getting distribution or interesting a paperback house. On other books, the problems loom like so many menacing claws.

For fear of attracting too many unsolicited manuscripts, I did not want Impact Press listed in the market guides. Nevertheless I receive many submissions. Some authors have read my book, in which I have a chapter on Impact. Others look into the telephone book and submit "blindly," not knowing, and seemingly not caring to find out, what we would consider and what we would not consider.

Impact Press is not an open house, one which will do many books per year. Dr. Lin's motive had never been an income-type investment. Had Impact flourished, she would have had a publisher. Dr. Dorn reasoned the same way. So did Di Witt, and so did I. In that sense, Impact is a family affair. Viewed another way, it is the most open house imaginable. We have utterly no restrictions. Having broken the ice with my book, we could move quickly on production and do a real professional job. It becomes a matter of *which* book. And that can be puzzling.

A chap in Canada proposed a sleazy sex book. I replied that, as an agent, I did not act as judge or censor. My job is to place books, whether I personally approve of the subject or not. But as a publisher, I can exercise personal taste. Sex, yes, most assuredly, but not anything from the basement. Far too many worthless books are being published now.

Contracts from Impact had gone out to Ken Edgar, whose first adult novel was published by Prentice-Hall, *End And Beginning*. Because my first responsibility is to a client, I kept showing the book to other publishers despite the contract, and finally I interested an editor. Impact Press cannot do what a large house can do; our special niche is to rescue the book which the large houses *won't* do.

Those who have read *Barnum-Cinderella* are familiar with Marjorie Holtzclaw's novels. Two are under contract to Impact, and it would delight me to put one into production. Miss Holtzclaw, doing what all dedicated writers must do, started a third novel, one which promises to be a stunner. *That one* should be published first, and it will be. And by a major house. Limitations remain limitations.

COSMEP

by Richard Morris

RICHARD MORRIS is coordinator for the Committee of Small Magazine Editors and Publishers, a must organization for the small-press publisher. The monthly News-letter *alone is worth the low membership fee. Morris is also a widely published poet. He heads his own press, Camel's Coming, which he founded in 1965. This article is an updated version of one that originally appeared in Len Fulton's* Small Press Review.

In May 1968 the Conference of Small Magazine/Press Editors and Publishers (COSMEP) was held in Berkeley on the campus of the University of California. It was organized by Jerry Burns, Len Fulton, and a number of other small publishers, and directed by Jerry. The organizers had long felt that such a conference was needed so that littlemag/small-press publishers could get together and discuss their common problems. Later the same year several of the editors who had attended the conference began the job of putting together an organization. It was called the Cooperative of Small Magazine Editors and Publishers (later changed to "Commitee" for legal reasons) in order to retain the acronym COSMEP. Len Fulton was chosen as chairman.

The first project of the new organization was to put together a catalogue which would list in one place all the magazines and books published by members and, hopefully, stimulate ordering by booksellers and librarians. As I look back on this, I can't help but feel that we must have been a little mad. The five-dollar membership dues and small catalogue-listing fees that we were collecting would have paid for ten thousand copies of a catalogue if we did most of the production ourselves (Jerry was going to do the printing--if he could get a press), but there would have been no money to keep an organization going afterwards. There was talk of the possibility of grant money, but at that point we weren't at all sure that we would get any.

I suppose that COSMEP would have survived one way or another. Things became easier, however, when Harry Smith (of _The Smith_) found COSMEP some grant support from a private trust. With the help of a small matching grant from the Coordinating Council of Literary Magazines (CCLM), we were able not only to go ahead

with the catalogue, but also to begin planning other
projects. Doug Blazek of Open Skull Press went to work
editing a bookstore list and survey, and Hugh Fox (Ghost
Dance Press) started organizing another conference, this
one to be held in Ann Arbor, Michigan.
     After some trouble with the printer, the catalogue
was finally published in June of 1969--just in time for
the second COSMEP Conference--and ten thousand copies
were distributed during the following year. Catalogues
were sent to every college, university, and junior college library in the United States and Canada, to every
city or county library with holdings of more than three
thousand volumes, and to selected foreign libraries.
They were also mailed to booksellers, to magazine subscription agencies, to State arts councils, and to any
individual or organization we suspected might have some
interest in knowing what was going on around the small-
press scene. In addition, two thousand copies were
given away free in bookstores.
     At first it was hoped that the publication of a
catalogue would bring in a large number of orders and
lead naturally to the setting up of some kind of distribution system. It soon became apparent, however,
that things would not be this easy. We saw that we
needed to make librarians, booksellers, and the public
more aware of littlemags and small-press books, and
that the catalogue was only a first step in this direction. Although it did contribute to making the small-
press scene more visible, and although it probably
brought in enough orders to compensate for the time and
money expended on it, it was felt that COSMEP could best
follow up by concentrating on other projects.
     We began publishing the COSMEP *Newsletter* in order
to give members information on printing, distribution,
selling to libraries, reviewers, and other subjects of
interest. The first edition of the COSMEP *Bookstore
Survey*, published in late 1969, contained annotated
listings of some 350 bookstores in the United States
and abroad which were reported to have ordered small-
press publications or littlemags at one time or another.
Since a great many members had experienced difficulty
collecting money from some stores, the *Bookstore Survey*
gave as much information as possible on the stores'
reputations for paying or for ignoring long overdue
bills. It also contained comments and recommendations

about dealing with booksellers. In early 1971, a second edition of the *Bookstore Survey*, listing approximately 450 stores, was published. A library list was published at about the same time.

COSMEP had become an organization that was engaged in getting useful information to members, and in representing the small presses in general. As its activities widened, it became apparent that it was also important to provide information about the small-press scene. There were requests for the catalogue (which was given away free as long as it remained in print), and inquiries about the address of this or that press. People wanted to know if there was a directory of littlemags and small presses available, and were given the appropriate information about the Dustbooks publication. A book jobber to academic libraries wanted a membership list, and expressed interest in handling more small-press books. A university library which wanted to start a littlemag collection of fifty publications said that its subscription agency did not want to handle irregular publications and asked for advice. Somebody in a school of library science turned out to be doing a thesis on COSMEP and needed to know where certain publications could be obtained. There were letters from kids in the boondocks who wanted to know where they could send their poems. Others did not bother to ask first and sent poetry to COSMEP. There were inquiries that could be answered, and some that were ridiculously inappropriate. At one point someone asked us to help him locate a pamphlet on butchering hogs and curing pork. At the same time COSMEP found itself receiving inquiries from members about printing, copyright, distribution, and availability of grants, and other subjects. Usually these were answered individually; sometimes they also suggested topics for articles in the *Newsletter*.

Just by answering the letters that appeared in the post-office box every day, something was accomplished. Nevertheless, there was still the more important task: helping to get small-press publications better known. Small-press publishers are always talking about the problems of distribution; they often forget that the problem lies deeper than this. There are a few small-press and littlemag distributors, after all. If small-press publications only sold better, existing distributors would take on more titles, and others would enter the field.

The Mad Ave publishers can afford to promote a book. They buy advertising, schedule appearances of the author on television talk shows, and make various kinds of special offers to booksellers. The book is reviewed in newspapers and magazines for the public; *Library Journal*, *Publishers Weekly*, and other publications get the word out to librarians and booksellers. If the book has any chance of becoming a best seller, or if its author is reasonably well known, it automatically receives various kinds of free publicity. And the public runs out to buy it. Books of a more scholarly nature, especially those brought out by the university presses, do not become as widely known, but they do receive their share of advertising and promotion. Mention in specialized journals frequently gives them more than their share of reviews.

The small publisher or littlemag editor can spend little or nothing on advertising. And if he receives any reviews at all, they are likely to appear in the littlemags. Since the circulations of these are so small and their audiences so inbred, this may not be much better than no reviews at all as far as sales are concerned.

COSMEP was not exactly in a position to spend millions promoting its members' publications. But it could do two things. First, it could help to educate librarians and booksellers. Hopefully, with the publications in more bookstores and libraries, more people would see them, and that small, select audience that seeks out littlemag and small-press books would be enlarged. The money added from library orders would, of course, be a benefit in itself. Hence, shortly after the publication of the catalogue, COSMEP began sending sample packages of member publications to libraries and bookstores. A copy of the catalogue was always enclosed-- just in case the copy previously sent had been misplaced. Second, we tried to help members get more reviews.

Bill Katz helped get the word out to libraries. He reviewed as many littlemags as possible in his magazine column in *Library Journal* and mentioned small-press books when he could. He included a chapter on littlemags in his book for librarians, *Magazine Selection*, and enlarged the littlemag section in his reference work, *Magazines for Libraries*. Since only a limited number of small-press books could be mentioned in his column, he agreed to write another column for *Library Journal* which would be devoted to them exclusively. And here and there other channels of information opened up. Len Fulton, then COSMEP chairman, wrote a long article for *American Libraries*, the journal of the American Library Association, which contained a 113-item bibliography of littlemags. Other librarians' publications, such as *Alternatives in Print*, contacted COSMEP asking for help in getting more comprehensive coverage of the small presses.

We also wanted to get the word out to the general public. At first the underground newspapers seemed the obvious medium for this. So every paper in the Underground Press Syndicate was put on the COSMEP mailing list, and we began running notes in the *Newsletter* on underground papers which would run small-press reviews. The results were not very encouraging. The underground press did not seem to be very interested in small-press publishing. Several papers ran reviews regularly for a while, but these brought in few orders.

We could not have foreseen this, but in retrospect it does not seem very surprising. The underground press and its readers tend to be preoccupied with such subjects as dope, politics, and rock music. They are much more likely to be interested in a book on one of these subjects that is released by Random House or Doubleday than in a small-press literary publication (unless it's a book by Snyder or Ginsberg). *Nola Express* in New Orleans is, as far as I know, the only underground paper which still continues to run regular small-press reviews. And *Nola Express*, unlike most underground papers, has always had something of a literary orientation. (John Wilcock's column, "Other Scenes," syndicated to the Underground Press Syndicate, often carries notices and evaluations of littlemags and small presses.)

When we finally began lobbying for better coverage in the commercial media, the results were much better. Virtually all the publications we contacted, including *The New York Times Book Review* and the *New York Review of Books*, at least expressed some interest. As I write

A bit of humor from the February 1972 issue of *COSMEP Newsletter*.

this, they have not yet begun to review many small-press books, and it remains to be seen how extensive their coverage will be. Nevertheless, the indications are that they are gradually becoming aware of the importance of the small presses, and that COSMEP will be able to continue to exert pressure on them in the future.

In writing this I have said nothing of the false starts we have made, of the disagreements we have had, or of the financial problems that COSMEP has had from time to time. If I were to include all this, it would probably be necessary to write a book. I should not, however, leave the reader with the impression that COSMEP is concerned only with the business side of small-press publishing. Thus I should probably say something about COSMEP's other major function: promoting dialogue among littlemag and small-press publishers.

There is no single center of small-press or little-mag activity. Magazines and presses are likely to spring into existence anywhere. There have always been quite a few in New York, but the New York publications are greatly outnumbered by those scattered around in Iowa City; Madison, Wisconsin; Putney, Vermont; Cerrillos, New Mexico, and like places. Because editors are so isolated from one another, they often do not have any opportunity for personal contact. This was one of the reasons why the first COSMEP Conference was organized in 1968, and it is the reason why COSMEP has held a conference every year since then. In 1969 the conference was held in Ann Arbor, in 1970 it took place in Buffalo, and in 1971 it was held at San Diego. In 1972 it was held in Madison, Wisconsin. And in 1973 the site was New Orleans.

There is also a certain amount of continuing dialogue in the COSMEP *Newsletter* which, by printing articles and letters sent in by members, provides a forum for the discussion of any topic of common interest. The *Newsletter* also keeps members in contact with happenings around the small-press scene. Not surprisingly, members often find things on which they can disagree. However, the arguments seem to have gotten more vehement at the conferences. The 1970 conference in Buffalo was particularly notable in this respect. In response

to a telegram from Lawrence Ferlinghetti, who was ill
at the time and unable to attend in person, the members
attending the conference passed a resolution to the effect that COSMEP should refuse to accept any federal
grant money while the war in Indochina was still in progress. Although the resolution was later defeated in
a referendum of the membership at large, it did have
the effect of creating a dialogue on the subject and of
clarifying the issues involved. Discussions continued
in the *Newsletter* for something like eight months after
the conference.

When the *Catalogue of Small Press Publications*,
COSMEP's first project, went to press at the beginning
of 1969, the organization had 150 members. At the end
of 1972, there were 450. It's hard to make any predictions about the future, however. COSMEP membership
generally increases by about 50 per cent during any giv-
en year. And then it drops when the year ends and it
comes time for members to renew. In addition to the
normal attrition experienced by every organization, a
number of member publications will have folded, and the
ones that have sprung up to replace them are not necessarily yet convinced that they should join COSMEP.
Still, the increase from 150 to 450 over a period of
several years should indicate a trend.
      Membership in COSMEP is open to any magazine,
press, or newspaper of limited circulation. The majority of the members are literary presses or periodicals.
Membership dues currently are fifteen dollars. Additional information can be obtained by writing COSMEP,
P.O. Box 703, San Francisco, Calif. 94101.

SOME CAUTIONS

by Dick Higgins

DICK HIGGINS published his own book in 1964 and from
that experience emerged Something Else Press, still
prospering with almost a hundred titles by many authors.
He lives, works, and writes in the clear, calm atmosphere of West Glover, Vermont.

The worst thing you can do to yourself as a writer and
as an artist is to allow your work to get cold, either
to yourself or in terms of its time. Not that everything you produce should be sent off tomorrow to be in
print a week from Thursday. Oscar Wilde said, "It's
very dangerous to be too modern. One becomes old-fashioned so very quickly." He was right.
     But works are nothing if they aren't read or seen
or played. They need their audience, and they need the
currency of their time. If you produce works "for the
future," you are kidding yourself. They will only have
a future if they have a present, if they are firsthand.
And the only time any of us will ever know at firsthand
is our own. The glory that was Greece and the grandeur
that was Rome are not our glories and grandeur. And
you can write for an intelligent Martian if you like,
but he, she, or it may not like.
     So you've read most of the articles in this book.
And you've decided to self-publish. I understand that:
I did it myself. A publisher accepted my manuscript,
but wanted to do it "a year from April." I was upset.
I went out and studied at firsthand the meaning of
the word *inebriation*. Then I went back, grabbed my
manuscript from my publisher's desk, took it to my studio, and studied the uses of a couple of bottles of
Gallo Chianti. I then went home and announced to my
wife, "We've founded a press." "Oh really," she said,
blasé. "What's it called?" I said something bland,
like "Shirtsleeves Press." "That's no good," she said.
"Call it something else." And I did, "Something Else
Press." The first book I did was my own, *Jefferson's
Birthday/Postface*, a collection of my happenings and
fluxus scenarios. I found I had an editorial position
(and to prove it wrote the Something Else Manifesto that

has now been published about seven times, in English, Dutch, and German). And so it went and so it went, till now the press has four employees, I no longer run it, we have ninety-six titles (only six of them mine, and these have paid for themselves), and while it's no money-maker, it will be. It takes at least ten years to make a literary- or art-oriented press pay for itself, and we're only eight. Furthermore, it's darn satisfying to see a whole organization, which does a lot of important books, evolve out of the one moment when I said no, if the old publisher wouldn't do it right and do it in a reasonable amount of time, I'd do it myself.

So you've made your decision. Now what? Well, in the first place, think about market. Not the market of publishers any more, since you've decided to become one. But the market of buyers of books. Looking out towards the dim and distant, there's you. Yourself as publisher comes next (you don't want to waste your money, do you?). Beyond this split ego of yourself, there are the mysterious salesmen and jobbers--the people who supply stores, the next vista. And beyond the stores, your actual public. Seems like an awfully long way to reach, and it is, and it's an outmoded system. You've already cut one link out of the chain by becoming your own publisher. What are the economics of the rest?

Let's start with the end link, the public. The book buyer gets a book because he wants it. He wants it for his Aunt Susan for Christmas (it must therefore look pretty), or because he has heard about it and figures it has something in it which he has to know (hence the importance of reviews), or because he noticed it in a store and it appealed to him, because of price or because he liked what he saw (this is again the importance of effective display).

The store is in an impossible bind. To sell, it needs a big stock, to stock something that every buyer will want for himself or for his Aunt Susan. It must therefore maintain an attractive location, pay a fairly literate staff, and keep a huge inventory of items bought from a vast array of suppliers. Each book requires an inventory slip, and a veritable ocean of mail results. The usual discounts range from the 20 per cent "short discount" for textbooks and technical books or for small orders, up to 45 per cent for large orders of

best sellers. And every day some nuisance requests
come in which have to be "special ordered" (and on
which the bookseller usually loses money) from the publisher (slow) or from a wholesaler, called a "jobber,"
who obviously can't offer the same discount as the publisher.
    The stores are supplied by commissioned salesmen.
(Larger publishers employ salaried salesmen.) If the
stores had to do it all themselves, their paperwork
would be even more untenable, so the salesmen do it for
them. They write up the orders and send them into the
publishers, who give them a 10 or 15 per cent commission of net (after discount).
    So now you're a publisher. Angie's Book Mart or-
ders ten copies of a photo book you've done, for $1.00
each. You give the store a 40 per cent discount, $4.00.
You give the salesman 15 per cent of the remaining
$6.00, or 80¢. If you pay someone to type up and ship
the order, this will cost maybe $1.00. To manufacture
each book cost you 15¢, $1.50 for the ten copies. This
is where you stand:
    List price of ten books, $1.00@, $10.00.
    Store gets $4.00, you get $6.00, except...
    Shipping and packing gets $1.00. Printer has al-
ready gotten $1.50. Salesman gets 80¢. Leaving $2.80.
    If you had other expenses to pay--royalties to the
photographer, permissions fee, an ad in your friendly
local underground newspaper or literary magazine, the
cost of giving away a few copies to friends and other
well-placed people--they must all come out of this.
And on top of it all, the salesman will be cross because he needs more than his 80¢ commission from you
every half hour to make a decent living, and he'll want
you to do deluxe editions (15 per cent of $60.00 would
be a lot more than 15 per cent of $6.00). The public
will be after you because no matter what price your
books are, they're always too expensive. Young people
will spend $45.00 a week on hash, $15.00 a week on records, but only 60¢ a week on reading matter, though
almost each of them considers himself literate and is
working on a book of some kind. The stores will receive
your bill to be paid in 30 days and pay it in 90 days
or 120 days, if then--but you can't do without them if
your purpose is to get your books to the people. And
if you can do any kind of book for just 15¢ a copy in

these 1970's, well hats off to you.

So how does anybody make money on books? Well, nowadays, nobody does. NOBODY MAKES ANY MONEY ON BOOKS! Except maybe the commissioned salesmen, and even *they* eat hamburger instead of steak and are a lean and stalwart lot at best. The stores operate on a 3 per cent profit level, less than the rate of inflation. Yet the publishers cannot give them more, because they make their money from secondary rights: movies, television, commercial property (e.g., sweat shirts), foreign editions, and magazines (though these too may be wiped out with the new postal rates).

College textbooks make money, some book clubs make money (not all), but basically books are considered dispensable, a luxury in our society. That is why our countrymen seem so universally moronic and lacking in ideas, compared to Italians or Germans or Netherlanders or Japanese or Maghrebi revolutionaries. It costs an Irishman a morning's labor to buy a paperback, the same book that an American could earn in a half-hour's time. Yet the Irish buy more books per capita. America is somewhere under thirtieth place in per-capita book consumption and reading. We only write so many books as a nation because there are so many of us--210 million people is a pretty large market, no matter how you look at it. But we have no reason to pat ourselves on the back on this matter, alas. And things are getting worse, not better (even the Europeans are reading fewer books, in spite of "mass education"). By the end of this decade, probably only one third of the bookstores that now exist will still be in business, and those that are will probably be using books as a prestige line to sell the more profitable greeting cards, chess sets, and novelties. Probably the number of magazines with any literary pretensions will be halved. And most university and trade publishers will have been swallowed up as appendages of the communications industry, so that their imprints will survive but without their independence.

Publishing and bookselling as we have known them are therefore probably doomed. Where does this leave a person who is an artist with words or whose medium, such as photography, lends itself to a book format? Well, often when the holocaust passes, we find it is the little ones who have survived. A generation which

doesn't think will be succeeded by a thinking generation, if only because the older generation left so much
mess that needed thinking through. A generation that
grinds up all its trees to print *The New York Times*,
which nevertheless goes unread--I've been told it takes
two thousand acres to print each Sunday edition, but
that's surely a slight exaggeration--is surely going to
be followed by a more literate one, which holds a tree
wasted if something worthwhile isn't printed on its
crushed fibers.

So by staying small, you lose less. You may even
profit, if you are quite clear just what kind of jungle
a writer must contend with.

My advice then, given the economics, is: DON'T
self-publish if there's any conceivable place you can
send to (book or magazine publisher) that already shares
your outlook and interests. Don't be too proud, too
lazy, or too afraid of an editorial NO to send your
work around. It's your own money you'll be saving.

And then too, much as you may want your work to
circulate, realistically, are there a million people
who want to buy your work in drugstores? Or even if
there are, will they know to do so?

Clearly the way to suffer least from the jungle
of publishing and the holocaust of economics that has
overtaken is to (a) tend to stay small, as small as
possible, and (b) to grow according to real possibilities, not according to what one would wish to be true.

If you are an economist specializing in 14th-Cen-
tury Arabic economic history, you probably know of most
of the specialists in your field. In that case, it is
foolish to try to get your local university press to do
your book--they will lose money on it, and sooner or
later you'll be frustrated by their experience. Better:
have it neatly typed, found a press and choose yourself
"an imprint," have it printed cheaply by electronic
duplication such as Itek Offset, send 150 copies to
the known experts in the field, and save 150 for orders
that drift in. The costs of the edition will be paid
by the lecture fees you get, and by the quotes you get
and their effect on your relation with others in your
field. That is to say, you'll probably get a raise or
a better job if you want one.

Some fields are even more deceptive. I notice in
the *Encyclopedia of Associations* that the Council on

Optometric Education is listed, but it has only seven members. Five gets you eight that a lot more than seven people are interested in teaching optometrists to supply glasses correctly.

So for a person working on optometric education, he would be well advised to go at it from the point of view of optometry and medical education in general, which is an awesomely huge field, rather than from the microcosm alone.

To come back to literature, a poet doing his own book can see to it that it is sold when he travels and lectures. This bypasses, as it did with the optometrist, an enormous proportion of the deadwood and dinosaur levels of publishing. Remember, the closer you are to your public, the more profitable it will be to sell each book. If you only write sonnets, how likely is it that you will find a sympatico editor on Madison Avenue who will promote your book in Barton, California, where there is a club of sonneteers? Only you can know such things.

I'd go even further: a poet who doesn't have a book of his own along to take orders on when he's giving a reading isn't a serious poet, because he doesn't really want to share his work with the people who come in contact with it. Every poet should therefore always have a book which he controls and can take orders for (the big publishers simply cannot do so), either by himself or via a friend by the entrance table where contributions are placed. The book should probably therefore be a self-published one. Or it could be a stock which the poet bought from some other publisher as remainders, overstock, or via a clause in his contract: "Author shall be recognized as a store, with all trade discount and return privileges pertinent thereto."

And suppose a film-maker gets a residency at the College of Consumption. He is in a weak position if he has to badger an outside publisher's sales department via his editor, but he can get the appropriate sales if he's at least co-published his book with his publisher or done it himself. The College of Consumption Bookstore may not pay its bills very promptly with the big publishers, and they therefore may not service the account very well or supply it faithfully. This would be true up my way, for instance, in northern Vermont, where our geography makes all of us in effect poor credit

risks. But the College of Consumption Bookstore will
certainly pay most very faithfully if the author is
the publisher and, for a while, a faculty member. *Every* film-maker should be a publisher, I would say,
since his is a public art, and he has the unique opportunity to expect a return from the books that contain
his ideas and that are sympatico to the enthusiasts in
the audience.
      Ah, but let's not forget a distinguished artist
(alas, he's not a fiction) who did a series of litho-
graphs in an off-format, 1 inch by 32 inches, and wanted silk-screened, plastic covers, to be held together
with rubber bands. It was a good project, I accepted
it. The more fool me. Because he wanted me to take a
gallery commission (he'd get one third, I'd get one
third, and one third would be used for promotion--this
is a common arrangement when a gallery does an edition).
Each copy cost $200, and there were, I think, one hun-
dred copies. So he expected a check from me, more or
less right away, for almost $7,000! You see, I had
made three mistakes. First, I had gotten involved in
a project in which the cost per item was more than I
could deal with. Secondly, galleries are the unique
source of supply for an artist's works, while bookselling looks to have as many books in as many stores as
possible, so the economic basis of the project was totally wrong. And third, I should have made it clear
from the outset that I could pay him only as I was
paid, in other words, on a consignment basis. Fortunately he was (and is) a very nice guy, and he let me
out; we printed his covers for him. BUT--what this
means to the self-publishing artist is: if you want
your work distributed widely, don't expect to make much
more than 10 per cent, and don't expect to get your
money back in a hurry. The art world is rich (and for
the rich), the book world is poor (and if not exactly
for the poor, at least *of* it).
      There is also a great advantage to doing a maga-
zine as part of a self-publishing program, rather than
starting right in with books. Usually a book, to attract attention, must be very formally presented, and
this means tying up a lot of money in the production.
But with a magazine the reader is much more flexible.
It should have a good cover (sell the artwork to raise
funds for the magazine), but the public will be indul-

gent with the interior production if the contents are vital enough. Cheap offset is now about at the same cost level as mimeograph was ten years ago, and it allows for much more design latitude. Handled intelligently, using good typewriting, cheap offset can be suitable not only for poetry magazines but for reference books, bibliographies, for the bulletin of the American Mongolian Society. It all depends on your imagination. My advice: don't spend more than you must on production.

And don't do a book if you can do a magazine. After all, the magazine can always release a series of books later, using its imprint. But the fact is, though stores don't like to sell little magazines, people will subscribe to them if they find out about them (more on that later), and that means both pre-selling (not having to wait ninety days for the bookseller to pay you)-- and this is almost impossible with a book--and bypassing the various discounts. While you may never get rich off a little magazine, you'll go broke a whole lot slower. But it isn't just cost: there are editorial advantages. First, you can surround yourself with work other than your own which is appropriate to it and gives it a good context. This is true whether you're doing *African Studies*, *Utah Poets*, *The History of Greenland*, or *Left-Wing Analysis*. By publishing top-notch work you associate with it, and you acquire a certain prestige that would be impossible if you simply did a book and all the copies cluttered your coat closet for the next eight years.

Secondly, if your magazine is a cheapy, you can even give it away--reaching the people you want to reach. Allen de Loach did this with his *Intrepid*, a quite good literary magazine. Without *Intrepid* we wouldn't have heard of Allen as young as we did, and we wouldn't have known just where and how to think of him, not having seen his context and only having seen a work here, a thing there. Of course, by giving it away, he was left with virtually no back copies to sell (very bad policy for a little magazine, where your first "rare" issues can cost as much as a four-issue subscription once they aren't current any more). But libraries wanted them, and along came a reprint house and paid him a quite substantial amount for the right to reissue them, leaving him with cash for other projects or for whatever he chose to do.

Finally, by doing a magazine you open a two-way exchange around the world with like-minded people. You tend to attract more new faces and see more new aspects of old ones than if you simply do books. My advice: never do a book if you can do a magazine (and this in spite of raised postal costs, which are an incredible impingement on our freedom to communicate-- after all, the "Continental Postal System" was founded in the first place to promote free communication among the "Colonies").

One final *Don't*, which brings me back to where we started all those pages ago: Don't sit on your work or your publications, whether from false professionalism or laziness or indefinable pride. Books age and fall apart, they look better on the shelf now than they will ten years from now. The ideas in them age too. The work should be out and circulating. Give it away, almost promiscuously, when there is even the slightest chance of a review. Send to reviewers, not publications. Find their home addresses and send your publications there. Remember, the old meaning of *publish* is proclaim. Well, proclaim then. If you have something to say or to show, say it or show it to all who will listen. That, not false modesty, is real professionalism.

Barton, Vermont
October 27, 1972

CCLM

by CCLM

THE COORDINATING COUNCIL OF LITERARY MAGAZINES, 80 Eighth Ave., New York, N.Y. 10011, is a tax-exempt, publicly supported organization devoted to the survival and growth of noncommercial literary publishing in America. Its main program is grants to noncommercial literary magazines.

CCLM was founded in 1967 by a group of writers and editors who recognized that literature had been largely neglected by American philanthropy and that literary magazines, the natural habitat of young writers and often the only forum open to them, were seriously threatened by the current economic climate.

Literary magazines--like symphony orchestras, museums, and theaters--have always operated at a loss. CCLM is the first organization to attempt to deal systematically with these facts of our cultural life by aiding the noncommercial literary magazines in this country through grants and select projects, thus making funds available to more than a few publications and available to literature on a scale comparable to the aid given the other arts.

At last count, there were about a thousand literary, noncommercial magazines in this country, many here to stay, some mushrooming for just a few issues. They are all very different, ranging widely in tone, aims, contents, look. Taken together, they are a symbolic institution in the sense that they represent the seriousness, the dedication, the openness, the adventurousness, the tentativeness, the precariousness behind all art. Much of the best of American writing has come up through these literary magazines, which reflect the diversity of American life as no other medium could. It is by now almost a cliché about our culture that these magazines, because they are open to new talent and keep the audience for it going, sustain the continuity of literary and intellectual work in this country, in both its traditional and its dissenting forms.

But these magazines have a common problem: how to stay alive. Out of the limelight of publicity and without the kind of support more "glamorous" ventures attract, they have had to depend on the persistence and dedication of their editors, who in all too many cases must scrape together the money to publish each issue, and on the patience of their writers, whose work remains unprinted (for a year or more in some cases) while the editor raises funds so he can take the magazine to press.

We feel the most important part of our program involves direct assistance to literary magazines, on the assumption that a live body is a prerequisite for any kind of publication or literary activity. Therefore, CCLM's major program provides general support grants to needy noncommercial literary magazines. These grants are designed to alleviate economic pressures, if only for a short time, to allow editors to edit and writers to write.

In addition, CCLM has also helped magazines by making grants for special issues, grants to enable a magazine to pay its contributors, if only nominally, and grants for experiments in graphics and printing.

The Coordinating Council also provides services on a national level to noncommercial publishing through sponsorship of special projects. It sponsors semiannual regional meetings of literary-magazine editors and writers with panel discussions which provide practical information in areas such as low-cost magazine production, problems of publishing experimental writing, printing costs and opportunities, and the role of the writer in the classroom. Other panel topics, such as the Northwest literary scene, have been more specific to the geographical area in which the meeting is held. The Council has recently made provision for these sessions to be taped and edited and we are hopeful that resources will allow reprints to be made available in the future to those individuals who were unable to attend.

CCLM also sponsors an annual contest of college literary magazines to encourage writers and editors in their formative stages, makes available to the public a library of noncommercial literary and arts magazines, and seeks to develop larger audiences for the new writer through project activities and sponsorship of magazine exhibits at such gatherings as the annual national meeting of the Modern Language Association. During the 1973-74 year the Coordinating Council will also implement plans for a library subscription project which is designed to make literary magazines available to a larger audience through the public library system. As a long-term benefit magazines will eventually increase their readership through subscriptions.

A summary of the Council's recent activities and project plans for the coming year includes a new emphasis on the advocate and supportive role the Council has taken in relation to the magazines. Each beginning magazine, regardless of editorial aims or concerns, must struggle with the basic problems faced by all noncommercial publications with respect to printing, distribution, and information services. It is hoped that with this increasing activity in our resource development program magazines will be able to refer to and to rely more heavily upon the Coordinating Council for information and consultant services.

Any noncommercial literary magazine which has published for one year and has put out at least three issues is eligible for a grant in support of its continued publication, authors' payments, or in support of a special need as may be requested by the magazine. A magazine is usually considered eligible to apply for a renewal grant after the grant funds have been spent and a minimum of one year since the last grant has been made. College literary magazines which are edited by college undergraduates, publish primarily undergraduate work, and have rotating editorships may enter the Annual College Literary Magazine Contest.

CCLM grants, unless earmarked for a specific purpose, are made for the general support of the grantee magazine and may be used to cover publishing or other normal operating costs, subject to certain guidelines to grant expenditures. In order to evaluate your need, CCLM needs the following information:

Name of magazine and address of editorial office;
What, in your opinion, distinguishes your magazine from other publications with similar aims;
A brief biography of the editor(s);
A list of several of the participating writers in recent issues;
A statement of magazine ownership;
Your print run for recent issues, including number of copies sold on newsstands, sold through subscriptions, and provided free of charge;

Average printing cost per issue;
What you pay contributors;
Gross annual publishing expenses (actual expenses
this year and projected for next year);
Gross annual publishing receipts (specify and include services and cash, actuals for this year
and projected for next year);
How you used your last CCLM grant if any. A completed Grant Fiscal Report form must be sent with
your renewal application unless one has already
been filed with our office.
Date your application and note by whom it is filed. It
is not necessary to request a specific amount. The
customary range of CCLM grants in the past has been
from one hundred to five thousand dollars. Together
with your application, submit six copies each of your
last two issues.

UPS

by UPS

THE UNDERGROUND PRESS SYNDICATE *is located at P.O. Box 26, Village Station, New York, N.Y. 10014. UPS performs a variety of services for alternative-culture newspapers and magazines. We especially recommend their* How to Publish Your Very Own Underground Newspaper *for its basic information about starting and printing publications. At one dollar a copy, this is the best elementary how-to pamphlet on the market.*

The Underground Press Syndicate is a nonprofit association of alternative newspapers and magazines begun in 1966. The original five members were the *East Village Other*, *Los Angeles Free Press*, *Berkeley Barb*, *San Francisco Oracle*, and the *Paper* (East Lansing). Their combined circulation was about fifty thousand. Since then UPS has grown to over two hundred twenty-five papers with a readership of over twenty million.

UPS has always been an anarchistic organization with an extremely diverse membership. Because of this diversity, UPS has concentrated mainly on seeing that the papers come out, via money, publicity, legal defense, and helping papers start and continue through providing information and reprint material. UPS also does things which require all the papers to work together--advertising representation, microfilming, a directory, a news service, exchange of papers, etc.

A main purpose of UPS is to increase awareness of the underground press. UPS constantly seeks and handles publicity for the underground press in daily newspapers and national magazines and on television and radio, to keep the underground press in the public view.

UPS is also a clearinghouse for information on the underground press. Each day, we answer scores of letters and phone calls and personal visits from reporters, authors, scholars, students, librarians, historians, and people who want to subscribe or advertise. We give them the information they need, or tell them where to get it.

UPS members have automatic free reprint rights from all other UPS members. To make this work, all members mail each edition to each other.

UPS conducts a continuous program to obtain national advertising for members. National advertisers are regularly serviced with up-to-date information, and UPS people are always available to consult with potential advertisers.

UPS puts out a list of all members with up-to-date addresses and subscription rates, which goes out to members for their exchange lists, to librarians and the general public, as well as advertisers.

UPS issues a biweekly news service with news of interest, news of what UPS is doing, and how we can work together.

UPS publishes the UPS Directory with complete information on all members: ad rates, mechanical specifications, publishing schedule, bulk distributor prices, address, editor, subscription rates, and founding date. The Directory is sent to all members free and given away to numerous places where it will do the most good. It is also sold to libraries and the general public to help finance UPS.

UPS maintains, services, and microfilms a library of all UPS papers and then, annually, sells the complete run for that year to libraries.

UPS holds conferences where underground-paper workers get together and exchange their experiences.

UPS does studies of underground-newspaper readership to help the papers sell more ads, serve old readers better, reach new readers, and identify readership.

The rules of UPS are traditional rather than statutory. They are:

(1) All members agree to free exchange of material. If any UPS member does not want another member to reprint his material for some reason, that member merely so notifies the other member and UPS. Specific articles may also be exempted from reprinting (as when copyright conflicts) by a simple notice, but this is very rare.

(2) An initiation fee of twenty-five dollars is paid with application for membership. New members may be objected to and brought to a general vote while they are associate members (first ten weeks). If vetoed, they are refunded their twenty-five dollars. Old members may be ejected by the same process.

(3) Members must send ten copies of each issue to UPS and one to each member paper. They are also requested to honor the UPS library subscriptions. The ten copies are used for advertising sales, publicity,

and the like.

(4) UPS members should list on their masthead
that they are UPS members. They also should publish
the membership list occasionally.

(5) When reprinting an article from another UPS
member, it must be credited, e.g. *Seed*-UPS. This is
not only fair but protects the other paper's copyright.

UPS is financed by the sale of library subscriptions to all UPS papers. Libraries pay us, and we ask
all UPS members to give those libraries complimentary
subscriptions. There are usually about twenty of these
subscribers. UPS also sells sample packets of a dozen
newspapers for five dollars. The UPS Directory is sold
for two dollars. Fifty per cent of the profits from
the microfilm sales go to UPS.

The illustration that accompanied the original publication of Jay Bail's article in *The San Francisco Book Review*. The drawing is from *Spinner Of Silver and Thistle* by Hannes Bok. Reprinted by permission of SISU.

ON BEING A PUBLISHER &

OTHER FEVERS

by Jay Bail

JAY BAIL is editor, publisher, and founder of **The San Francisco Book Review,** *a monthly started three years ago as a review source for all books, including those published by little presses (P.O. Box 14143, San Francisco, Calif. 94114; subscription: $6.50 per year). This article originally appeared in the November 1972 issue (Number 25) of* **The San Francisco Book Review.**

Copyright © 1972 by Openings; reprinted by permission of the author.

The first time I thought about being a publisher I had a fever and was hallucinating freely. I recovered some two weeks later, and strict orders were left for my recovery (keep him warm, plenty of rest, and call me if he talks about publishing).

Years passed, as they occasionally do. I married, unmarried, lost a few jobs, wrote stories and novels, and got sick again. My family: "It's bad enough he's a writer, now he wants to be a publisher." My friends: "What's that mean, publishing?" My doctor: "Who did you say you were?" What really decided me to break with everything I knew was a little old man, a Jewish peddler, who tried to sell me five nubby pencils. When I refused to buy them, he looked at me curiously and then whispered, "Mister, you're cheap enough to be a publisher."

Alas (as *Fortune* magazine said upon returning my recent manuscript, *Down and Out in Sodom and Gomorrah*), he was so right. Publishing is a thrifty enterprise where, unless you have the backing of a bank's clerks, officers, and manager's daughter, is apt to be a money-pinching profession. Yes, as I often say to my creditors (and usually I let it stand at that), publishing is done by the skin of one's illusions. The only luxury publishers can afford is to maintain their obsession, which is publishing. I have myself (and let this be recorded) seen a young man just in his twenties, with all of life before him, give up everything to become a publisher. Indeed, this young man I speak of had only two years before publishing took such a toll of his time and energy that he passed on, out of sheer exhaustion, to motorcycles.

For it is exhausting; there is little doubt of that (or a few other things I have in mind). It is work where you put in every dollar you have, all your hours, and, most importantly, energy. For it is human energy, as Schopenhauer was noted not to have said, that drives the Will to Live, and this in turn is the main motive force behind publishing (Bergson also did not say anything about this, and often). What woman could compare to the fair day when the finished magazine comes back from the printers with halftones all wrong and lines blurred and the printer nobly looks you in the eye and coughs gently? What children and home and security could conceivably measure up to the wild excitement of finding that sales are lower this month by 30 per cent, which means that twenty more copies will be able to be sent out free? And what--I say, what--madness could be more exhilarating than falling off the edge of your chair (and, of course, acting as if you had planned it all along) after pasting up and typesetting for forty straight hours?

For three years I have lived in the eye of the hurricane of publishing (this is exactly the same comment Swift made in his *On The Ethics Of Sneezing* [see page 31, Standard Revised Edition, 1637, Keoghegan and Matchlick Publishers, $5.95] and kindly brought to my attention by Professor Ellison Cartwright of Idaho State University at Moscow, 3165 70th Avenue, Moscow, Idaho 21501, and a self-addressed, stamped envelope should be enclosed). It has not been an easy three years. Everything I have has been put into the venture. Fifty to sixty hours a week of work, training myself in typesetting, layout, design, billing, bulk mailings, editorial, and closet-sweeping. It was indeed in this latter capacity that I was able to survive the maelstrom of publishing, the welter of opinions, the madness of the times, and an occasional flu epidemic. For closet-sweeping (or, as we say in the trade, Reading) has proven to be the bane of my bone or, if you will, the strength of my professional indecision. Once one is able to understand through closet-sweeping that one, in his publishing obsession, is indeed in the highest tradition of life, it is quite helpful. For only through closet-sweeping can one find that Ortega y Gasset believes publishing to be as fateful as the revolt of the masses; or that C. S. Lewis admonishes us to go into publishing with the same vigor that we lose sight of life; or that Virginia Woolf, while not mentioning publishing directly, had the foresight and the understanding to note, "Lord, these moods come and go ..."

So, in conclusion, let me note that publishing is not easy. Not everyone was made for it. It helps if you know how to type seventy words a minute for hours on end, can talk pleasantly with a telephone operator who is about to disconnect your phone, can pay the printer incredible sums of money while living on a pittance, can talk your parents into willing you their money *before* they die, and can avoid the expense and the distraction of women, stereos, friends, dogs, and thoughts that go bump in the night.

Drawing by Rochelle Holt and D. H. Stefanson in *To
Make A Bear Dance*.

FROM A DREAM

TO VALHALLA

by Rochelle Holt &

D.H. Stefanson

ROCHELLE HOLT *has been a painter, dancer, translator, printer, and poet. When she met D. H. STEFANSON, a bibliographer and student of 18th-Century literature at the University of Iowa, they began issuing finely made books under the imprint of Ragnarok Press. The press is headquartered in Sioux City, Iowa. The "I" in the following article is Rochelle, while "we" refers to Rochelle and D. H.*

I remember being in Bienvenido Santos' office one time when a woman student from the International Writers' Workshop came in to show him her first book of poems printed by the Windhover Press. I forget the title of the book--it had something to do with a red umbrella-- but I do remember how beautiful it looked. The black type was set evenly on rich white paper, and the whole effect was one of impressive craftsmanship. After that, whenever I wrote poems or thought of poetry, I remembered that small, hardbound book. Someday I, too, would have a beautiful book of poems. Other young poets must feel the way I did, and perhaps my experience with printing my own books may encourage them to do the same.

Because I was accepted by the Iowa Writers' Workshop in fiction rather than poetry, I became even more resolved to publish my first love, poetry. I enjoyed seeing my poems appear in magazines; yet, I still wanted a book. A book of poems should not be just a certain number of poems printed and bound together; it must be complete in itself, a unity. The kind of poems, their length, their order of appearance, plus the paper, binding, and typography create a setting for each poem that illuminates and enhances it. The poem, like a jewel, exists by itself, but is more precious and beautiful in its proper setting. In the big magazines, a poem is likely to be juxtaposed with a full-page ad for Johnny Walker Black Label and to vie for attention on its own page with a four-column article. The poem looks like filler on the page. The layout does everything to discourage reading of the poem. That was not the ideal for my book.

While reading *Madame Bovary* for my first writers' workshop, I discovered the passage that would become the epigraph and title of my first book of poetry,

"...and human speech is like a cracked kettle on which
we strum out tunes to make a bear dance, when we would
move the stars to pity." At that time I did not even
think about the book as being published by anyone other
than myself, knowing that commercial publishers print
only established poets.
        The idea of printing my own book remained dormant
for a year and a half; then everything came together
when I met D. H. Stefanson. He was completing a Ph.D.
in 18th-Century English literature, but his love of
books had led him to work in analytical bibliography.
Bibliographers are by nature and training people who
are interested in studying books, variations in editions, their authorship, format, and imprint. In January 1970 we decided to audit a typography course with
the intention of printing a limited edition of my first
book of poetry, *To Make A Bear Dance*. D. H. selected
the poems and wrote the introduction, and both of us
designed the book and printed it on a Vandercook press,
a simple press for novices. Ours was the most ambitious and lengthy project in the class, and by the end
of May 1970 we had fifty copies of a 6.5- by 10-inch
hand-printed book. I remember the completion of this
first book very well. I had intended to dedicate it to
my mother and father, but then the trouble at Kent State
was going on in protest of the incursion of the United
States into Cambodia. I decided to dedicate the book
to my mother and father and Peace, and we printed the
dedication in red to signify the bloodshed and the
killing of students at Kent State. It was a feeling of
elation at the thing of beauty which we had created and
a sense of dismay and consternation at the rejection,
denial, negation of life around us. We also had been
bitten by the printing bug, and even before we finished
To Make A Bear Dance, we were making plans for our own
press. The first book showed us that it was possible
to print our own books, and we were determined to continue.
        Courses in typography are available around the
country and offer the best opportunity for one's first
efforts. Setting up a private printing shop requires
considerable time and expense and also a permanent resi-
dence to house the equipment, something most students
and writers either lack or avoid. By taking a course,
however, we had the use of type and presses; we had a

teacher to explain the mysteries of the craft; and we
gained enough experience to decide whether or not we
wished to pursue our own printing. We had one book completed which was sufficient reward for our efforts; yet,
in spite of the difficulties and our own ignorance, we
were resolved to have our press.
       The name for our press came from D. H.'s Icelandic
heritage. D. H.'s grandparents on his father's side and
great grandparents on his mother's side came from Iceland, and what always appealed to him about the Iceland-
ic people was their love of books and literature and
their independent spirit. Iceland is perhaps the most
literate and literary country in the world, a place
where ordinary citizens edit scholarly journals and
where almost everyone reads the old eddas and sagas,
the main source of Germanic and Scandinavian myths and
legends. Their democratic parliament dates from the
10th Century; and in spite of their viking heritage,
they are a peaceful nation. Their history of struggle
against a harsh environment reflects the ancient Norse
belief that life is a battle of human heroes and the
gods against the forces of darkness and evil. The heroes and gods will ultimately be defeated in a great
final battle, but they nevertheless continue to struggle
against the coming darkness. Indeed, that struggle is
what creates heroes out of mortals. We like the idea
of working along with other private printers, poets,
and artists who are engaged in that struggle to keep
truth and beauty alive. Thus the name *Ragnarok*, signi-
fying the final battle of the heroes and gods against
the powers of darkness, was selected as the name of our
press, and a Norse funeral ship, the Gokstad ship, as
our emblem. Norse mythology also offered us a whole
world to draw upon for names for the series of varied
books which we planned to do.
       Our first series was of Rochelle's poetry, the
Valkyrie Series. The Valkyries are the handmaids of
Odin who ride through the air to battle and choose the
heroes who are to be slain and taken to Valhalla, the
hall of immortality. Valkyrie 1-4 are *To Make A Bear
Dance*, *The Human Omelette*, *A Seismograph of Feeling*,
Wing Span of an Albatross. We are now printing Valkyrie 5, *A Ballet of Oscillations*. *Eidólons*, the first
anthology in the Valhalla Series, will be followed by
Children of the Moon, an anthology of women poets which

315

will be ready for distribution in the summer of 1973.
As our plans include publishing individual poets, we
have named the series for women poets after Freya, the
goddess of fruitfulness and sexual love. The series
for men is named after Balder, the god of the summer
sun and called the god of good. *Bragi*, the god of poetry, is the name we use for the occasional broadsides of
individual poems; and *Thor*, the god of thunder who
wields a mighty hammer, is reserved for the scholarly
books, of which the first is now in progress. *Midgard*,
the abode of humanity joined to heaven by the rainbow
bridge of the gods, designates art books, of which the
first, *A Peaceful Intent*, is in the planning stages.
My haiku will be juxtaposed with the photographs of nature in peace by Randall W. Hummel.

Dreaming about a press is one thing; acquiring one
is another. Yet to make our dream a reality, we had to
gather the equipment, then print and bind and distribute
the books. Except for one small printing project and a
theoretical knowledge gained from studying the history
of printing, we were totally ignorant of what we were
about to do. This lack of knowledge and experience
caused us a great deal of needless trouble and expense.
Although many of our troubles were amusing, our successes are probably more valuable for other beginning printers.

After an initial error in buying a 1,200-pound
10- by 15-inch Chandler & Price press when we had no
place to put it and no equipment to operate it, that is,
no quoins, furniture, or composing stone, we bought a
5- by 8-inch handpress and a case of type that we could
operate in our small house. We later learned that Virginia and Leonard Woolf also started printing with a
small press in their living room and then later gained
a larger press which was used in their basement. That
first year we printed two books and several small items
on that little press in our living room and gained much
practical experience since printing is a craft that must
be learned like any other craft. By the second year
we were ready to begin in earnest although we still had
a lot to learn. We contacted a person who sold used
printing equipment as a sideline. From him we bought an
old 8- by 12-inch C & P press (only a half of a ton in
weight), type, cases, quoins, and cabinets, almost everything we needed. Although part of the fun of private

316

printing is visiting shops that are going out of business or are switching to offset, we discovered that paying for used equipment in good condition was better than relying on the cases of old type or furniture that can be picked up free or at a low price. Now after two years of buying and gathering equipment, we have a small shop in our basement and after three years of practice are becoming much more proficient in producing books.
In planning a book, we usually start with a title or group of titles. Then poems are selected according to the way they fit together to form a movement and a feeling. Thus, the title usually comes first and helps mold the shape and form the book will take. For example, *To Make A Bear Dance* had to be tall like an upright dancing bear, but then again, because it was our very first book, it had to be traditional in style and format since we were learning from the beginning the process of making a book. After the poems are chosen, a mock-up is made so that we know the order of the poems, the page size, type to be used, and the titles. More and more, the title of the book, which is indicative of the poems inside, determines what kind of book we will print. *The Human Omelette* was a looseleaf book, poems printed on one side and unbound in a folder, a bright red one. Like an omelette, the poems could be scrambled and mixed in any order, a very modern book. *A Seismograph of Feeling*, a collection of short love poems, by necessity, we thought, had to be a small and delicate book with no experimenting with inks of different colors or multicolored paper. No, it should be almost Oriental in effect, with a simple, suggestive frontispiece ink dripping to set the tone. Our one light touch was a cupid's ornament after the final poem. *Wing Span of an Albatross*, on the other hand, was envisioned as a humorous book of poems, an alphabet dictionary to be enjoyed by adults first and children next. The letters of the alphabet would be at the top on small index tabs, and the cards could be pulled out of a box, rather like a crayon box without the lid. Yellow, orange, and blue was the color scheme. Illustrations by a neighbor artist, Susan Jennings, interpreted the poems, and the cards were put into a special gold box.
When it came to the anthologies, we sought something more classical. We wanted *Eidolōns*, the first, to be hardbound and rather regal, elegant, with a large

format, like a William Blake book, so we chose a royal
purple bookcloth for the binding. This was the first
book we had bound by someone else, perhaps the only man
left in the Midwest who is carrying on this lost art.
We are printing the second anthology, which we will bind
ourselves. Since this is to be an economical book, using paper that we had left over from other books, we
have also decided to sew and bind this edition in soft
covers.

First then in the matter of production is long and
hard thinking about what kind of book is desired: size,
shape, tone. Next, the mock-up is mandatory so that one
knows what pattern to follow, the order of the poems to
be printed, whether poems are to be centered, set to the
left or the right, and at what distance from the top.
And then a beginning can be made. We choose the measure
and set the poem from the California job case, the standard type case. The type is transferred from the composing stick to the galley tray and eventually to the
chase, which is on a steel composing stone. Furniture
is put around the type to hold it together and then
quoins lock the wooden furniture into place so that the
type is solid and not able to fall out when the chase
is put into the bed of the press. There's a whole new
vocabulary to learn when printing, but it is easily
learned.

The press is made ready for printing. That is,
the rollers are put on and the plate is inked. The
platen is prepared with tympan paper and backing, and
measurements made on the top in pencil lines with the
aid of a ruler or good judgment. In our case, we use
no motor for the press, which is operated by a foot ped-
al and the lever at the side of the press where the
large wheel is. We print one sheet at a time and are
able to print only about three hundred sheets in an hour
and a half, since we have to stop to reink and occasionally to readjust something, like the type or the rollers
or the gauge pins which act as guides for the paper.
Usually we print only twice a week, so that it takes
about five months to finish the printing of the book.

Then the sheets have to be sorted and those that
are not perfect removed. The book is gathered before it
is sewn by hand with a needle and thread. If we bind
ourselves we put on the covers with a strong glue and
then trim the books in a Challenge hand paper cutter.

If we're having someone else bind them in hardcover, we sew the books by hand first. The whole process requires enormous amounts of patience, fortitude, energy, and love.

Distributing the books has been the least successful, yet in many ways the most rewarding part of the press. Poetry is written, and books are printed with an audience in mind; when that audience is pleased, the endeavor has been successful. That is why most private printers produce only a few copies as, for example, we do in the Valkyrie Series, where we print only 50 to 100 copies and now seldom more than 150 copies. For the anthologies, however, we wanted to reach a larger audience, which then brings up the problem of distribution. If a person is going to print small editions of a work, then distribution is simply a matter of giving the copies to friends as we did with our first book, *To Make A Bear Dance*. Once we began paying for presses, new founts of type, paper, and binding, we had to begin selling the books to meet expenses. Otherwise, we wouldn't be able to do the next book or the next.

Selling is often the most difficult part for any artist, made more difficult by an artist's natural tendency to concentrate on the art and not on remuneration. Yet sales are necessary if we are going to continue printing, and although at first we disliked being commercial, we discovered that the best praise we could receive was if someone liked our books well enough to purchase them. Those who like what we are doing buy, and the books end up in the hands of those who want and appreciate them--although part of the job is convincing people that a limited edition of a handmade book can be just as artistic and enjoyable and valuable at $5 or $10 per book as a lithograph or print at $40. If the price is reasonable, the exchange is worthwhile.

Because of the concentration on printing the books, we have not devoted as much time to distribution as is necessary. So far our methods have been simple: small publication parties and mailing notices to friends and friends of friends. Some libraries have begun buying our books, and that pleases us. Still, the best has been the names given us by those who have bought our books or by friends of the contributors to our anthologies. We have recently completed forms to have ourselves included in the *Directory of Little Magazines*

and Small Presses and *Small Press Record of Books*. We
also have been included in *Under the Sign of Pisces*,
the Anaïs Nin newsletter, since our anthology *Eidolóns*
contained an entry from Anaïs Nin's diary of summer
1971 and work by other members of the modern circle.
We plan to put a classified ad in *Ms*. magazine as soon
as our women's poetry anthology is ready. So far, we
have named two ways of distribution: friends on a mailing list and advertising in other publications.

We plan to exhibit in a downtown bank and recommend small-press printers seek out these ways of exhib-
iting their work. Fortunately, we were able to exhibit
our presswork when I exhibited my paintings at the
Sioux City Art Center. Also at that time, we put some
of our books in the art center's gift gallery, which
might be another good outlet for printers. Distribution, then, is a job apart from producing the books.
That is why most private printers print only a few copies and distribute them to friends.

Either way provides its satisfactions. Because
there are two of us and because the printing gives us
knowledge and experience that is useful in D. H.'s work
in analytical bibliography, we decided to do more printing than we might otherwise have done. The rewards of
private printing are many, not the least of which is
the knowledge that others around the country are also
printing and are continuing a craft and a tradition that
has presented some of our finest poets to the world.
It is truly wonderful to hear praise for each book that
we do. Right from the beginning, we have been told how
professional we are, and how dedicated to the fine art
of printing we are, which makes us feel quite good since
when we do something, we like to do it as well as we
can. People who buy our books are truly amazed at how
original and creative each book design is. Perhaps
the greatest compliment we have received came from Anaïs
Nin, who had *Eidolóns* included in a special library exhibit at the University of California at Los Angeles.
But as we progress, we still are working to fulfill the
wisdom of our first printing teacher, Harry Duncan, a
perfectionist who teaches excellence as well as printing
and whose first printed lines were ours also: "Simpli-
city is the last thing learned. It comes from simple
thinking, not from a conscious attempt to be simple."

TRACKING THE

SMALL PRESSES

by Len Fulton

LEN FULTON journeyed from Maine to Paradise (California). He now does for the littles what LMP *does for the bigs.* His Directory of Little Magazines, Small Presses and Underground Newspapers; Directory of Small Magazine/Press Editors and Publishers; Small Press Record of Books, *and* Small Press Review *are keystones of the do-it-yourself scene. Subscriptions are available from 5218 Scottwood Road, 95969.*

It is the smell of fields I remember as we cut them
down in the northern Vermont summer. She was a hard
land and the late Forties were hard times. The winter
was white--I remember that too. We broke through ada-
mantine snow and the ice to get the animals to water.
In the morning the only warmth came from the cows we
were milking, and the manure had to be pickaxed out of
the gutters. The nights were long and tuneless and
marked the days with ghosts. One winter as we huddled
in that farmhouse under the northern shadow of Mount
Mansfield my father took to writing. I think he had
always coveted the enterprise--or at least possessed
some prideful hint of a secret talent. A Canadian Scot,
he was (and is), whose people were northern lumberjacks
with a literacy hard-won and carried high. In those
few bleak months as the temperature edged to 30 and 35
below he bent seriously to it, wrote poems, stories a-
bout the region, and an allegorical novella called *Our
Town*. I think what touched me most and first was his
privacy of self, the luxurious loneliness of his own
world of mind. I sensed what he was up to those hours
and nights and weeks behind the keys--just as I had come
to sense him as a man of the soil and as a hunter. He
was making a hard world over according to his own pas-
sions; he was putting his private mind (and his loneliness) into a *form*. I had an almost immediate and or-
ganic faith in the effort, as I had in the beauty of
those deep Vermont woods--which could be any place you
wanted to make them.
     Writing then for me grows out of the private self
and gives form. Publishing is (or *should* be) a further
natural step in that formation--which is why I feel the
small magazine, for example, is itself an art form. It
presents a life-style, a personal bout with some devil

or dolphin. The form of the work determines its published shape as it slips from its private to its public world. The form must be true to its private ori-
gins and the shape to its formal ones. You then have
the craft of publishing keeping faith with the art.
And this is, it seems to me, a rather personal business.
I can't imagine publishing a magazine, book, or newspaper that lacked a continuity, or in whose continuity
I took no part. Well, yes, I can *imagine* it, but it
jars.
        I mention the newspaper because that's where I
really began. After the Army I edited a college monthly
for two years, still clinging to that bleak north New
England homeland (this time Maine) and keeping alive
and fit by shoveling snow, parking cars, and cutting
burned-off pine in Maine's southern wastes. In 1957 I
started a weekly tourist paper at Kennebunkport with my
friend, Bob Fay, and that fall, by one fate or another,
we found ourselves with a small letterpress plant in
the town of Freeport. We ran three local weekly newspapers out of that shop and spent a bitter cold winter
doing it. The best we could allow was that it *seemed*
to beat cutting dead pine in waist-high snow. (Bob
still carries a chainsaw scar on his shin; me, a few
years back I came across my old Army boots bearing
tracks where a chainsaw had clawed its way at me. I
threw the boots out.) The art of writing was not a
very critical factor in the craft of *that* kind of small-
time publishing. This was 1957, a half dozen years before the onset of the weekly-underground-press movement.
I struggled in Maine with newspapers of 800 or 1,500
circulation, newspapers that had belonged in the community for years. Local news items were the big fea-
ture--no one talked about dope or war or national politics or civil rights. The nation slept, under the pro-
tective order of John Foster Dulles. I was twenty-two,
and my generation was still worrying its fate from Hi-
roshima and Massive Retaliation.
        Bob and I hit the streets to sell advertising--no
more beautiful words until the Sixties came round to
read them. We started with nothing and ran downhill.
The key to a local backwoods weekly was food advertising, just as the key to an alternative (underground)
weekly is the full-page record ad. We went together
in our best clothes one frosty day to visit Mr. Plummer,

a taciturn old codger who owned the local food store.
Plummer ran a full-page ad a week; our mission was to
coerce him into *two*. We found him marking cans. He
ignored us so studiedly, and we were in such desperate
shape, Bob and I, that we looked at each other and one
of us cut a grin. The other emitted a bleat, and it
was all over. We quite literally laughed our way out
of Plummer's store, *all* his ads, *and* the newspaper business. A few days later the linotype man hit me for a
raise seconds before all the payroll checks bounced.
Next day as I walked into the place I met a stranger
coming out. He was carrying the belt which drove our
big old flatbed press. That was the paper supplier's
last act. We closed up shop and farmed out the printing
until we could find someone to take over all the papers.
That someone turned out to be the mayor of Lewiston
and publisher of a French daily, *Le Messager*.

In the fall of '58 I was working for one of the
world's first offset dailies just outside New York, and
I made one last trip to the Maine wilderness. In one
night I got my life clean again: found an accountant in
a dim store front to do my income tax, paid off a lawyer for a divorce, drove my car back to Commercial
Credit Corp and left it as a final balloon payment,
signed over every interest I possessed in newspapers,
and shook hands with a man who held a note against me
for five thousand dollars. Goodbye Maine, and a year
later the East, forever. I would be a professor; I
could write and read and teach--let someone else sweat
the publishing, the presses, the ads, the linotype
operators.

And always, for me, there was a strange, almost
mythic geographic imperative. I came to *resent* the
rolling, deciduous East, and covet the flat and cease-
less plains of the high West where the sky was grand
and the people sparse. Today even, there is in me a
kind of cognitive map with the bleeping light of my own
locus moving on its face. I cannot long stay east of
the Mississippi. In New York for a year on that daily
paper I worked out two novels. One was a violent newspaper story called *Press Run to Hell*; the other a draft
for what has turned out to be my major, single creative
effort: a saga of Wyoming's territorial cattle days. I
have carried it with me these years, forgetting about
it, remembering it, rewriting it. I suppose now I have

actually come to fear publication of it, for it would be taken away from me, would no longer require my work or my thoughts to have its own life.

I fled west in the summer of 1959, away from the need to publish, and from the nagging forces of heritage and prudence. I took a new wife with me, whom I would love forever, and a new (or renewed) passion for literature and the privacy and solitude I had lost in newspapers. In 1961 I took a B.A. degree at Wyoming and came into the graduate psych department at Berkeley. In those years on the plains, as the decade turned, I had enjoyed plumbing the academy and ignoring the world. I had thought, too, that the study of literature, and especially the *writing* of it, had to be embedded in a grasp of the human mind in its conscious and nonconscious states. The grand study for me, then, was literature and psychology, especially psychology since that was where my own ignorance lay. Psychology should be the study of art and artists.

But it was not, is not. Modern psychology--at least at that time and, I suspect, at this time too-- sees itself as a science, a study of organismic behavior after the manner of John Watson's 1913 manifesto, "Psychology as a Behaviorist Views It." Psychology is reductive and manipulative, and I found myself confronted with statistics, laboratory paraphernalia, mice, monkeys, and dying frogs. At Wyoming I could ignore this because the study parallelled for me a program in literature; and because I must admit to some fascination with the games the statisticians played. At Berkeley, though, it all possessed a kind of menacing seriousness, an insularity born of the need for research grants and guarded by some mental manacle called "experimental rigor." No art leaked in. It was pure something else. And so you can guess how I struck them with my whim to write a dissertation on Freud's literary roots. As fate would have it, I caught for an advisor a monkey psychologist from Maine--with the accent to prove it. He told me no one there cared how Freud "felt"--only how he "stated" or "postulated"--"so don't write 'Freud felt blah blah.'"

I didn't stay around long after that--two years I guess. But I had found in Berkeley a home, a place as alive as that psych department was quiescent. Things were rumbling under the Berkeley earth. The Sixties were upon us, and America's visions were on calamitous divergence from her realities. Berkeley was tense and refulgent with promise and vitality. We had added another member to the family, a son; so I took up work in that talent and learning that seemed most lucrative: statistics. Psychology had given me that much. Until 1968 I worked as a biostatistician for the California State Department of Public Health.

I had made some compromises, to be sure, for once I drifted from the notion of a doctorate in psychology my life broke from certain comfortable moorings I'd fastened to on my way west. I needed to earn money to live in Berkeley; and I needed to write another novel and put some touches on the Wyoming saga. Not to make too close a point of it, the business of statistics, systems development, and computer technology is fairly crummy most of the time, fairly dull, and fairly impersonal. Yet there does exist somewhere inside the whole slavish, empirical turn of it all some limited chance for modest creativity and theory. Furthermore, VD morbidity tables, rapes with sex-specific breakdowns, and population fluctuations can be interesting. Some distributions of data have graphs of pleasing visual quality. I felt myself always a force for the humanization of it and inevitably wrote reports in the first person, active voice. I did in fact write another novel, a somewhat autobiographical story of the sexual-intellectual maturation of a Vermont farm boy. I did in fact get to a final draft of the western saga and sent it to Alan Swallow (who died before he ever got a chance to respond, though our correspondence had been hopeful and fulfilling). I began to develop too an aesthetic theory called "The Psycho-geometric Form of the Novel," and discovered Samuel Beckett. I was writing. I was working.

In 1963 came Mario Savio and the Free Speech Movement (FSM) on the Berkeley campus. What Savio said about academe--its insularity and irrelevance--I had experienced only months before in that very institution. And so that spirit, which flamed and spread as the Sixties unfolded, caught me up. The University was a microcosm for what ailed the country--I knew that, and so did Savio. "Sometimes the machine becomes so odious, so impersonal," he said, "that you just have to put your body on the wheels and on the gears and stop it."

I saw it, saw that first issue: the relevance of all
else to the self and being, the sanctity of body in
charge of its extension in mind, reversing the root ingredient of western rationalism and so seeming to make
chaos itself a value to cherish. I was a long way from
Freeport and Maine and burned pine pulp. I had to get
back into publishing.

Through 1963 I served on the Board of Directors of
The Berkeley Citizen, a co-op newspaper just starting.
But the wheels were too slow. Some issues eventually
got published, but as a co-op corporation, a "reader-
owned" periodical, it was subject to the constant har-
assment of the California Corporations Commissioner.
Local merchants eschewed it, and readers came and went
as the content pleased or outraged them. And further,
it ran headlong on the streets into something called
the *Berkeley Barb*, and the *Los Angeles Free Press*, and
subsequently into the whole underground-press movement,
against which few citizens' newspapers of that era could
stand. *The Citizen* struggled for a year or more with
organization and no sign of publication. I *had* to get
something *going*. The magazine appealed to me more and
more as a format, but I had not yet come fully to the
imperative of doing it alone. In late 1963 I started
Dust Magazine with five other people.

These early cohorts were unlikely, as things in
those days with little magazines were bound to be: a
geneticist, a composer, a journalist off the Berkeley
streets, a psychiatric social worker (Andrew Curry),
and my old friend and partner, Bob Fay, with the scar
on his shin from another era. We thought to do a mimeo
mag, but found it just as cheap to go offset because we
had no equipment anyway. The name *Dust* emerged from the
polite but mistaken notion that we could maintain an
open posture which would not violate any of our editorial proclivities. The name existed in literature without regard to style or age--from "dust into dust" to
"fear in a handful" of it. The name *Dustbooks* was con-
cocted by poet Gene Fowler one night in writing an ad
for his book, *Field Studies*, brought out under the imprint in 1965. And as things are often depleted by
their own excess, that openness which brought the editors together ripped them ultimately apart. Before the
first six issues got out Curry and I were alone at it--
he to edit *Dust* until 1970.

Intense as were the editorial disadvantages in having six editor-publishers, the production and other costs were spread that many ways as well, and so an eighty-page, $600 issue could be prorated at $100 each, minus subscription receipts. The latter were also boosted by having six people with private circles as disparate as their artistic biases. By Volume 1 Number 4 *Dust* had over 500 paid subscribers, virtually all individuals, no institutions. Subscriptions covered roughly two of the first four issues, so that when postage and clerical costs were added to printing and other costs, we were spending about $250 each--considerable when the final product was not, and could not be, satisfactory to all. Subscribers were as fickle as editors. At first renewal paid subscriptions plunged to 300, and with each succeeding issue more atrophy occurred, with huge gouges at Number 8 and Number 12 when new volumes began. Moreover, after three or four issues libraries began to subscribe, which they do in an often mechanical fashion; and they renew automatically--all of which can convert the subscription list into a higher sales than readership function. When *Dust* suspended publication in 1972 it had less than 350 paid subscribers.

Those early days were exciting to me because it was a *doing*. America had come out of its long sleep and had taken to the streets. There was turmoil across the country in good causes, obliterating a certain deadly dullness and recalcitrance of the Fifties. One editor quit because we published a lesbian poem, "A Pretty Story," by a college coed, Lake Purnell. Another left because we voted not to do one of his own short stories. We interviewed Louis Simpson, 1965 Pulitzer Prize poet; Alan Watts, the Zennist; Booker T. Anderson, a Bay Area black organizer; poet Gene Fowler; street poet Doug Palmer; Cleveland's d. a. levy, and others. We published Frank Lapo's crazy "roor," which brought mail; my own short stories, "The Line" and "The Ellipsoid;" stories by Ed Franklin, Ed Bullins, Gary Elder, and many others. I worked with Gene Gracer through four drafts of his story, "Shadows of Dawn," before publishing it in Number 5. Number 13 was all prose. And the poetry was constant: Bukowski, Cashen, Daruwalla, Finch, Hitchcock, Krech, Lord, Neylon, Schevill, Wantling, Young--150 poets in the first twelve issues.

Alone now as publisher--Curry editing *Dust*--I
learned that a small press is essentially a one-man
life-style, the essence of that private world of the
mind of an individual, just as the single work of art
is, which I had known since those Vermont winters. The
small press is an outgrowth of a person's experience
and outlook. As a result, in trying to publish *Dust*
with six people, though we intended to be cosmic in our
implications, we broke down; ultimately *someone* imposed
his viewpoint. And then I was aware of movement all a-
round not unlike my own, as the individual began a des-
parate reassertion of his integrity against Savio's im-
mutable machine. Journalism was in the streets in the
underground newspapers, and there were little magazines
starting up everywhere. In some electric way we saw
that Godot would not come and save us if we only clowned
and waited, for *we* were Godot and it was out of our
primal reality--movement--that saving had any meaning
at all. The small-press movement, freed from academic
subsidy and principle, was a phenomenon pushed directly
out of this awakening of the sound of self.
      That sound was of the blood and lymph. It was in-
decipherable, nonlinguistic. I doubt that many, if any,
of us who got into it back then knew exactly what we
were up to in any transcending way. We knew only that
with the dawn came a long and rumbling noise that drove
us through the day and into the night, cranking the
mimeo machine and using the mails with an angry will.
Literary principles? The imperatives of art? Tran-
scendence to a god (unknown) of culture, taste, and
intellect? A Shakespeare maybe, lurking, waiting, hurt-
ing, for us to find? Shit! We were trying to get into
a people's literature. We were a people working. We
had our moments of critical passion to be sure--and who
of us could escape thoroughly the aesthetic regulations
of Eliot and Ransom, who escape altogether the arche-
type Christ inside our very blood stream? But these
moments were more passionate than critical. Mainly we
were taking what we probably thought then was the whole
thing into our hands. The one directive was: DO IT
YRSELF. We judged the state of literature and more,
literary publishing, to be top-heavy with finished,
proven, saleable, high-market material. We judged the
bottom (as we were in it) to be in disastrous diminu-
tion, an inverted pyramid or iceberg, to use two

structural analogs; or to use a more operant one, and
one to illustrate the greater reality of process over
structure, a *food chain* with that high-demand, low-
yield consumer at the top looting the whole world's
garden to sustain his minority self and appetite. Like
the big eaters, the big publishers and their affluent
clientele gobbled down a share of the culture a thousand times that allotted them out of their natural number. Worse yet than straight food gluttons, the big
publishers undermined and exploited the early, localized
stages of the ecological web that supported them. They
took much, returned little. And as with food there were
(as there are) distinct signs of diminished and dimin-
ishing quality, an austerity of meaning in the products.
We were at a stage as early as can be located in the
culture chain. No altruisms drove us, no conscious and
general effort to enlarge the base resources. It was,
as I've suggested, a sound low down and in back. Perhaps the sound of hunger.
    By 1965 I had become self-consciously interested
in this whole production of literature. My concerns
enlarged on me, almost without my knowing it. I found
it terribly agreeable to be in touch with other small
pressmen, to know what they were doing. Something dis-
permitted my holding exclusive focus on my own things
any longer. My sights rose unremittingly. The human
drama of *how* literature got produced was fascinating
and vital as an art form laid over other art forms.
And I began to plot the publishing process. You can't
do anything without knowledge, and the first thing to
know about the little magazines and small presses of
the day was who they were, and where. Hence, that year
(1965) I brought out the first edition of the *Directory
of Little Magazines*, which later added to its title
Small Presses and Underground Newspapers. (The ninth
edition of this publication has just been released.)
In 1966 I got help in England from Cavan McCarthy of
Locations Press, who scoured Europe for small mags and
presses to include in the *Directory*. The third edition
reflected his great efforts. It was no easy matter to
locate and list these often clandestine and evanescent
publications. In the first *Directory* I likened it to
counting fry under a waterfall. James Boyer May--who
was to become the *Directory* co-editor in 1970--had been
running the "evolving directory" in *Trace* since the

early Fifties, and warned me of the difficulties.
But I felt inevitably that the *Directory* gave only
standing room each year. I needed something that would
be more fully a part of the process it plotted. I needed to know stages, energies, directions in the process.
For the main point of disjunction between what I thought
of as *old* and what I though of as *new* was a vision of
man as an extension of form, of structure on the one
hand, and a vision of him as energy, or process, on the
other. In late 1966 I started the *Small Press Review*,
got the first issue out in early '67 after a struggle
that became more the rule than the exception for the
magazine. Since then *SPR* has published hundreds of reviews, and dozens of essays, features, and reports, all
calculated to track the energies of the small-press
world internationally. I said in that first issue:
"Small-press books and mags are primary victims of a
'thing' culture, caught against matters of high postage,
high printing, bad distribution, and fearful legisla-
tors. Without deluding itself as to its possible and
probable dominions, *SPR* will throw in every time on the
side of the little, the side of the new, independent
literature and thought, however it is delivered. But
SPR believes in dialogue, will not be drawn into anybody's suicidal bags, and does in fact reserve the
right in its world view to *encompass* cliques--despite
their need to be rejected by outsiders. *SPR* will not
respect international boundaries." I have felt since
then through sixteen issues that *SPR* has been true to
its intention. In the first several issues I ran a
"Record" of small-press books published, which in 1969
I incorporated separately into the *Small Press Record
of Books*, with plans to do one every year or two. In
1970 I brought out the first edition of the *Directory
of Small Magazine/Press Editors and Publishers*.
And so, I plotted a drama. Beginning in 1965 with
Fowler's *Field Studies* I brought out a dozen chapbooks
of poetry and prose, books by Hilary Fowler, William
Wantling, Andrew Curry--even one of my own. In 1969 I
made an attempt to resurrect the long poem, bringing
out Gary Elder's *Arnulfsaga*, L. C. Phillip's *Love Ode*,
Romiossini by Yannie Ritsos, and *Once* by Wally Depew.
Depew also took over *Dust* in 1970, edited four issues
until I suspended publication in 1972. He turned the
magazine toward the "new poetry" (concrete), and put

out some very fine issues. But my own interest had been exhausted, and I was simply unable, with all else that was happening, to mediate between editor and printer.

Remember that publishing during this earlier time was for me, technically, a part-time endeavor. I was still employed as a statistician, now for one Governor Reagan, and breath was coming in gulps. In late '67 Jerry Burns (Goliards) and I cooked up a gala meeting of the country's small pressmen, to be held the following May in Berkeley. It got so big so fast that as the year turned we had more mess on our hands than anything else, except determination to see it through. On January 8, 1968, I fell neurologically ill ("cracked up" might be better) in Los Angeles, and got back to Berkeley just before notions of physical and mental collapse set in. For three weeks I did little but hover between things which I did not understand, and when next I arose in one piece again I knew something had to give: the statistics, the publishing, or the nerves. My wife agreed that it should be the statistics, and so we cut ourselves loose from Berkeley and spent that summer finding a place in the mountains. Significantly enough, the move to Paradise occurred on January 8, 1969. Here we came and here stayed, with our horses and trees and garden. Here my health renewed itself, and I have resurrected that archetypal sense of the earth which I knew as a boy on that Vermont farm. Here I have been able to fill my life with small-press publishing--and I wonder how I ever did otherwise. Here, too, on a fateful Mother's Day in 1970, I lost my wife and most treasured companion in an auto accident. The moorings of my soul were again wrenched loose.

The conference came off in May 1968, Jerry Burns moderating. I chaired a panel on distribution, with Hugh Fox, D. R. Wagner, Doug Blazek, and Harry Smith sitting too. It was out of this panel that the Committee of Small Magazine Editors and Publishers (COSMEP) was born. The five of us sat in Larry Blake's Rathskeller on Telegraph Avenue and wrote up a $15,000-grant proposal (which we didn't get) to set up a distribution agency for little magazines. Harry Smith took the proposal back to New York, rewrote it and submitted it to the Coordinating Council of Literary Magazines, which had partially funded that first conference. Later

that year Burns, Richard Morris, and I set the org up
formally, and by the next conference (Ann Arbor, 1969)
had produced a *Catalogue of Small Press Publications*
and a *Bookstore Survey*.

COSMEP's history is covered in another chapter by
Richard Morris, and my own history since then would
take another chapter or two. But this one must close,
and here is a good place, save for a word about printing. From that old flatbed press in Maine until November of 1972 I owned no machinery. I had seen my small-
press friends around the world go mad trying to survive
with a 1250 or a 320 or what have you. I wanted none
of that, nor of the necessity to do "job printing" for
others so I could afford a press for myself. Consequently I have spent much energy and money and many
hours with printers--and that is a madness of itself.
In 1972 I took one last musty gulp of that air and set
up my own shop out back. In the process of building
the shop, finding the press and its accessory equipment,
I lost my fear of the machine. The secret for me seems
to have been to wait it out. And waiting *anything* out
in the small presses, as I've noted, is not an easy
thing.

IN DEFENSE OF NYLE

humor by Gordon Lish

GORDON LISH *is an indication that the establishment is good for something.* As Esquire*'s fiction editor for several years, he has consistently insisted on quality before commerciality.* Prior to joining Esquire, *he was editor of a California literary magazine,* Genesis West, *and published several books.* He is currently assembling a collection of Esquire *fiction for publication by Doubleday.* Lish rarely leaves Gotham City and tries to answer all his letters on his own typewriter.

Three times to date I've made a formal statement of my
fondness for what the whiners call the New York Literary Establishment or maybe the Eastern Literary Establishment, but what I call *home*. Each time the thing
I spoke was a piece of impeccably styled persuasion,
eloquent and commanding even in its commas. I convinced the bejesus out of people who didn't want to be
convinced. They came there (this was always on some
campus somewhere!) to sneer behind their dirty finger-
nails and have a confirming look at a for-instance of
their loathing, but of course left with their moronic
notions busted in twain. These were people pretty
scruffy in their tiny hatreds, glassy-eyed ruffians,
every one of them *types*, if you follow my meaning.
But it's a routine business to wipe smirks off faces,
to turn brutes into lovers, such sissies this kind to
a man are, even in the rough embrace of their stoutest
principles. All I had to do was pronounce the speech,
flash a few ironic inflections, close off with a shade
enough of the funny hoarse thing I can do with my voice,
and the rabble were trampling one another in this mad
break to kiss my hem. All of which proves everyone
would be nuts about the New York Literary Establishment if only it put in an occasional afternoon on public relations.
      But none of this really interests me, of course.
It's easy to sell people something they don't like, especially if it costs them up the giggy to buy it. It's
not that I'm not proud of the New York Literary Establishment or not proud of my part in merchandizing it.
I'm as happy as a clam with both. But what gets me is,
how come I got this way? Because *before* I arrived in
New York, at *Esquire*, and thus upon the heights of my
current station, I held the literary establishment of

the same name in as low opinion as any of your average
crybabies do.
Ah! you say, *we* know what gives with *him*. The
punk hates himself for selling out, so it's your standard *reaction formation* thing...!
Excuse me, but that's crap.
I stick up for the New York Literary Establishment because it's a *terrific* literary establishment.
And the reason I didn't have any use for it when I
didn't have a hand in it was I was too dumb to know
better.
How come I got this way? I got smart, is how!
Now, to get down to the premise of this book: ha,
ha!--because, any way you look at it, the thinking in
here is: *they*'re not deep enough, *they*'re not sensitive enough, or thoughtful enough, or courageous or
sophisticated or artistic or reckless enough, or contemporary or inspired or un-American enough to print
the deep, sensitive, thoughtful, courageous, sophisticated, artistic, reckless, contemporary, inspired, un-
American stuff I wrote--so I guess I'll just have to do
the really righteous thing and print it myself.
But I can't be bothered with the whole affair.
What's wrong with publishing your own stuff nobody with
my serious work in life has time to discuss.
I do, however, have a few moments to crush this
haughty attitude toward the New York Literary Establishment, which I do now, with exquisite pleasure. So
pinch up your skirts; here goes.
The virtues of the New York Literary Establishment are as follows:
(1) The people who constitute it are deeper, more
sensitive, more thoughtful, courageous, sophisticated,
artistic, reckless, contemporary, inspired, and un-
American than are those who constitute any other literary establishment going. Besides, they're better
drinkers--and it goes without saying that their sexual
conduct is compatible with the libertarianism we like
to see in a truly creative environment.
(2) In this literary establishment you get to
eat better French food than I ever got in the San Francisco Literary Establishment.
(3) The whole idea of a literary establishment
is that you have a force which makes judgments, hurts
people's feelings, and gets a few things done. Well,

338

consistent with that idea, the New York one does more of all of it. Accordingly, logic insists this establishment is a better one than the one in Iowa City. And if I fancied myself a writer, for sure I'd sooner have George Steiner telling the world my book is a twist of dog than have Mrs. E. Ellingsworth Twitbrain putting me down to her Thursday evening pottery group.

(4) All of my friends are in *this* literary establishment. (The other friends I had, customers in the Chicago Literary Establishment and the San Francisco one, don't want to be my friends anymore.)

(5) This literary establishment has improved my emotional health. Before I came here I used to pick at my scalp a lot. I think it was nervousness that made me do it, nervousness I got from not being sure how good I was. The New York Literary Establishment, bless its big mouth, has made my excellence clear to all the nation and, best of all, to me.

(6) My wife Barbara likes this one better, too. So does my son Atticus. You should see them smile with pride when I wear my NYLE uniform with the leather patches at the elbow.

Now, those are all the virtues--and just to keep the record straight and put perfect balance to what fuss-budgets will probably regard as a unilateral viewpoint, let me set down every single rotten aspect of the New York Literary Establishment.

(1) The French waiters you hereabouts run into are a genuine achievement in arrogance. (Not unlike some noncommercially-published writers you also run into.)

(2) Right now the Establishment isn't heartless enough. It's still letting a lot of those lower-case books by. I certainly would like to see more cruel censorship slammed around in that direction.

(3) There ought to be a regular Establishment-sponsored, participation-free exercise program set up. The food and drink here in the big time are delivering me to flab.

(4) It's true; the New York Literary Establishment does indeed discriminate against certain kinds of writing: writing that proceeds from a rural experience (William H. Gass' stuff, for example). My God, the way these boys have turned their backs on a Western writer like Kesey, or a playful one like Barthelme,

or a tricky one like Barth, or a recondite one like
Hawkes, or an obscurantist one like Nabokov, or a
strange one like Purdy, or an old-fashioned one like
Robertson Davies, is a downright scandal! Something
should be done about this, I agree.

(5) Another thing wrong with the New York Literary Establishment is that it doesn't do much about the
lousy condition of the streets here. If you could have
a squint at my block, you'd see what a war zone looks
like.

I for one think the New York Literary Establishment should begin to exert its terrible power in an effort to clean up the streets of this city. And if this
is what you think too, then I am glad to see we have
finally come to an opinion we can hold in common.

Because if New York looked like San Francisco,
the national literature would be a lot easier on the
ears.

And if you can't figure that last one out, then
it goes to show you're as dumb as I've been hinting
throughout. Which must be the case anyway because,
after all, here you are wasting time "self-publishing"
(ooch, the ear flinches no less than the brain) when
you might have better used what little life you have
learning how to write good enough to get up there where
a person of my eminence will want to toast your existence over the *plat de jour*.

ASSORTED TIPS: HOW-TO

Having read this far, you realize that in publishing nothing is true or false. Most is uncertain. Some of the following tips may be contradicted or supplemented by the preceding articles. Make up your own mind.

BOOK SIZE. Size is important because bookstores and libraries are in the habit of shelving certain sizes. Odd sizes cause manufacturing problems too. The basic size for hardbound books ("hardbound" usually means cloth over cardboard) is 5.5 inches wide by 8.5 inches high, give or take an inch either way. Paperbacks tend to be smaller. Your book may be any size you desire, from postage-stamp to room size, but you may pay a penalty in manufacturing costs and sales.

HARD COVER VS. PAPER COVER. A paper cover is cheaper; you can charge less for your book and maybe sell more. But most libraries (a major source of sales) balk at ordering paperbacks because they receive a battering in circulation. Some libraries will order paperbacks and stock them or have them rebound--but don't count on it.
  Since most publishers issue books first in hardbinding, major review sources are accustomed to (programed to) reviewing hardbound books.
  Solution: do at least some of your edition in hardbinding.

LETTERPRESS VS. OFFSET. Check our bibliography about books on printing. Check costs and manufacturing problems with your printer. Whatever method you use, make sure you end up with a printed page that is worthy of what is said on that page. Sloppy books receive prejudiced scowls from buyers and reviewers.

TYPEFACE. Make sure your reader can read it. Ten point is basic for the text. Easy solution: go to your library or bookstore and pick out a book or books with type you like. Go to a printer and offer that as a sample. The same goes for layout, size, and binding. If you wish to follow a more complicated approach to choosing type,see the bibliography listings on type.

PRINT ORDER. Be cautious. Save your initial money for publicity and promotion. Tell your printer to keep the type or plates standing for new runs after the first printing (you may have to pay a storage fee). What's a cautious print order? Enough copies to send to review sources plus a few hundred for early sales.

PRICE. Check the prices of books that are similar to yours in genre, length, quality of manufacturing, and market. Consider distributor's cut, discounts to bookstores (usually 40 per cent) and libraries (usually 25 per cent or less). Or maybe you expect mostly full-price orders from space advertising with a coupon or direct mail promotion. Or maybe you will give your books away. Make a sane, informed, sober estimate of demand. Then guess.

LISTINGS. It is important to get your book listed so that people will know the title, subject, price, and where to order.
  National Union Catalog. See "Library of Congress Catalog Cards" under "Title Page Verso."
  Books In Print: An Index to Publishers' Trade List Annual (R. R. Bowker, 1180 Avenue of the Americas, New York, N.Y. 10036). Reaches just about everybody interested in books. Published in October of each year in a two-volume set, listing over 330,000 in-print books from over two thousand U.S. publishers. Volume one classifies books by authors; volume two classifies books by titles. (*Subject Guide to Books In Print* lists 245,000 books classified by subject.) Closing date for listings for the following year's issue is May 15. Free or at a slight expense. Contact R. R. Bowker Co. for information about these listings or listings in *Paperbound Books In Print*, *El-Hi Textbooks In Print*, *Medical Books In Print*, *Children's Books In Print*, and other publications.

Publishers Weekly (R. R. Bowker, 1180 Avenue of the Americas, New York, N.Y. 10036). *PW*'s "Weekly Record" lists books recently published in the United States. *PW* reaches more than 27,000 bookstores, libraries, and other markets. Send them a copy of the book with price, publication date, publisher, and publisher's address. This copy is in addition to review copies or galley proofs brought to the attention of *PW*'s review department (see "Review Sources").

Cumulative Book Index (H.W. Wilson Co., 950 University Ave., New York, N.Y. 10452). Request their information slip. Fill it out and send it back with a copy of your book for listing in the *Index*, published monthly through the year. The *Index* lists all books printed in the English language and is distributed to approximately ten thousand libraries and bookstores.

Small Press Record of Books (5218 Scottwood Road, Paradise, Calif. 95969). The second edition (1969-1972) is in print. Send your book for listing in the next edition.

Contemporary Authors (Gale Research Co., Book Tower, Detroit, Mich. 48226). Ask for their information form. If you are an author your biography can appear here with a listing of your book.

REMAINDER DEALERS. If you strike out these people will buy your leftover books for next to nothing. Check *Literary Market Place* for names and addresses. You may prefer to give your unsold books to libraries, prisons, hospitals, and others who need them.

TAXES. If you make a profit you have to pay taxes. Keep good records. Business expenses include printing, copyright fee, typing cost, stationery, postage, and travel expenses, even a portion of household and apartment bills if your office is at home. Check with your income-tax man. Don't forget to tell him how much you lose too, if this is the case.

AUTOGRAPH PARTIES. If you can interest your local bookstore, give it a try. Advance publicity will help. Providing wine, cheese, invitations, and a real party atmosphere may coax in the crowds.

DISTRIBUTION. This means getting your books placed with

bookstores, libraries, and wholesalers. For lists of bookstores and wholesalers, see *American Book Trade Directory*; for lists of libraries, see *American Library Directory*. (More information about these books may be found in our bibliography under "Directories.") Your local library will probably have a copy of each. COSMEP (see our listing under "Associations") supplies its members with a selective, updated listing of bookstores and libraries that are friendly to small-press people.

There are several ways to distribute your book or books.

The Personal Visit. This worked for Walt Whitman and others. Concentrate your visits where they will do the most good. If your book is specialized, concentrate on visits to bookstores dedicated to your specialty (*American Book Trade Directory* lists such shops in its general listings). If your book is of wide interest, don't forget to visit the headquarters of the larger chains if geographically feasible: Doubleday, B. Dalton, Brentano's, Walden, and Pickwick are a few of the more important. Don't ask for an appointment because you will be given excuses. Just drop in and ask for a minute of the buyer's time. In all cases offer the standard 40 per cent bookstore discount, with a better discount for generous orders. Agree that books may be returned for full refund after three months on the shelves.

Wholesalers tend to stock books, sit on them, and wait for orders. But a visit with and/or a sample copy to Baker and Taylor Co., 50 Kirby Ave., Somerville, N.J. 08876, may get your publication listed in their various catalogs. Another wholesaler of good small-press repute is Richard Abel and Co., P.O. Box 4245, Portland, Oregon 97208. Wholesalers expect larger discounts than bookstores.

A visit with libraries in your area may help; so would a booth at your State library convention. However, your best national library-selling device is a key review in *PW* or *LJ* (see "Review Sources"). Libraries depend on reviews in placing orders. Using Bowker's assorted mailing lists or compiling your own from *American Library Directory*, send your reviews to the libraries. Standard discount here is 25 per cent.

Commissioned Sales Representatives. Located in

346

various parts of the country and requiring exclusive rights in their territory, some of these people call on bookstores and wholesalers while others call on libraries. *Literary Market Place* lists bookstore and wholesale reps. You might also advertise for reps, including library salesmen, in *PW*'s classified section. But be cautioned: these people are very hard-nosed about sales potential. From a mere 10 to 15 per cent commission (more for library reps) they pay all their travel and living expenses and must of necessity work for many publishers at once. A long shot, unless you have a very commercial property.

Commercial Publishers. Sometimes they will be willing to distribute your books for you. But again, you must have a hot commercial item.

Small-Press Distributors. Probably the best bet for most small-press people. The following distributors are friendly to small publishers. COSMEP's *Newsletter* updates this list frequently.

Book People, 2940 Seventh St., Berkeley, Calif. 94710 (415-549-3033). Distributes books from commercial publishers and small presses. Emphasis is on quality paperbacks and titles of interest to the alternative culture.

B. DeBoer, 188 High St., Nutley, N.J. 07110 (201-667-9300). Long in business, distributing university reviews such as *Partisan Review*.

L and S Distributors, 1161 Post St., San Francisco, Calif. 94109 (415-771-0330). San Francisco area only. Long-established distributor of little mags.

RPM Distributors, 5862 Wicomico Ave., Rockville, Md. 20852 (301-770-4228). New in the distribution of small-press paperbacks and magazines in the eastern United States.

Serendipity Books, 1790 Shattuck, Berkeley, Calif. 94709 (415-841-7455).

FULFILLMENT. Means receiving orders and mailing out the books. You can probably handle this yourself. It's more fun that way. If not, *Literary Market Place* lists services that do it for a fee.

Several firms make padded shipping bags, necessary in assuring that books arrive undamaged. Jiffy Manufacturing Company, Hillside, N.J. 07205, is the most popular. Also check out U.S. Box Crafts, 67 Metropolitan Ave., Brooklyn, N.Y. 11211.

The U.S. Mail provides the best deal for smaller shipments. Mark your packages, "Special Fourth Class Book Rate," and they go for fourteen cents the first pound and seven cents each additional pound, as of this printing. Usually the person who orders the books pays the postage, but you may wish to absorb the cost for the sake of non-complication.

Individuals should pay in advance. Bookstores and libraries usually won't pay in advance: include the invoice with their shipment. Unlike bookstores, libraries generally pay promptly. Bookstores and wholesalers may take up to three months to pay and then merely ship back unsold books using their three-month return privilege. Even if they sell a few copies your monthly statements of money owed may be ignored while they pay off the big commercial houses. Be polite for a while. Then a letter on your lawyer's stationery or a threat to tell Dun and Bradstreet or the Better Business Bureau may help.

ASSOCIATIONS. COSMEP, CCLM, and UPS are described elsewhere in this book. *Literary Market Place* lists over one hundred more associations, most of slight interest to the small-press publisher. Here are two more: The Association of Little Presses, 262 Randolph Ave., London W.9, is Great Britain's equivalent to CCLM; New England Small Press Association, Box 512, Amherst, Mass. 01002, seeks to promote literary life in New England, provides readings and lectures for members, and finds outlets for members who run small presses or little magazines. Founded in the fall of 1969, NESPA membership is limited to New England residents, and the fee is five dollars annually. Associate memberships are available to nonresidents, who enjoy the same rights as members.

BOOK CLUBS. There are as many types of book clubs as there are types of books. *Literary Market Place* has the best listing. Some book clubs like to receive galleys in advance of publication so that their publicity can be timed with the publisher's pub day promotion. However, a bound book after pub date is also acceptable to others. Best to check with individual clubs for preference.

ADVERTISING AND PROMOTION. Advertising is expensive and can be unproductive. Advertise wisely and selectively. If your book is on a specialized subject, advertise in media dedicated to that subject. If you are trying to reach a general audience, the usual choices are *Publishers Weekly*, *Library Journal*, and *The New York Times* (*Times*' rates are very high).

A postcard to any periodical will bring you batches of ad-rate information, plus phone calls from space salesmen--if not the salesmen in person.

Often you or an artist friend can design an ad just as well as an ad agency. Although agencies get a usual 15 per cent discount from media, they will often bill you for production costs in designing your ad. The chances are that you or your friend, since you care more about the ad, can do it better and cheaper.

Don't forget to use your reviews. Buyers are more interested in what somebody else says about your publication than what you say--especially if they recognize that somebody else's name.

Direct mail is often as productive as space advertising. You can buy just about any list of names and addresses broken down into subheadings. Often magazines will rent you their subscription lists. *Literary Market Place* includes a variety of sources under "Mailing Lists," but some of the most reputable lists come from *LMP*'s publisher, R. R. Bowker. If you don't care to buy addresses and labels, check *American Library Directory* (library addresses and information) or *American Book Trade Directory* (bookstores and wholesalers) in your local library.

REVIEW SOURCES

Pick your review sources carefully. If your publication is of general interest, send review copies to the general-audience reviewers. If your publication is of specialized interest (beekeeping, stamp collecting, or the like), concentrate on reviewers in that field. Later we list *general* review sources. If your book is specialized or technical, don't try to get reviewed in these journals. Select your sources from the books listed in the "Directories" section.

Don't forget your home-town television and radio

stations and newspapers. You may rate a feature and a review, or both.

Don't waste review copies. A descriptive announcement with the notice, "Review copies available on request," to less likely review sources will save you books and postage.

Do tell reviewers your publication date so that they will know approximately when to run the review. Include all other pertinent data, such as price, author's biography and bibliography, and illustrations planned.

Do make good use of advance-of-publication-date comments to influence chances of post-pub-date reviews, especially if your comments are from reputable individuals. Splashing your advance reviews across the back of your book's jacket or cover may help gain the reviewer's attention. Remember that the average reviewer is inundated with a good portion of the more than 37,000 books published annually.

Do request a clipping of the review when it appears. Most reviewers will send you a copy automatically, but it helps to ask. Clipping services will snip out your reviews for you, but their services are unnecessary and expensive for the small publisher.

DIRECTORIES OF REVIEW SOURCES. *Literary Market Place* (R. R. Bowker, 1180 Avenue of the Americas, New York, N.Y. 10036). *LMP* contains the best selective list of newspaper, magazine, syndicate, television, and radio review sources, plus columnists, commentators, and book-review services. Public-relations, promotional, and consulting services are listed. Most libraries have a copy. Recommended.

Directory of Little Magazines, Small Presses, and Underground Newspapers (5218 Scottwood Road, Paradise, Calif. 95969). The publications listed in this directory may lack the influence and circulation of other review sources, and some don't review. But if your book will appeal to the alternative culture, a review in one of these publications may sell many books. This is the best directory of its kind.

Ulrich's International Periodicals Directory (R. R. Bowker, 1180 Avenue of the Americas, New York, N.Y. 10036). Two volumes. Lists magazines of all countries. Useful as a supplement to *LMP*.

Ayer Directory of Newspapers, Magazines, and Trade

Publications (N. W. Ayer and Son, W. Washington Square, Philadelphia, Pa. 19106). Comprehensive supplement to *LMP*.
  Catholic Press Directory (432 Park Avenue South, New York, N.Y. 10016). Complete list of U.S. and Canadian Catholic magazines and newspapers.
  Associated Church Press Directory (343 South Dearborn St., Chicago, Ill. 60604). Complete list of all Protestant magazines and newspapers in the United States and Canada.
  America's Education Press (School of Journalism, Syracuse University, Syracuse, N.Y. 13210). Classified list of U.S. and Canadian educational publications.

IMPORTANT GENERAL REVIEW SOURCES. Library Journal (1180 Avenue of the Americas, New York, N.Y. 10036). The most comprehensive and democratic book-review journal in publishing. Librarians depend on *LJ* reviews in determining acquisitions. A good review here will result in many orders. Send two books or two sets of galleys followed by books, preferably in advance of pub date. Another copy of your book or little magazine should go to *LJ*'s Bill Katz, School of Library Science, State University of New York, 1400 Washington Ave., Albany, N.Y. 12203. He writes *LJ* reviews and articles on the small-press world.
  School Library Journal (1180 Avenue of the Americas, New York, N.Y. 10036). Same importance as *LJ* for books of interest to children and young adults.
  Publishers Weekly (1180 Avenue of the Americas, New York, N.Y. 10036). Not as comprehensive or democratic as *LJ* but just as important. *PW* will review the books of do-it-yourself publishers if you can attract their attention (with advance comments, for instance) and if your book is of general, nonspecialized interest to book buyers, booksellers, and librarians. Send two sets of galleys or two books three months before publication date (*PW* reviews only in advance of publication) to the nonfiction, fiction, paperback, or children's book departments.
  The Kirkus Reviews (60 W. 13 St., New York, N.Y. 10011). Important pre-publication reviews. Send galleys, page proofs, or bound books two to three months in advance of pub date. Kirkus says they are reviewing more small-press material of interest to a general

market. Many libraries and some bookstores rely on Kirkus.

The New York Times (229 W. 43 St., New York, N.Y. 10036). Rumors have it that more than half the book buyers in the United States subscribe to the daily and the Sunday *Times*. Consequently, the *Times* is bombarded with review copies. For most small publishers this is a long shot, but well worth the attempt. The *Times* does occasionally come through--especially if your book is of general interest and brought to the editors' attention by advance comments from established types. Both daily and Sunday departments like two sets of bound galleys (i.e., don't send loose sheets; staple them together) or books two months in advance of publication date, but they have been known to review from bound books after pub date. Send galleys or books to *both* the daily and Sunday book-review sections.

Saturday Review Syndicate (380 Madison Ave., New York, N.Y. 10017). More newspapers subscribe to this service than to any other. Send a review copy to John Barkham at 27 E. 65 St., New York, N.Y. 10021.

Choice (100 Riverview Center, Middletown, Conn. 06457). The review source for books of academic importance: adult fiction and nonfiction, reprints, reissues, and paperbacks.

Small Press Review (5218 Scottwood Road, Paradise, Calif. 95969). Len Fulton, editor, has long been dedicated to small-press people. His *SPR* features news, reviews, and essays about small presses. Lacks the sales clout of the more-establishment-type review sources, but worth a review copy and a subscription.

The Booklist (50 E. Huron St., Chicago, Ill. 60611). Both juvenile and adult books. The American Library Association's magazine. Try it.

The Horn Book Magazine (585 Boylston St., Boston, Mass. 02116). For juvenile and young adult books only.

San Francisco Book Review (P.O. Box 14143, San Francisco, Calif. 94114). A good review source, sympathetic to small presses. See editor Jay Bail's chapter earlier in this book. Again, none of the sales influence of *PW*, *LJ*, and others, but worth a review copy and subscription.

TITLE PAGE VERSO

The other side of your title page is one of the most important pages in your book. Here is some information usually printed there.

COPYRIGHT. The copyright notice indicates to the public who holds the copyright. The notice should read: "Copyright © (year of publication) by (name of copyright owner)." It is essential that you comply with the wording required by the copyright office or your copyright will be invalid.

At present the copyright in a published book lasts for twenty-eight years from date of publication and can be renewed for another twenty-eight years. But this situation is under review by Congress and will probably change in the near future.

For information and copyright application form, write to the Register of Copyrights, Copyright Office, Library of Congress, Washington, D.C., 20540. Ask for Form A, "Application for Registration of a Claim to Copyright in a published book manufactured in the United States of America." (If your book is manufactured outside the United States, another form is required.)

Steps: (1) Print your copyright notice in the proper place. (2) Publish your book (publication occurs when copies of the first authorized edition are placed on sale, sold, or publicly distributed by the proprietor of the copyright or under his authority). (3) Register your copyright claim promptly after publication by sending the completed, notarized Form A, plus two good copies of the work and a fee of six dollars, to the Register of Copyrights at the above address.

LIBRARY OF CONGRESS CATALOG CARDS. For no fee to the publisher, the Library of Congress prepares a Catalog Card and sends copies to more than 19,000 libraries that subscribe to the Library of Congress Catalog Cards. Some larger libraries buy copies of each book recorded. All books currently acquired and cataloged by the Library of Congress are listed in *The National Union Catalog*, subscribed to by practically all public and private libraries.

Before you print your book notify the Chief of the Card Division, Library of Congress, Navy Yard Annex,

Building 159, Washington, D.C., 20541, and include the following information: (a) full name of author or editor; (b) title of book; (c) if the book is a first or later edition; (d) date of publication; (e) name and address of publisher and/or printer; (f) if the book is part of a series, the series title and number in that series; (g) if the publication is a serial (a periodical or an annual); (h) if it is to be copyrighted; (i) approximate number of pages; (j) type of binding.

If the book is to be added to the Library's collection, a catalog-card number is preassigned and returned to the publisher. The publisher prints this number on the verso of the title page as follows: "Library of Congress Catalog Card Number: (the number)." After the book is manufactured, send an advance-of-pub-date copy to the Library so that Catalog Cards may be printed.

The Library does not usually assign numbers to certain types of books such as vanity-press books, workbooks, laboratory manuals, pocket-sized books, pamphlets of less than fifty pages, portfolios, brochures, calendars and record books, precollege textbooks, and paperback reprints.

INTERNATIONAL STANDARD BOOK NUMBER. ISBN is something new. If you want your title page verso to have one, write to R. R. Bowker, 1180 Avenue of the Americas, New York, N.Y. 10036, before printing and they will send you information. Not obligatory. Mostly of interest to large commercial publishers. The purpose of ISBN is to coordinate and standardize internationally the use of book numbers so that each ISBN identifies via computer one title, or edition of a title, from one specific publisher, in a specific national, geographical, or language group.

HERE'S HOW your title page verso might be set up:

    Library of Congress Catalog Card Number:
    Copyright © 19__ by _____
    All Rights Reserved
    Printed In The United States of America
    First Edition
    ISBN:

SELECTED MANUFACTURERS

The manufacturers listed below are interested in short-run editions. Most of these companies also jacket and bind books or can recommend a bindery. A more comprehensive list of book manufacturers can be found in *Literary Market Place*, but many do not produce short-run editions and also cannot compete with short-run manufacturers in cost estimates. Printing and binding estimates, plus samples of previous work, should be secured from a variety of the firms listed below before signing a contract.

You might also find the manufacturer you need in the Yellow Pages of your local telephone book. Or like a number of contributors to our book, you may wish to buy your own press and make your volume yourself (see bibliography listings for how-to books).

Adams Press
30 W. Washington St.
Chicago, Ill. 60602

Ray Freiman and Co.
60 E. 42 St.
New York, N.Y. 10017

Theo. Gaus' Sons, Inc.
30 Prince St.
Brooklyn, N.Y. 11201

Graphicopy, Inc.
175 Franklin Ave.
Franklin Square, N.Y. 11010

Harlo Printing Co.
16721 Hamilton Ave.
Detroit, Mich. 48203

Multiprint, Inc.
28 W. 23 St.
New York, N.Y. 10010

Pine Hill Press
700 E. 6th St.
Freeman, S. D. 57029

Edwards Brothers
2500 S. State Street
Ann Arbor, Mich. 48104
(Offices in New York,
Boston, Washington, D.C.,
Cleveland, Chicago, and
San Francisco)

David R. Godine
282D Newton St.
Brookline, Mass. 02146

Halliday Lithograph Corp.
Circuit St.
West Hanover, Mass. 02339
(Offices also in New York)

Key Printing Co.
1369 Solano Ave.
Albany, Calif. 94706

Northbrook Press, Inc.
601 Skokie Blvd.
Northbrook, Ill. 60062

The Print Center
194 State St.
Brooklyn, N.Y. 11201

The Print Shop
333 Terry Road
Smithtown, N.Y. 11787

BIBLIOGRAPHY

This is a selective listing of in-print books of interest to do-it-yourself publishers which have appeared or been reprinted in the past three decades. Reviews, when helpful, are also quoted. Prices are accurate as of this printing but should be rechecked before ordering. "Recommended" books are of outstanding general use to small publishers.

BOOKBINDING.

Bookbinding in America. Hellmut Lehmann-Haupt. Bowker. $12.00. A history of bookbinding.
Bookbinding, Its Background and Techniques. 2 vols. Edith Diehl. Kennikat. Reprint. $27.50. "...both a historical record, and, more important, an eminently practical guide." *The New York Times.*
Creative Bookbinding. Pauline Johnson. The University of Washington Press. Revised edition. "Photographs, line drawings, and diagrams are to be found on almost every page. They are uniformly excellent and contribute to the straightforward step-by-step instructions. *Library Journal.*

COPYRIGHT.

A Copyright Guide. Harriet F. Pilpel and Morton Goldberg. Bowker. 4th edition. $5.50. Legally sound, nontechnical advice.
A Manual of Copyright Practice. Margaret Nicholson. Oxford University Press. 2nd edition. $7.50.

DIRECTORIES.

American Book Trade Directory. Bowker. Issued annually. $38.50. Lists over 16,000 booksellers, wholesalers, and publishers in the United States and Canada with information about each. Recommended.
American Library Directory. Bowker. Issued annually.

$35.00. Lists over 26,000 libraries in the United States and Canada with information about each. Recommended.

Books In Print. 2 vols. Bowker. Issued annually. $44.50. Lists 330,000 in-print U.S. books by title and author.

Bowker's Medical Books In Print. Bowker. $22.50. Lists 24,000 medical books in print.

Children's Books In Print. Bowker. $15.95. Lists 42,000 in-print children's books.

Directory of Little Magazines, Small Presses, and Underground Newspapers. Edited by Len Fulton and James Boyer May. Dustbooks (5218 Scottwood Road, Paradise, Calif. 95969). 8th Edition. $3.50. Best and most comprehensive information about small publishers. Recommended.

Directory of Small Magazine/Press Editors. Dustbooks (5218 Scottwood Road, Paradise, Calif. 95969). 3rd edition. $3.50. Small-press editors with information about each.

COSMEP Bookstore Survey. COSMEP (P.O. Box 703, San Francisco, Calif. 94101). Free to COSMEP members. A listing of bookstores interested in small-press publications, with credit ratings, plus hints on dealing with bookstores. Updated periodically in COSMEP's *Newsletter.* Recommended.

El-Hi Textbooks In Print. Bowker. 3rd edition. Lists 14,000 textbooks in print.

Literary Market Place. Bowker. Issued annually. $16.50. Information that is of practical use to the publishing and literary trades. Everything that you may need to know is here. Recommended.

Paperbound Books In Print. Bowker. Issued twice a year. $18.95. Lists over 90,000 titles per volume, indexed by author, title, and subject.

Small Press Record of Books. Dustbooks (5218 Scottwood Road, Paradise, Calif. 95969). 2nd edition. $2.50. Lists small-press books and pamphlets published throughout the world.

Subject Guide to Children's Books In Print. Bowker. $15.95. Lists 42,000 in-print children's books under more than 7,000 subject headings.

Subject Guide to Books In Print. 2 vols. Bowker. Issued annually. $39.50. Classifies 245,000 in-print U.S. books by 63,500 Library of Congress subject headings.

UPS Directory. Free Ranger Tribe. (Box 26, Village

Station, New York, N.Y. 10014). $2.00. Lists under-
ground newspapers, editors, rates , and deadlines.

MANUSCRIPT PREPARATION.

The Elements of Style. William Strunk, Jr. with E. B.
White. MacMillan. 95¢. "Watch a craftsman work...You
can write like that. Here are the tools." *The Last
Whole Earth Catalog.* Originally self-published.
Jacques Barzun on Writing, Editing, and Publishing.
Jacques Barzun. The University of Chicago Press.
$1.35. "...a feast of witty, well-pruned writing, as
well as valuable practical advice on how to produce."
Freelancer's Newsletter.
A Manual of Style. The University of Chicago Press. 12th
edition. $10.00. Since 1906, the standard tool for au-
thors, printers, proofreaders, and editors. Recom-
mended.
Preparing the Manuscript. Ulda Olsen. The Writer. $3.95.
Words Into Type. Marjorie Skillin and Robert Gay. Appleton. Revised edition. $7.50. A complete guide for
manuscript preparation, including proofreader's marks,
style, typography, illustrations, and grammar.
Writing, Illustrating, and Editing Children's Books.
J. Colby. Hastings. $7.95. All phases of juvenile pub-
lishing, from writing to production.

PAPER.

Papermaking Through Eighteen Centuries. Dard Hunter.
B. Franklin. $19.50.
*Papermaking: The History and Technique of an Ancient
Craft.* Dard Hunter. Knopf. 2nd edition. Illustrated.
$20.00.

PRINTING.

Basic Typography. Ruedi Ruegg and Godi Frohlich. Hastings. $30.00. Current typesetting systems, typogra-
phic principles and concepts, practical application of
typography, development of type forms.
Book Jackets and Record Covers. K. Weidemann. Praeger.
$15.00.
Books and Printing: A Treasury for Typophiles. Paul
Bennett, editor. Peter Smith. $4.25. A collection of

articles by foremost English and American bookmakers. Includes articles by and for amateur printers. "Anyone...who has any urge to know what lies behind the making of a book, or about the art of printing in general, will find this his kind of reading." *San Francisco Chronicle.*

The Book: Story of Printing and Bookmaking. Douglas C. McMurtrie. Oxford University Press. 3rd edition revised. $15.00.

Calligraphic Lettering With Pen and Brush. Ralph Douglass, editor. Watson-Guptil. $5.95. "...presents a lot of different forms of lettering...but it's up to you to do them right: he just shows you what the letters should look like." *The Last Whole Earth Catalog.*

The Encyclopaedia of Type Faces. W. P. Jaspert, W. T. Berry, and A. F. Johnson. Barnes and Noble. 4th edition. $18.50. A collection of 2,000 type faces with their histories.

First Principles of Typography. Stanley Morison. Cambridge University Press. $1.75. Guiding principles for the amateur.

How To Publish Your Very Own Underground Newspaper. UPS (Box 26, Village Station, New York, N.Y. 10014). $1.00. A good, elementary primer on small-magazine and newspaper printing.

Ink on Paper. Edmund Arnold. Harper. $10.95. Practical, fundamentally accurate, elementary advice on all phases of printing.

Printing for Pleasure. John Ryder. Branford. $3.25. "A practical guide for simon-pure amateurs...will answer the questions of readers and librarians who have or want to have a press of their own." *Library Journal.*

The Printing Industry. Victor Strauss. Bowker. $27.50. A comprehensive encyclopedia of printing.

Printing It. Clifford Burke. Ballantine. $2.95. "Claims to tell you everything you need to know...However, it is not necessary to follow his advice on every point. Burke often makes things seem too complicated." COSMEP *Newsletter.*

Practice of Printing. Ralph and Edwin Polk. Bennett. Composition, presswork, inks, paper. An introduction for the amateur printer.

Printer's Supply Book. The Kelsey Co. (Meriden, Conn. 06450). 35¢. "Kelsey sells only letterpress equipment.

But they have a full line--everything. Good and reasonably priced. For the holdout who still prints letterpress." *The Last Whole Earth Catalog.*

Printing Types: An Introduction. Alexander Lawson. Beacon. $9.95. An introduction for the neophyte typophile.

Printing Types, Their History, Forms and Use: A Study In Survivals. 2 vols. D. B. Updike. Belknap Press, Harvard University. $18.00. Illustrated history with bibliographic references.

Printing With The Handpress. Lewis and Dorothy Allen. Van Nostrand-Reinhold. $9.95. Originally issued privately, a definitive manual to encourage fine printing through hand craftsmanship. Advice on selecting and assembling the press, clamping the paper, and choosing the ink. "Once the printing equipment is in running order, the reader need only follow a chapter 'A Day at the Press,' perhaps the most skillfully-worded description of how to make a handproduced book...this book may someday be a classic." *Library Journal.* "A beautiful, explicit book on how to handprint beautiful books. Seeing the book makes you want to do it, and the contents can indeed get you there." *The Last Whole Earth Catalog.*

A Short History of the Printed Word. Warren Chappell. Knopf. $12.50. From pre-typographic printing to the present.

Sources of Illustration: 1500-1900. Hilary and Mary Evans. Hastings. $12.50. Details reproductive techniques and sources of pre-photographic illustration.

Type and Lettering. William Longyear. Watson-Guptil. 4th edition. $6.95. Elementary instruction for students of typography and lettering.

The Typographic Book. Stanley Morison and Kenneth Day. The University of Chicago Press. $30.00. A study of fine typography through five centuries. Some 378 examples of title and text pages drawn from the presses of Western Europe and America.

PRODUCTION AND DESIGN.

Bookmaking: The Illustrated Guide to Design and Production. Marshall Lee. Bowker. $14.00. "Probably the only existent reference for someone who needs to deal with printers and publishers and isn't sure he knows

an offset from a castoff...by the time you finish
reading it you'll probably know enough to start criti-
cizing its design." *The Last Whole Earth Catalog.*
"Its nontechnical approach will make it acceptable to
general readers as well as those whose careers may be
the production and distribution of books." *Library
Journal.*
The Design of Books. Adrian Wilson. Van Nostrand-Reinhold. $15.00. General reference book for the contem-
porary book designer.
Heritage of the Graphic Arts. Chandler Grannis. Bowker.
$17.50. Twenty-two lectures about graphic design by
various experts.
Making of Books. Sean Jennett. Praeger. 4th revised edition. $18.50. "An introduction to the various stages
of printing and binding." *Publishers Weekly.*
Methods of Book Design. Hugh Williamson. Oxford University Press. 2nd edition. $11.25. Discusses the indus-
trially-produced rather than the handmade printed
book.

ADVERTISING AND PROMOTION.

Advertising Graphics. H. W. Bockus, Jr. Macmillan.
$7.50. "Drawing, rendering, and on through the pro-
duction process." *The Last Whole Earth Catalog.*
Printing and Promotion Handbook. D. Melcher and N. Lar-
rick. McGraw. $15.95. For everybody who has to buy
printing and direct-mail services; for people who
have to plan or prepare advertising, publicity, or information of any kind. "Immensely useful." *Library
Journal.*

PUBLISHING.

The Art and Science of Book Publishing. Herbert Bailey,
Jr. Harper. $7.95. For those interested in how the
commercial business operates.
*Book In America: A History of the Making and Selling
of Books In The United States.* Helmutt Lehmann-Haupt.
Bowker. 2nd edition. $15.95. "Anyone interested in
the making of American books...will have to read this
volume." *Library Journal.* "An invaluable study." *Publishers Weekly.*
Book Publishing In America. Charles Madison. McGraw.

$12.50. The emergence of book publishing in America from 18th-Century beginnings to the present.

A History of Book Publishing in the United States: The Creation of an Industry, 1630-1865. John Tebbel. Bowker. Price not set. Just published, this is the first volume of a three-volume history. Volume two, *The Expansion of an Industry,* is planned for fall 1973. "A splendid contribution to the literature of American publishing." *Publishers Weekly.*

How To Publish, Promote and Sell Your Book. Joseph Goodman. Adams Press. $2.00. Basically a promotion piece for Adams Press but contains some good elementary information.

How To Run a Paperback Bookshop. S. Gross and P. Steckler. Bowker. $7.95. In case you want to know what a paperback-bookstore owner goes through. Read it to improve your empathy.

Imprints on History: Book Publishing and American Frontiers. M. Stern. AMS Press. $20.00. "A scholarly yet necessarily romantic investigation of 19th-Century publishing." *San Francisco Chronicle.*

Publishing and Bookselling: A History from the Earliest Times to the Present Day. Frank Mumby, Max Kenyon, editors. Bowker. Price not set. The fifth edition of this standard book about British book history.

Publishers on Publishing. Gerald Gross, editor. Grosset. $2.95. An anthology of self-portraits by American and British commercial publishers.

Scholarly Reprint Publishing in the United States. Carol Nemeyer. Bowker. $12.50.

The Small Publisher's Book. COSMEP (Box 703, San Francisco, Calif. 94101). Free to COSMEP members and any other noncommercial or literary publisher. $2.50 to libraries. Tips from other small publishers. Recommended.

What Happens In Book Publishing. Charles Grannis. Columbia University Press. $10.00. A look at commercial publishing.

COLOPHON:

HANDBOOK HOW-TO

This book was published by Bill and Nancy Henderson.

The distributors are Book People and RPM.

The book was copy-edited by Nancy and designed by Bill and Nancy.

The type was set by Nancy, using an IBM Selectric with Letter Gothic and Light Italic attachments. Delivery and rental for two months: $75.

Display type was set by Bill, using Letraset press-on type at $3 a sheet (Tactype is another good brand) and a 29¢ plastic T square.

The printers are Edwards Brothers, Inc. of Ann Arbor, Michigan.

The contributors to this book have agreed to share 25 per cent of profits rather than share 10 per cent royalties or receive a flat fee as they would under the usual commercial agreement.

Bill arranged for *Publishers Weekly* to publish sections of the Introduction together with information on the book and Pushcart.

Our office is a studio apartment in Yonkers, N.Y.

The bookkeeping is done by Nancy.

The budget for the first printing is $3,500: $1,500 for the printing and binding of 1,000 copies (900 paperbound and 100 hardbound) and $2,000 for do-it-ourselves advertising and promotion.